Post-Apartheid Fragments

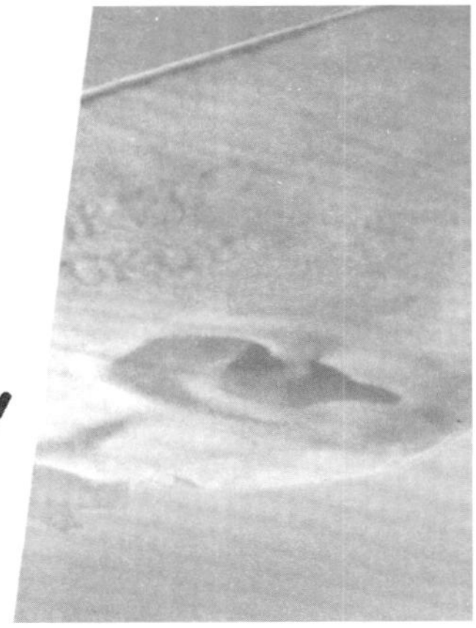

Imagined South Africa

Unisa Press celebrates ten years of democracy in South Africa with a range of books entitled *Imagined South Africa*. To publish is to name reality; it is to mark identity and to confer the status of valid knowledge on the opinions, views and knowledge of a mass of voices once denied a hearing. This series chronicles the multiple ways in which South Africans of all colours and ideological persuasions have been responding, either critically or creatively, to the numerous contradictions in ten years of democracy.

Abebe Begeye
Series Editor

Chabani Manganyi (Ed.)
On Becoming a Democracy:
Transition and Transformation in South African Society

Dial Ndima
The Law of Commoners and Kings:
Narratives of a Rural Transkei Magistrate

Reitumetse Mabokela and Zine Magubane (Eds)
Hear Our Voices: Race, Gender and the Status of
Black South African Women in the Academy

Devarakshanam Govinden
'Sister Outsiders': Identity and Difference
in the Writings of South African Indian Women

Peter Stewart
Segregation and Singularity: Politics and Its Context Among White
Middle-Class English-Speakers in Late-Apartheid Johannesburg

Ari Sitas
Voices that Reason: Theoretical Parables

Ashraf Jamal
Predicaments of Culture in South Africa

Leon de Kock, Louise Bethlehem and Sonja Laden (Eds)
South Africa in the Global Imaginary

Michael Titlestad
Making the Changes: Representations of Jazz
in South African Literature and Reportage

Chris Ledochowski
Cape Flats Details: Life and Culture
in the Townships of Cape Town

Andries Oliphant, Peter Delius and Lalou Metzer (Eds)
Democracy X: Marking the Present
and Representing the Past

Louise Bethlehem
Skin Tight: Apartheid Literary Culture and Its Aftermath

Greg Cuthbertson and Alan Jeeves (Eds)
Fragile Freedom: Democracy's First Decade in South Africa

Post-Apartheid Fragments

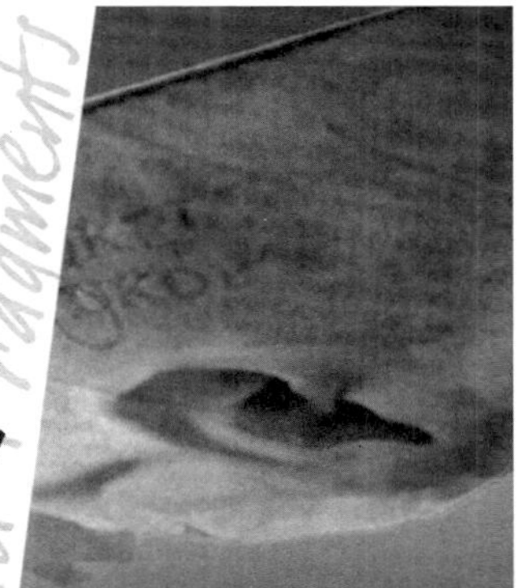

Law, Politics and Critique

Edited by

Wessel le Roux and Karin van Marle

UNIVERSITY OF SOUTH AFRICA PRESS
PRETORIA

KONINKLIJKE BRILL NV
LEIDEN

First edition, first impression
© Published by arrangement with Koninklijke Brill NV 2 Plantijn Street, PO Box 9000, 2300 PA, Leiden, The Netherlands

ISBN 978186888105-6

Published by Unisa Press
University of South Africa
PO Box 392, Unisa 0003

Book series designer: André Nel
Cover design: Andri Steyn
Electronic origination: Compleat Typesetters
Printer: Jakaranda Printers

Cover image: *The Lost Men Project* by Paul Emmanuel. This outdoor, site-specific memorial installation was launched at the National Arts Festival, Grahamstown, South Africa in July 2004. The technique involved printing; lead type, blind embossed on the surface of the artist's skin; and photography.

CONTENTS

FOREWORD: THINKING AGAINST THE GRAIN

Drucilla Cornell

The new South Africa has been both an inspiration and a source of watchful concern since the African National Congress came to power in 1994. The kind of apocalyptic Hegelianism that has dominated so much political and economic theory in the last ten years since the new South Africa was brought into existence after years of struggle is well known. In the most dramatic version of this story, people like Francis Fukuyama not only claim the victory of neoliberalism, but describe it in the glorious terms that Hegel used for modernity: freedom has finally been realised and 'man' has finally overcome his alienation and realised his destiny in neoliberal capitalism. Fukuyama cheers as one country after another in the globalised world takes its place in what he sees as the ultimate form of political and social organisation – ultimate in that it purportedly realises 'freedom' and stands as the ultimate sign of progress.

Socialism is dead, he contends. And the socialists who remain are at best wayward dreamers and at worst outright psychotics railing against the direction of history. And then in 1994, in a relatively peaceful transition, Nelson Mandela was elected president of South Africa. Many of us socialists watched with anticipation as the post-apartheid South Africa came into existence. Yes, there have undoubtedly been concessions in South Africa to privatisation and other neoliberal forms of social organisation. Many socialists and progressives who held out such hope for South Africa have watched in despair as South Africa has seemed to confirm Fukuyama's claims that the end-of-ideology times we live in make resistance itself futile. And yet, there continues to be struggle across multiple layers of society, including at the level of the Constitutional Court, over the ultimate future direction of South Africa.

In a deep sense, then, South Africa – and the struggle to create a new South Africa by trying to find institutions that can shelter the best aspirations of socialism – belies the basic mistake made by Fukuyama. We must not fail to learn from Hegel that without the struggle for such institutions actually to give shelter to the spirit of Absolute Freedom, this force turns against itself by becoming only the empty raging of Absolute Terror. Indeed, in the actions of the United States of America in its ongoing war against Iraq, which has caused so much unnecessary suffering, we see the aggressive aspect of freedom defined as 'absolute lack of moral limitation'. Perhaps, this explains why the struggle in South Africa to create those institutions is so important, not only for South Africans, but for the rest of the world, who can learn from a country in which basic questions such as property rights are actually put on the political and social agenda as ones that could be addressed in a new way rather than under the forms of property that have been developed in the West.

In the deepest sense the essays in this volume show how the struggle continues and why the struggle for social justice cannot follow the easy path of social progress predicted by some Marxists. Each essay addresses the fact that a jurisprudence adequate to the aspirations of the Constitution of South Africa can only develop if it dares to address the most pressing philosophical issues of our time. The questions raised in these essays range from a sophisticated examination of the meaning of reconciliation, to reconfigurations of what kind of property could guarantee some of the poorest South Africans access to both land and basic resources. Indeed, at the heart of these essays is an appeal to address the very idea of what is new about the new South Africa and what might be its future, other than Fukuyama's vision of the ultimate triumph of capitalism.

The essays do not offer easy answers or give facile promises. In fact, they take seriously the task of moving beyond the narrow-minded assumptions made by those who put so much hope in South Africa as the one country that could bring socialism into the world, by forcing us to take up deeper questions and prodding us to think again about ideals such as progress, the future and even ideals themselves. Yet each one of the thinkers in this collection does in fact address the promise and responsibility of developing jurisprudence adequate to the task of the new South Africa. Perhaps, justice is preserved, then, in the aspiration for such jurisprudence and what ultimately unfolds as an unconventional path beyond Western notions of positivistic law and calculable harm is charted toward the sort of dignity that needs to be called into existence to give shelter to the spirit of freedom.

INTRODUCTION

Karin van Marle and Wessel le Roux

Friendships

The wider context of the essays that have been brought together in this collection can be traced back to a series of constitutional events in post-apartheid South Africa during the second half of the 1990s. The first democratic elections had taken place on 27 April 1994. The newly created Constitutional Court had heard its first case on 15 February 1995 and was slowly making its way into uncharted constitutional territory. The first fully democratic South African Constitution had been adopted on 8 May 1996 after many years of colonialism and apartheid (the so-called interim Constitution of 1994 was still promulgated by the apartheid parliament). The Truth and Reconciliation Commission[1] had survived a constitutional challenge on 25 July 1996[2] and was beginning to hear harrowing evidence of past human rights abuses. These institutional events shook the South African legal community to its roots. A sense of expectation hung in the air. Spurred on by the energy released by the anticipation of new possibilities, a few colleagues and friends came together once a week to read texts, and discuss themes and issues of the day.[3]

These meetings and discussions did not form part of a bigger academic or theoretical agenda. It was left to the members of the reading group to select and propose, without any programmatic pressure, texts that could form the basis of the discussions. These personal choices became the contingent events that eventually fostered and sustained both new and already established friendships. This collection of essays is the result of those friendships, and, as such, continues to bear the marks of those little contingencies amidst a series of over-determined constitutional events of global significance.

The weekly meetings eventually came to an end as some of us moved to other universities; the discussions and friendships, however, continued.[4] Towards the end of 2003, the friends decided to organise a panel at the Law and Society Association annual meeting, which was

1 The South African Truth and Reconciliation Commission was established in terms of the Promotion of National Unity and Reconciliation Act 34 of 1955.

2. *AZAPO v President of the Republic of South Africa* 1996 (4) SA 671 (CC)

3 André van der Walt and Johan van der Walt started with these discussions in the early 1990s, Henk Botha joined them later and eventually, during 1997, Karin van Marle and Wessel le Roux. Danie Goosen, although not a regular member, gave much direction to some of the discussions, in particular the reading of Hannah Arendt. At some stage all members of the group were working in various departments at the University of South Africa (Pretoria).

4 The annual conference of the Research Unit for Legal and Constitutional Interpretation (RULCI) is one example of a space where most members of the reading group came together and where the early discussions were continued in a wider context.

to take place in Chicago during May of 2004. The organisers accepted the proposed panel – loosely billed as a session of, or on, fragments from post-apartheid jurisprudence – and Jonathan Klaaren kindly agreed to chair it. This collection of essays is the direct result of the papers that were presented at that event. The brief was nothing more than an engagement with, and reflection on, texts and themes that were originally of concern during the discussions in the late 1990s and the years thereafter. The aim was in no way to limit the focus or restrict the imagination by forcing a particular theme or framework onto the individual contributions, the session itself or, finally, this collection of essays as a whole.

Given this history, it would be extremely reductive suddenly to reconstruct a single unifying theme or closed conceptual framework for this collection as a whole. The various chapters are reflections of engagements with many of the diverse texts, themes and thoughts that featured in the group discussions over a decade. This is not to say that those engagements are merely abstract, disembedded and disembodied contemplations. Each chapter is in its own way marked with material concerns of a specific context, time, space and place. The title of the collection captures the spirit and aim of the collaboration: to put forward reflections – which are by no means representative, but nevertheless examples – of the becoming of post-apartheid jurisprudence.

Texts

Fragments of the weekly discussions that took place among the contributors to this volume (Stewart Motha excluded) can be located to a lesser or greater degree in all of the chapters, as they can between them. A closer look at these fragments reveals one of the larger themes that animated many of the earlier meetings and discussions: a critical concern with the relationship between law and politics within the context of constitutional democracy and the discourse of constitutional rights. The more contingent interpersonal context of the collection also reveals itself in the nature of the texts that became focus points during some of the discussions and still remain so for most of the contributors today. Karl Klare's article on 'transformative constitutionalism' from 1998 is one such example.[5] It became the vehicle for a return to the different ways in which the American Realists[6] and (US) CLS[7] had exposed the politics of law; or, as it was described by Klare, to the tension between freedom and constraint in legal interpretation. The advent of the South African Truth and Reconciliation Commission during those years placed the theme of reconciliation

5 Karl Klare 'Legal culture and transformative constitutionalism' (1998) 14 *SAJHR* 147.

6 These texts included, among others, Oliver Wendell Holmes 'The path of the law' (1897) 10 *Harvard LR* 457; Thomas Grey 'Holmes and legal pragmatism' (1989) 41 *Stanford LR* 787; Felix Cohen 'Transcendental nonsense and the functional approach' (1935) 35 *Columbia LR* 809; Robert Hale 'Coercion and distribution in a supposedly non-coercive state' (1923) 38 *Political Science Quarterly* 470; Joseph Singer 'Legal realism now' (1988) 76 *California* LR 467; Charles Reich 'The new property" (1964) 73 *Yale LJ* 733; Jürgen Habermas 'How is legitimacy possible on the basis of legality' and 'On the idea of the rule of law' in *The Tanner lectures on human values VII* (1988).

7 These texts included, among others, Duncan Kennedy 'Form and substance in private law adjudication' (1976) 89 *Harvard LR* 1685; Mary-Joe Frug 'A postmodernist feminist legal manifesto (an unfinished draft) (1992) 105 *Harvard LR* 1045; Peter Gabel 'The phenomenology of rights-consciousness and the pact of the withdrawn selves' (1984) 62 *Texas* LR 1563; Mark Tushnet 'Anti-formalism in recent constitutional scholarship' (1985) 83 *Mich* LR 1502; Gary Peller 'The metaphysics of American law' (1985) 73 *California LR* 1151.

on the table.[8] From the very first discussions a prevailing concern was the possibility of a (re)construction of a public sphere. Hannah Arendt's *The human condition* provided a central focus for the discussions in the group and for the research of individual members of the group.[9] For us as legal scholars, language is central to everything we do and because of the effect of the interpretive turn,[10] our discussions were also marked by what can be described as certain postmodern or poststructuralist tendencies.[11] Feminist concerns were also voiced.[12]

This eclectic choice of texts and reading material soon impressed on everybody's work the understanding that post-apartheid legal scholars, facing the failures of positivist as well as natural law approaches of the past, had to think about the relationship between law, politics and critique in new ways while they confronted the shift from authoritarianism to democracy, parliamentary sovereignty to constitutional supremacy, inequality and discrimination to equality.

Our tentative attempts to this end have resulted in this collection of essays. The collection is no more than a fragment of a larger ongoing debate about the nature and place of law in post-apartheid South Africa. It does not represent a single position in this debate. There are to be found here fragments of a vision of post-apartheid politics; or what Karin van Marle describes in chapter two as 'bits and pieces' of a post-apartheid politics of action. The collection is also marked, finally, by the fragmented nature in which it draws on two frequently opposed philosophical and jurisprudential traditions, most notably 'post-realist' American constitutionalism (i.e., Klare and Michelman) and 'post-structuralist' French thinking (i.e., Nancy, Derrida, Lyotard and Kristeva).

Traces

All the chapters are animated by the attempt to rethink the idea of the public, politics and democracy in a post-liberal manner, that is, as qualitatively different from the administration of an aggregate of private interests. From this perspective the discourse of constitutional rights is rethought beyond its traditional liberal confines: not as pre-political bounded spaces of individual freedom, but as something inherently contested

8 The South African Truth and Reconciliation Commission was established in terms of the Promotion of National Reconciliation and Unity Act 34 of 1995. The Act survived a constitutional challenge on 25 July 1996, when the Constitutional Court held in *AZAPO v President of the RSA* 1996 (4) SA 671 (CC) that the widespread amnesty provisions of the Act did not violate the interim Constitution of 1994. The commission started its proceedings shortly thereafter. For an account of the early days of the Commission's proceedings see Antjie Krog *Country of my skull* (1998).

9 Hannah Arendt *The human condition* (1958).

10 See for example Rosemary Coombe 'Same as it ever was: Rethinking the politics of legal interpretation' (1989) 34 *McGill LR* 604.

11 These texts included, among others, Jean-François Lyotard *Just gaming* (1985); Jacques Derrida 'The force of law' in Carlson, Cornell and Rosenfeld *Deconstruction and the possibility of justice* (1992); and Chantal Mouffe *The return of the political* (1993).

12 Such as those raised by Drucilla Cornell 'The doubly prized world: Myth, allegory and the feminine' (1990) 75 *Cornell LR* 644.

and political. The relationship between rights and politics is complex, however. Two different sets of questions can be distinguished in this regard. How can the politics of legal interpretation be fashioned into a politics of legal transformation? How must the traditional doctrinal engagement with the right to property and the right to equality, to take the two examples discussed in chapters four and five respectively, be rethought in order to open the constitutional rights discourse to the possibility of transformative politics or public action?

Henk Botha argues in chapter five that the politics of interpretation is at work, not only when subjective preferences inform legal judgments, but also where a reliance is placed on apparently neutral legal principles. The critical task is to force open the interpretive politics of legal formalism in order to reshape the hidden politics of interpretation into an open site of democratic contestation and transformation. To this end, Botha argues that the 'dignity-based concept of equality' that dominates the post-apartheid constitutional equality discourse should be doctrinally replaced with a 'complex conception of equality'.

André van der Walt explores a number of water disputes in chapter four in order to illustrate that the dominant private law doctrine of property rights fails to give proper expression to the public or political dimension of property law. He argues that the classical liberal view of subjective property rights, from which the post-apartheid property rights discourse has largely been derived, will have to be doctrinally reworked if it is to support the possibility of post-apartheid transformative politics. The task of property law is not (exclusively) to create wealth, but to constitute a specific social or political order, that is, to contribute to an aspect of public life without which individual life is unthinkable; an aspect that transcends both the private interest and the public interest (understood as the harmonisation of individual entitlements).

The first set of questions dealing with the politics of legal interpretation also opens a second. Karin van Marle argues in chapter two that the post-apartheid constitutional rights discourse can never become the medium of political action and revolt. Law is precisely for this reason not politics. From her perspective the drive towards the politicisation of constitutional rights must also confront the limits of law's ability to doctrinally or theoretically reconstitute itself as a medium of politics and transformation. What the limits of law constitute and how those limits should be registered combine to form a second set of questions which animates this collection.

Johan van der Walt takes up these questions in chapter one. Relying on the work of Derrida and Nancy, he urges us to be attentive to the aporetic difference between the subjective intentionalities of politics (the Schmittian pull of unity) and the in-tensionality of the political (the Arendtian pull of plurality). He proceeds to interrogate critically the threat that mercantilism, religious moralism, multicultural language politics and the politics of the unitary state pose to the 'complexity of the political' and to the time of reconciliation in post-apartheid South Africa. These phenomena all tend to reduce the complexity of the political to some form of unity. Van der Walt finds the 'obnoxious solidarity' of these attempts just as problematical as the 'placid plurality' of political liberalism.

Karin van Marle argues in related terms in chapter two that constitutional rights are, and will always be, caught up in their own monumentality and closure. This poses dangers in the post-apartheid context, where constitutionalism and human rights have seemingly become all-pervasive. On the one hand, rights have tended to become monumentalised and are not open to continuous questioning; on the other, rights have become the only legitimate avenue of politics. The result of this reduction is an absence of action, thinking and revolt, as is evident in the mainstreaming of gender politics. Relying on the work of Arendt and Kristeva, Van Marle argues that in this context critique should take the form of a memorial life or an 'ethical engagement with the limits of the law'. It is only in its memorial moments (moments of failure) that the constitutional rights discourse is able (if at all) to recall the possibility of a politics of becoming.

In chapter three Wessel le Roux explores a number of spatial metaphors that are associated with the architectural design of the new South African Constitutional Court building. He does so in order to interrogate the limits of a republican politics of constitutional rights. Relying on the work of Lyotard, he argues that constitutional rights mark an aporetic boundary between the ethical and politics, between obligation and norm. The aporetic structure of rights necessitates a constitutionalism of negative representation, such as that which Lyotard associates with the aesthetics of the sublime. The constitutional rights discourse can therefore never simply be approached as the normative gathering of the political community. It is always and also the moment that marks the limits and the labyrinthian dislocation of all laws, norms and communities.

Traces of these and other arguments cut across the borders of all the individual chapters. Johan van der Walt, for example, tackles reconciliation explicitly in chapter one, but the theme also resonates in Karin van Marle's discussion of action in chapter two. The former author's exposition of mercantilism is echoed by the latter's discussion of Mamdani's critique of reconciliation. Van der Walt's warning against a Schmittian totalisation of politics likewise recalls Van Marle's criticism of the monumentalism of constitutional and human rights politics. Le Roux's insistence on justice as *differend* (following Lyotard) or *differance* (following Derrida) in chapter three resonates with Johan van der Walt's reliance on Nancy's empty or inoperative community in chapter one. Hannah Arendt's understanding of politics and the public flows through the collection, from Johan van der Walt's reliance on her notion of plurality, through van Marle's commitment to the centrality of life in her thought, to André van der Walt's explicit use of her exposition of the public/private distinction in chapter four. Henk Botha similarly develops the Arendtian notion of politics into the concept of complex equality in chapter five. Botha shares Le Roux's concern with the spatial metaphors that structure the post-apartheid rights discourse, as well as Le Roux's critical response to the Constitutional Court's decision in *Jordan*.[13] Botha's exposure of the claim to neutrality that lies at the heart of the post-apartheid dignity jurisprudence, is at the same time echoed by van Marle's concern with a monumental approach to rights that seemingly

13 *S v Jordan* 2002 (6) SA 642 (CC) 2002 (11) BCLR 1117 (CC)

ignores the politics of the past. These traces are marked in the respective chapters by short cross-referencing footnotes.

The concluding chapter by Stewart Motha provides a critical reflection on some of the key themes and tensions in the collection as a whole. It is written by somebody outside the immediacy of the post-apartheid context. The chapter formulates its own challenge to critical legal thought in post-apartheid South Africa and elsewhere. At the same time it begins to assess the way in which each of the individual chapters in this collection tries to respond to this challenge. As such it reformulates many of the questions that have been raised in the course of those chapters. The focus here, as in the rest of the collection, is not on what has been achieved, but on what remains to be thought in the ongoing debate on the relationship between law, politics and critique.

Images

The photographic images that appear on the front and back covers of this collection of essays are from The Lost Men Project by South African artist Paul Emmanuel. This outdoor site-specific memorial installation was launched in July 2004 at the National Arts Festival, Grahamstown, South Africa. The images interrogate the fragility of public memory and constitute a site of resistance to fixed and monumental representations and the closure of meaning. As such, the images and the whole project resonates closely with some of the central themes that inform the essays in the collection as a whole.

The artist himself explains the background to, and spirit of The Lost Men Project in the following words:

> The installation has a delicate, fragile presence and invites the viewer to contemplate the work against the surrounding landscape. This project is a development from a previous series of works dealing with memory and loss, namely the Air on the Skin series. Traditionally, war memorials have idealised and/or emphasised the glory of war. Usually, the materials chosen for memorials, for example, granite, marble and bronze, signify the permanence of the memory of those who have died. To make the ultimate sacrifice for one's country or ideals is perceived as a noble concept, as is that of the 'glory of war'. This project emphasises the complete opposite. The Lost Men talks about loss, the pathos of impermanence, the fragility of life, the memories that remain and how in time they fade, and questions traditional notions of masculinity. The materials specifically emphasise and speak of delicacy and transience, and use the ephemeral quality of the imprinted silk to contrast with the use of lead type used by the artist in a process of blind embossing.

Our hope is that the images will inspire a desire to read the printed texts in this collection from the inside outwards. Temporarily bound together by the images on the covers, but ultimately, like them, mere fragments; impermanent and fragile.

ONE

The Time of Reconciliation

Johan van der Walt

1.1 Introduction

This chapter endeavours to take further the thoughts on the time of reconciliation that I developed in an earlier essay.[1] The first essay took Kant's definition of law as its point of departure. The definition turns after all on the notion of the reconciliation (*Vereinbarung*) of the external liberties of individuals. Law is to effect this reconciliation under a general system of rules.[2] Colleagues who responded to the essay suggested that the Kantian definition was a bad place from which to start an inquiry into the time of reconciliation.[3] The reason for this, it was argued, was that: the rather generic conception of reconciliation between individuals in the ordinary course of life that is envisaged by the Kantian definition of law, does not address the exigencies of the more exceptional and specific question of reconciliation that the four workshops aimed to address, namely, the reconciliation at issue in the aftermath of markedly traumatic disruptions of the social bond or social fabric, such as genocides and other deeply disruptive human rights abuses. In other words, my earlier essay did not pay sufficient attention to the fundamental difference between the two kinds of reconciliation invoked here: the resolution of a conflict of individual interests in the ordinary commerce of life and the resolution of severely traumatic social disruptions. Breach of commercial contracts

1 Johan van der Walt 'Psyche and sacrifice' (2003) *TSAR* 635-651. The section on cultural politics in post-apartheid South Africa was presented as a paper at the May 2004 Law and Society Association meeting in Chicago. I wish to thank Karin van Marle and Wessel le Roux for organising the session on 'Post-Apartheid legal fragments' in which it was presented, and all the participants in the session for further insightful comments. Thanks are also due to Drucilla Cornell for coming in at the end with generous and incisive comments. See also the acknowledgements in(n 3) below. Remaining errors and shortcomings are of course strictly mine.

Readers may wonder about my 'liberal' or 'progressive' convictions when they find in what follows, remarks that are sympathetic to political stances that are not reconcilable with a typical liberal or progressive politics. This is not the first time that I feel the need to remark on this (Johan Van der Walt 'Horizontal application of fundamental rights and the threshold of the law in view of the *Carmichele* saga' (2003) 19 *SAJHR* 521). The problem with the typical progressive or liberal political stance, to which I invariably subscribe spontaneously whenever gut reactions are at play, is its tendency, all too often to regress to very conservative and reactionary ways of thinking when confronted with conservative and reactionary politics. A deeper liberality is at stake when we wish to think about reconciliation; no, when we wish to think at all.

2 Immanuel Kant *Metaphysik der Sitten in Werke in 10 Bänden* (Weischedel edition 1983) Band 7, 337.

3 I am especially indebted to Scott Veitch and Bert van Roermund in this regard, but I also wish to thank Emilios Christodoulidis and all the other participants in a series of workshops on the Time of Reconciliation held at the universities of Edinburgh, Glasgow, Tilburg, Johannesburg and Cape Town for their valuable comments on Van der Walt 'Psyche and sacrifice' (n 1). Parts of this chapter were also presented at one of these workshops.

cannot be compared to the breach of the social contract, so to speak, assuming here for a moment that *breach of contract* is at all an accurate phrase to rely on with regard to a breach of the social contract.

The earlier essay may indeed be said to have unduly levelled the difference between ordinary commercial and deeper cultural or political crises. The following passage could be a clear indication in this regard:

> The historical encounter with the failure of the free market to make good its promise of social justice gives us reason to believe that Kant's definition of law is much more contentious than it appears at first sight. The definition turns on the assumption that the reconciliation between external liberties is possible. The historical encounter with the failure of free markets suggests that it is not. This does not apply only to the free market of commercial transactions governed by private law systems. It also applies to the free market of cultural expression and social or political identity in multi-cultural and multi-ethnic societies governed by systems of constitutional law.[4]

Now, I am still rather inclined to argue that the difference between economic and political crises, between the ordinary breach of commercial contracts and the breach of the social contract, is not all that clear-cut. My cue in this regard is again Derrida's insistence that the distinction between the private and the public, the distinction between the economic and the political, is linguistically unstable.[5] And this cue can also be taken from Schmitt. The political is not, for Schmitt, something that exists or occurs entirely apart or separate from other spheres of social life such as the economic, the cultural and the religious. According to him, the political is an *intensification* of one or other of these non-political spheres of social life.[6] However, if this chapter aims to take things further, it will have to take issue with the difference between commercial and political crises. What fundamental element of the political can be identified as evidently absent from the commercial and vice versa? Well, if one were to take one's cue from Schmitt, it is precisely this *intensification* that demands attention when coming to terms with the difference between the commercial and the political. *Intensification*, in other words, is not only the bridge that links commerce and politics, it is also the abyssal void that in the first place allows for the span of the bridge, and thus fundamentally brings forth what is absent from the commercial and only comes into presence with the political. So, intensification as link or bridge draws its very span from intensification as abyss. Intensification is an *abyssal link*. Perhaps it is not so much the linking of the commercial and the political that is so troublesome in 'Psyche and sacrifice', but the failure to take issue with the abyss spanned *by* the link, the abyssal span *of* this link.

Intensification will therefore be the focus of this chapter. Intensification, I shall argue, *resists* reconciliation. It lies at the heart of resistance to reconciliation. What is intensification? What is resistance? These are the questions that must be addressed

---

4 Van der Walt 'Psyche and sacrifice' (n 1) 635.

5 Jacques Derrida *L'autre cap* (1991) 110–11.

6 Carl Schmitt *Der Begriff des Politischen* (1996) 38: 'Das Politische ... bezeichnet ... nur den *Intensitätsgrad* einer Assoziation oder Dissoziation von Menschen, deren Motive religiöser, nationaler (im ethnischen oder kulturellen Sinne), wirtschaftlich oder anderer Art sein können und zu verschiedenen Zeiten verschiedene Verbindungen und Trennungen bewirken.' (in original).

in order to come to terms with the precarious time of reconciliation in the wake of traumatic disruptions of regular social life or *sociality*.[7] I shall use the word *sociality* to denote the regular and relatively amicable co-existence of people in all the various spheres of social life; commerce, culture, religion and so forth. Sociality could also be described provisionally by invoking Bakhtin's notion of a body politic in which sufficient dialogue and humour relativise social tensions and thus prevent them from becoming so *tense* or *intense* that they give rise to *intentional* political disruptions of the body politic.[8] Understood thus, sociality could also be described in terms of the corporality of social existence and the *corporality* of the law (the *Corpus Iuris*) that Nancy[9] describes in terms of an extension. He refers in this regard to a note that Freud wrote shortly before his death: '*Psyche ist Ausdehnung, weiss es nicht.*'[10] Psyche is extension, knows nothing thereof. One could elaborate as follows: Psyche is *unaware* of her extension. Her extension is *non-intentional*. Her extension is not *that* intensive. Sociality, it would seem, cannot be conceived in terms of the intensification that occasions sovereignty according to Schmitt, an intensification that Derrida in fact suspects to be a subjectivist *intentionality*.[11] Psyche's extension nevertheless remains *in tension*. Her extension is a matter of existence in and with tensions. Her extension is matter in-tension. This is why the matter of Psyche matters, albeit not intentionally so, or *so* intentionally so. The post-metaphysical or postmodern condition (in the strictly Lyotardian sense of the word) in which we live can no longer conceive of sociality in terms of an integrating or super narrative that could figure as the overall intention of sociality, hence the need to move away from the sovereign intentionality that Schmitt infers from the intensification of the political.

But sociality continues to matter. And the fact that sociality matters, and sometimes matters rather seriously and critically, cannot be understood without regard for the intensification that, according to Schmitt, occasions the political. One can therefore also not move too far away from Schmitt. Perhaps one should not move away from him at all. Perhaps one should simply provide the considerable weight of his thought with a sufficient counterweight. Doing so may well help one to come to grips with the difference between Schmittian intensifications that give rise to intentional sovereignties that are bound to disrupt sociality, on the one hand, and Schmittian intensifications that take part in the regular political tensions or in-tensionality of sociality, on the other. The homonymic resonance or inaudible semantics at play between these two intensifications simultaneously disclose and conceal what is at issue here. It discloses the frailty of the distinction between the two intensifications, but it also conceals or hides the abyssal crossing between them, the abyssal crossing that is guarded by this very frail distinction

---

7 The theme of 'resistance' is also taken up by Karin van Marle in chapter two of this collection when she enters into a discussion of 'revolt'.

8 Michael Bakhtin *Rabelais and his world* (1968).

9 Jean-Luc Nancy *Corpus* (2000) 22.

10 Sigmund Freud *Schriften aus dem Nachlass in Gesammelte Werke* (1999) 152; JLCI; Jacques Derrida *Le toucher, Jean-Luc Nancy* (2000) 22.

11 Jacques Derrida *Politiques de l'amitie* (1994) 86–87.

between them. Giving Schmitt a counterweight in what follows will draw attention to the frail guard-rails of an abyssal crossing so as to sound an alert to the abyss itself.

1.2 Two concepts of the political and the movement from social contract to social contraction

Another Nancyan theme can be invoked to explain the corporal *extension* and *in-tension* of sociality. Nancy distinguishes between a community of which the element of communality would consist in an *être en commun* and one of which the communality would consist in an *être commun* or in a *communion*.[12] The *être en commun* would *consist* (literally: exist with or exist together) in a togetherness of a plurality of singular political voices that do not amount to, culminate in, or return to, *an operative unity*. The *être commun* or *communion* would, however, *insist* (exist emphatically *in*) on a self-referential, self-related or internal oneness to which Nancy also refers as *immanence*.[13] These themes clearly resonate with Lefort's analysis of totalitarianism in terms of its insistence on unity and absence of internal divisions.[14]

The argument that follows does not relate Schmitt's understanding of the political directly or simplistically to the totalitarian logic of unity that Lefort highlights or the *être commun* or *communion* that Nancy brings to bear on the argument. A sympathetic reading of Schmitt (and I would argue that reading is or should as such be a sympathetic endeavour) cannot but notice a certain complexity in his thinking regarding the political and sovereignty. The intensification that, according to Schmitt, gives rise to the political clearly occasions a moment of plurality. It occasions the encounter between the friend and the enemy, the engagement between or coming together of at least two political voices. The challenging question with which this moment of plurality in Schmitt's analysis of the political confronts one, is whether plurality can at all be contemplated without a moment of antagonism or agonising conflict.[15] But there is no point in denying the fact that Schmitt ultimately understands the political in terms of the unification of the political unit in the encounter with the enemy. The intensification that marks the political for Schmitt occasions a moment of plurality, but it is not the sustenance of this plurality that ultimately interests Schmitt. The moment of plurality is for him at most a phase in the dialectic return, rise to oneness or unification that marks the political. The *political intensification* of regular spheres of social life is for Schmitt ultimately a matter of *political unification*.[16]

The moment of, or movement towards, unification, the fixing of boundaries and borders, may well be an inevitable and irreducible aspect of the political as it is known. One would therefore be naive to dismiss it simply as necessarily indicative of a totalitarian politics. A realistic critique of the political as defined by Schmitt would therefore

---

12 Jean-Luc Nancy *Être singulier pluriel* (1996) 64; *La communauté désoeuvrée* (1999) 201–234.

13 Jean-Luc Nancy *La communauté désoeuvrée* (n 12) 35–42, 88.

14 Claude Lefort *L 'invention démocratique* (1994) 101.

15 Chantal Mouffe *The return of the political* (1993) 109–115.

16 Johan van der Walt 'The (im)possibility of two together when it matters' 2002 *TSAR* 462 at 466–467.

not dismiss it as such. A realistic critique of the political would at most question the complete reduction of the political to an intensification that amounts or gives rise to unification. Such a critique would want to contrast the Schmittian concept of the political with the one that Hannah Arendt articulates in *The human condition*. This concept of the political emphasises plurality as the very condition of politics. Arendt writes:

> Action, the only activity that goes on directly between men without the intermediary of things or matter, corresponds to the human condition of plurality, to the fact that men, not Man, live on the earth and inhabit the world. While all aspects of the human condition are somehow related to politics, this plurality is specifically *the* condition – not only the *conditio sine qua non*, but the *conditio per quam* of all political life.[17]

This passage from *The human condition* evidently prioritises the element or moment of plurality in the movement of the political. It would be implausible to argue that Arendt would simply dismiss or deny the moment of unity and unification that political action also occasions. But one can plausibly argue that she stresses, at least here, a different direction in the movement of the political; one that always returns to plurality as the fundamental condition of politics.

A critique of the political that would contrast the emphasis on plurality in Arendt's understanding of the political, with the emphasis on unification in that of Schmitt's, would do so not in order to dismiss the one in favour of the other, but to identify and sustain two distinct but perhaps inseparable directions in the moment or movement of intensification that occasions the political. The political would thus come to be understood as an intensification directed simultaneously towards both plurality and unity. The political would thus come to be understood as an irreducibly complex event of plurality and unity or 'pluralising and unifying'. Within the play of this complex event, but only *within its play*, one may well replace the words unity and unifying with singularity and singularising, thus invoking what is really at issue in the political, namely, the plural-singular existence that Nancy expounds in *Être singulier pluriel*.[18] I stress the 'within its play', because outside the play of the political event singularity again gets displaced by unity.

Reductions of this complexity of the political to either one of its directions cannot but destroy the political. Reductions of this complexity in favour of unity may well give rise to the totalitarian logic analysed by Lefort or the obnoxious solidarity that Michelman invokes in 'Law's republic'.[19] Reductions of this complexity in favour of plurality could well give rise to a denial of the political as a very specific mode of, or event in, social life; namely, a mode or an event of intensification that disrupts the placid plurality that is regularly associated with facile and politically complacent versions of political liberalism. The Michelman of 'Law's republic' refers in this regard to "the vice of plurality".[20]

---

17 Hannah Arendt *The human condition* (1989) 7. Arendt's understanding of 'action' as definitive of 'politics and 'the public' is also explored by Karin van Marle in chapter two of this collection and by André van der Walt in chapter four.

18 Nancy *Être singulier pluriel* (n 12) 23–24.

19 Frank Michelman 'Law's republic' (1988) 97 *Yale LJ* 1496.

20 *Idem* 1526–1528.

I would like to argue that it is this complex tension intrinsic to the political that Nancy aims to articulate with his notion of the *être en commun* of the inoperative community. The notion of sociality invoked above cannot be contemplated without a regard for this intrinsic complexity of the political. The social, interactive and communicative element and erotic eventfulness of sociality cannot be understood without a regard for the complexity of the political. The complexity of the political is the very matter of sociality or the very reason why sociality matters, why sociality *attracts* and *contracts* (but nevertheless does not enter contracts, as will become clear below). Or perhaps one should rather say that the political constitutes or embodies the complexity, attraction and contraction of sociality. Let us invoke Nancy's (and Derrida's) Psyche again. Unlike the Psyche that Greek mythology relates, Nancy's Psyche is prepared to remain ignorant of the ultimate identity of Eros. She is prepared to know Eros as her lover only. But Psyche can nevertheless not be dispassionate, because Eros has the art of the caress.[21] She cannot and will not enter into contracts; marriage contracts that define the *intention* of their co-existence, but ultimately only envisage an eventual breach of contract. But she remains *in tension*. Her extended body contracts under the caress of her unknown lover.

Reconciliation would thus not involve the question of how a community deals with breach of contract, social or commercial. Breach of contract is a hard (and fast) depiction of social disruption. It is bound to harden the terms and thus frustrate further the event of reconciliation. The phrase 'breach of contract' could, in fact, indicate the problem at the heart of reconciliation when one reads the 'of' as a subjective genitive instead of reading it as an objective genitive, as is usual when one refers to breach of contract. At issue is not the contract breached, but the breach caused if not committed by contract, that is, the breach effected by the exacting terms of a social contract that would suspend further contractions of the social.

Reconciliation would thus rather involve the question of how a community deals with traumatic breaches that suspend the political contractions of its sociality. It would involve the question of how a society returns to in-tensionality after a disastrous slip into intentionality. One would think that some deliberative restoration of, or a return to, sociality would be a prerequisite for reconciliation. One would think that this deliberative restoration or return would capture the 'essence' of reconciliation, but 'essence' and 'deliberate' are again very tense and perhaps just too intentional notions to be helpful here. They smack of intensifications that are bound to repeat and perpetuate the traumatic breaches of sociality that suspend the contractions of sociality. There are indeed those who conceive of reconciliation and the return of sociality by way of very essentialist and intentional notions of reconciliation. They will be introduced in section 1.5. The argument will be that these essentialist conceptions of reconciliation in their own way constitute resistances to reconciliation. However, let us first take a closer look at the phenomena of resistance and reconciliation themselves.

---

21 Derrida *Le toucher, Jean-Luc Nancy* (n 10) 79.

1.3 Resistance and reconciliation

Freud and Nancy enable one to trace the shifts from sexualisations to eroticisations of the political and the social. These shifts would in a way always involve a move from politics, understood in terms of an 'irregularly' or 'exceptionally' monopolised social sexuality, dominated by a father figure, to an understanding of politics in terms of a regular social sexuality that would allow for a plural and dispersed erotic togetherness of sons and lovers and daughters and lovers. This is the move from a (Hobbesian) *social contract*, which institutes or always *re-institutes* the father (as Fitzpatrick points out so well)[22] and thus establishes the truth or blueprint of an operative community, to *social contractions* that constantly displace and subvert this truth or blueprint. We know from Freud that the social *contract* comes back to haunt sociality by means of a system of regulated sexuality that re-institutes the taboos of the father in some lesser form. It is, however, not these lesser returns of the taboo and the contract that concern Nancy in *La communauté desoeuvrée*. What bothers Nancy is, in fact, the return of a monopolised sexuality that re-institutes the taboo of a shared sexuality or shared corporality (*corporalité partagée*, to invoke here in one phrase the two concerns of *partage* and *corpus* so central to Nancy's thought) in an absolute way. It is, however, not with reference to Freud but with reference to Bataille that he addresses this re-institution of sexual monopoly.

At issue in *La communauté disoeuvrée* is again a contract, but this time the contract does not institute or re-institute the father. Or let us say that it does not re-institute the father *as directly* or *as evidently* as in the case of Freud's analysis, for the father may very well still be the ominous background here too. At issue is the suicide pact between lovers, the pact through which lovers consummate their desire to exclude all others effectively and eternally, and unite absolutely in death.[23] At issue in this pact, argues Nancy, is the desire for a return to a sexual and social immanence that would finally eradicate the exteriority of the erotic, the exposure to the irreducible risk of otherness and others, without which the choice of two (or more) to *come together* and *stay together* simply loses its existential, if not breathtaking, quality.

It is against the background of the two concepts of the social, social contract and social contraction, and the concomitant notions of monopolised sexuality (which is at most marginally erotic) and the dispersed plurality of the erotic (i.e., to be sure, never entirely free from the pull of the sexual) that I shall endeavour to explain the relation between, and move from, resistance to reconciliation in what follows. In doing so, I shall have to adjust another setting in the essay 'Psyche and sacrifice'. In that essay I related reconciliation directly to the erotic contractions of love that can never be captured as, or in terms of, a fixed presence. I consequently explained reconciliation in terms of the interminable movement of a *never fully reconciled* sociality. In other words, I equated reconciliation, albeit incomplete reconciliation, with sociality. Following the suggestions made during the third workshop on Time and Reconciliation mentioned above,[24] I shall in what follows restrict the meaning of reconciliation to that which is

22 Peter Fitzpatrick *Modernism and the grounds of law* (2000) 25.

23 Nancy *La Communauté disoeuvrée* (n 12) 36–37.

24 See (n 3) above.

required to restore sociality in the wake of severe disruptions of sociality. I shall retain the idea that sociality is never *fully* reconciled. But this incompleteness of social reconciliation should not be confused with the interminable contractions (and relaxations) of the social that constitutes a regular sociality. The incompleteness of reconciliation should not be confused with the indefinite deferral of a fully contracted society, that is, with the indefinite deferral of a fixed social contract that would finally terminate or at least suppress or frustrate social contractions. No, the rather fortunate prevalence of regular social contractions and the indefinite deferral of a social contract would be indicative of a quite fully reconciled sociality. Would that that had been all that had to be contended with! However, the incompleteness of reconciliation, the interminable returns of a real, distinctive and acute need for reconciliation, relate to something else. The incompleteness of reconciliation relates much rather to the fact that traumatic disruptions of sociality by a patriarchal social contract, *invariably in view of some distinct identification of the enemy of the social*, remain a real possibility or potential of sociality that has all too often materialised in the history of humanity and can be expected to materialise all too often still in the future of humanity.

To invoke again the two concepts of the political outlined in section 1.2, the incompleteness of reconciliation and the interminable need for reconciliation relate to the undeniable social fact that the Schmittian political moment, which is, as argued above, always part and parcel of sociality, always also threatens to disrupt sociality by suppressing and displacing the Arendtian political moment. The disastrous return of the social contract, which is invariably a patriarchal social contract, invariably relates to a displacement of the Arendtian by the Schmittian concept of the political. The move from resistance to reconciliation must therefore be understood to inhere in the return from contract to contraction, the return from a patriarchal disruption of sociality in which the Schmittian concept of the political plays the exclusive or at least all too dominant role, to a restored sociality in which the Schmittian political takes its place alongside the Arendtian.[25]

Adjusting the setting of the move from resistance to reconciliation concerns a certain reduction of the abyssal nature of the Schmittian political moment invoked in the introduction above. However, it does not reduce the politics of sociality to a mere play of platitudes. The plateau of regular politics can and should never lose sight of its abyssal edges. When it figures as part and parcel of sociality and not as the disastrous displacement and disruption of sociality, the Schmittian political moment retains and must retain a vertiginous quality that sustains the exhilaration and thus also the energy of the politics of sociality. The politics of sociality would lose its political quality should it preclude completely a certain brinkmanship and a certain approach to or approximation of the *brink*. It thus always retains an abyssal element. It retains a real sense of the abyss, the abyss that can always precipitate an entirely different politics (and an entirely indifferent politics at that), an entirely Schmittian politics in which Arendt no longer has any say. It is this real sense of the abyss, this real sense of vertigo, that

25 This allusion to Schmitt and Arendt as the father and the mother of the politics of sociality is rather coy, but not all that far-fetched.

ultimately keeps the politics of sociality from going *over the brink*. It knows the abyss is no place to go. The abyss is a *non-place*. The politics of sociality does not go there. The politics of sociality is not devoid of utopian dreams, but again, it does not go there. It at most approaches and approximates utopian dreams and it does so acutely aware of the precarious nature of this very approach and approximation.

Resetting the move from resistance to reconciliation in this way thus allows one to come to terms with the irreducible abyssal span of this move, an abyssal span that was correctly found lacking in the concept of reconciliation expounded in 'Psyche and sacrifice'. Going *over* the brink concerns a first *resistance*. It concerns the disastrous resistance of the extreme brinkmanship that is prepared to take, and does take leave of the politics of sociality. From thereon it is not turtles,[26] but resistances all the way down, spiralling into the gaping voids of the abyss, resistances provoked by and, in turn, aggravating the first resistance (if one can at all talk about 'a first' resistance, to invoke Fitzpatrick again). Resistance is another name for the abyss. Resistances are the voids of the abyss in which the politics of sociality can only fail to find footholds. Hence the abyssal span of reconciliation. It is a matter of returning to sociality from where such return is quite impossible.

What is resistance? What is this intensive and ultimately intentional void where sociality finds no foothold? What is this anti-social thing that is capable of such catastrophic disruptions of the social?[27] Psychoanalysis informs us of a whole range of resistances evident in the process of therapy. There is the resistance of the patient to the analyst. There is the resistance of the analyst to the resistance of the patient. There was a time when Freud believed that the responsibility of the analyst stopped with the finding and offering of a meaning of the pathology or the dream. Then it was up to the patient to accept the meaning and be healed or relieved by it. Only later did he realise that the responsibility of the analyst also extended to overcoming the resistance of the patient itself.

But then there is the more fundamental or deeper resistance of the pathology or the dream to analysis. Freud distinguishes between two kinds of resistance. There is the temporary resistance that can increasingly, if incrementally, be outflanked by the analyst. Then there is the impenetrable, insurmountable and thus interminable resistance to all analyses of the navel or *Nabel* of the dream, the *omphalos*. Freud refers in this regard to an absolute limit of knowledge, *der Unerkannte* that cannot be gauged. *Unergründlich*, he calls it. But the navel at issue here also involves a knot (*un noeud*) that is also a cloudy matter (*un nouage*). It is thus a cloudy knot that ties up the umbilical cord. Derrida emphasises this cloudy knot, in contrast with Lacan who puts more emphasis on the hole or opening or gap (*le trou or la béance*) of the navel that is closed or tied up by the knot.[28]

---

26 Frank Michelman 'Constitutional authorship, "Solomonic solutions" and the unoriginalist mode of constitutional interpretation', in Paul Bradfield and Derek van der Merwe (eds) *'Meaning' in legal interpretation* (1998) 216.

27 See also Johan van der Walt 'Interrupting the Myth of the Partage: Reflections on Sovreignty and Sacrifice in the work of Nancy, Agamben and Derrida' (2005) 16 *Law and critique* 277

28 Jacques Derrida *Résistances* (1996) 23–24.

At issue then is that which forever eludes the analysis of the dream, a knot that cannot be untied.[29] Every dream, says Freud, has such a dark place that is unfathomable, *unergründlich*,[30] a place that one must leave in the dark (*den man im Dunkel lassen muss*), a place where analysis must stop (*le lieu même où l'analyse doits' arrêter*).[31] Derrida stresses the responsibility of law, politics and ethics to take into account psychoanalytic knowledge.[32] I would suggest that it is this very limit of psychoanalysis or psychoanalytic knowledge that he wants law, politics and ethics to take into account; this unfathomable desire of the dream. The rupturing and disrupting knot in the umbilical cord that ties up the very navel of the dream is also the precipice beyond which the politics of sociality will no longer enjoy the footholds from where it can kick in and pull itself up from the gaping abyss, should it decide to venture there. At issue in any attempt to venture there is nothing but the desire to return completely to the origin of the self, the desire to return completely to the complete unity or oneness of the self.

At issue is indeed a Schmittian sovereignty severed from the Arendtian concern with plurality. At issue is a Schmittian sovereignty severed even from its own fleeting experience of plurality, its momentary engagement with an other, albeit a hostile other, *facing* the self. At issue is a Schmittian sovereignty stripped of the last and least Levinasian encounter with the face of the other that even Schmitt's own analysis of the political could not avoid fully. Schmitt had to traverse the face of the enemy before he could invoke the unity of the political subject or agent. It is the friend who keeps the self from sinking into his own abyss, proclaims Zarathustra,[33] but the encounter with the enemy may well be the very last opportunity for the self not to venture into its own nothingness. It is not without reason that Zarathustra wanted the friend to be able to be an enemy.[34] When sociality runs into real crisis, the enemy may well turn out to offer the last opportunity for a friendship that could save the self from drinking madly from its own heart.

How to return from the madness at the heart of the dream, having once ventured there? How to find foothold again in the sanity of sociality when the madness of the dream is too dark for even psychoanalysis to illuminate, when even psychoanalysis must leave it in the dark? This is the abyssal span of the question of reconciliation that any discourse on reconciliation must address. At issue is the forgiving of, or at least the reconciliation with, the unforgivable that Derrida invokes in *Cosmopolitanism and forgiveness*.[35] At issue is also an impossible rest of time that begins after the time is already up, of which *Donner le temps* makes mention.[36] At issue is a radical concept of

---

29 *Idem*. 24 'Or ce qui à jamais excède ici l'analyse du rêve, c'est bien un noeud qu'on ne peut délier, un fil, qui, pour être coupe, comme un cordon ombilical, n'est reste pas moins à jamais noué, á même le corps, à la place du nombril.'

30 Ibid.

31 Ibid.

32 Jacques Derrida *États d'âme de la psychoanalyse* (2000) 78.

33 Friedrich Wilhelm Nietzsche *Also sprach Zarathustra in Kritische Studienausgabe 3* (1999) 71: 'Ich und Mich sind immer zu eifrig im Gespräche: wie wäre es auszuschalten, wenn es nicht einen Freund gäbe? Immer ist für den Einsiedler der Freund der Dritte: der Dritte ist der Kork, der verhindert, dass das Gespräch der Zweie in die Tiefe sinkt.'

34 *Idem* 72: 'In seinem Freunde soll man seinen besten Feind haben'.

35 Jacques Derrida *Cosmopolitanism and forgiveness* (2001).

36 Jacques Derrida *Donner le temps 1. La fausse monnaie* (1991) 11–15.

grace of a non-sovereign god that would come to save us from the abyss *and* not save us from the abyss invoked in *Voyous*,[37] the grace of the non-sovereign god who would save us only *incompletely* from the abyss, since any notion of a complete salvation would merely restore or re-instate the mad dream from which we have to be saved. The return to a regular sociality after traumatic disruptions of sociality concerns an inexplicable graciousness that simply befalls us, a graciousness that nourishes, and is nourished by, an awareness of how easy it is to fall back into the madness from which we have come.

1.4 The time of reconciliation

This, then, is the time of reconciliation in the wake of traumatic disruptions of sociality: it is the time marked by a grateful and gracious acknowledgement of mortals that their time has actually already been up, that it is still up and will always have been up, but that they are inexplicably saved for this impossible while, incompletely saved for a while that is not guaranteed to last. It is a time marked by a Heideggerian 'whiling' or lingering (*Verweilen*) with fellow mortals and the things that call forth the world of mortals, the fourfold engagement of gods and mortals, and heaven and earth without which no sociality can ever be conceived, not to mention restored.[38] It is also a time of charity, suggests Derrida.

1.5 Resistance and reconciliation in post-apartheid South Africa

One would expect an investigation into the time of reconciliation in post-apartheid South Africa to deal extensively with the proceedings of the Truth and Reconciliation Commission. This is not the case in what follows. I shall deal only marginally with the Truth and Reconciliation Commission (TRC), and to the extent that I do so, will express some serious doubts about the religious, clerical and moralistic identity given to these proceedings by especially its president, Bishop Desmond Tutu. I nevertheless wish to make clear that neither the merely marginal engagement nor the criticism expressed in the course of this engagement should be understood as a denial of the important, if not indispensable, work done by the Commission and the invaluable role played by Bishop Tutu in this process.

The reason for dealing merely marginally with the TRC can be explained as follows: the activities of the commission can for all practical purposes be said to have come to an end. The process of reconciliation required for long-term peace and stability in South Africa is something that largely still lies ahead. The TRC proceedings occasioned real instances of personal reconciliation between victims and perpetrators of human rights violations that took place during the apartheid years. The undeniable and unfathom-

---

37 Jacques Derrida *Voyous* (2003) 160–161.

38 Martin Heidegger *Vorträge und Aufsätze* (1985) 165–166, 173. Heidegger's meditations on 'dwelling' and 'the fourfold' are further explored by Wessel le Roux in chapter three of this collection as part of his attempt to distinguish between 'buildings' and 'dwellings' as spatial metaphors.

able moral significance of these instances of personal reconciliation cannot be stressed enough. The public record of these human rights violations and of the instances of personal reconciliation between victims and perpetrators embodied in the TRC Report and in works such as Antjie Krog's *Country of my skull,*[39] may also eventually turn out to be of immense significance as regards the development of a credible and persuasive symbolism of reconciliation in a future South Africa. However, it would be naïve to assume that these relatively rare and isolated instances of personal reconciliation and the public record of these instances translate directly into the broader event of national or social reconciliation on which peace and stability in a future South Africa would come to turn. To rephrase in terms of the concepts thus far developed in this chapter: the proceedings and public records of proceedings of the TRC are not as such indicative of a restored sociality in post-apartheid South Africa. Hence the emphasis in what follows on the factors that quite obviously will affect the process of reconciliation or the restoration of sociality in post-apartheid South Africa much more fundamentally than the history and historical records of personal reconciliation occasioned by the TRC, factors that can, in fact, easily undo the significance of this history and historical records.

The mistaken assumption that the instances of personal reconciliation between victims and perpetrators of human rights violations occasioned by the TRC proceedings somehow translate into a broader event of national reconciliation, constitutes in itself a first factor that may come to undo the future significance of the TRC's work. This is not only so because the assumption would induce a complacency about the huge responsibility regarding reconciliation that still lies ahead. It is also so because the discourses of personal or individual and religious morality through which one makes sense of instances of successful or unsuccessful personal reconciliation all too easily translate into an offensive moralism when they are transposed into a discourse of national reconciliation; not that is, when it becomes a discourse that is also meant to apply to individuals and groups of people who were not directly or personally involved in traumatic violations of human rights. Hence the criticism expressed below regarding the *moralistic or clerical understanding* of social or national reconciliation that was quite evident in the rhetoric of the TRC. This moralistic and clerical rhetoric, I shall argue, itself constitutes a certain sovereign resistance to the restoration of a regular sociality in South Africa, a sovereign resistance that is bound to provoke further sovereign resistances.

The second factor that significantly affects the process of reconciliation in a future South Africa is the still all too evident division of rich and poor along racial lines. The symbolic significance of the TRC proceedings will eventually be reduced to an empty and offensive myth if the process of reconciliation cannot be seen to translate – perhaps slowly but at least surely – into a socio-economic reconstruction of South African society; a reconstruction that increasingly erases the racial basis of the division between rich and poor, if not the division between rich and poor as such, hence the critical analysis of the *mercantile resistance* to reconciliation below.[40]

---

39 Antjie Krog *Country of my skull* (1998).

40 Derrida (n 35) 14.

The third and fourth factors that may well come to undo the future significance of the TRC's activities is the political desire for cultural and/or ethnic autonomy, if not sovereignty, on the one hand, and the resistance to this desire in the name of the ideal of non-ethnicity in a unitary South Africa endorsed by the African National Congress (ANC) government, on the other. The desire for cultural autonomy is especially evident among the Zulu people and Afrikaans-speaking whites. In what follows, I look specifically at recent developments relating to the aspirations of cultural autonomy of the Afrikaner people.

1.5.1 Reactionary and non-reactionary mercantilism

Apparently the most innocent or least threatening resistance to a new sociality in South Africa is the withdrawal of the European or white population into a materialist privacy that has no, or very little, concern with, and interest in, the political process of restoring a regular sociality in all walks of life in post-apartheid South Africa. This would seem to be a purely economic reaction to post-apartheid South Africa, one that appears to have no connection with the intensification that occasions the political or the moment of Schmittian sovereignty. However, to the extent that this withdrawal into a materialist private life or the resort to the pursuit of private wealth is marked by an element of *reaction* to or a *reactionary deliberation* regarding the post-apartheid political dispensation, it is certainly not a purely economic phenomenon. The element of *reaction* marks this withdrawal into privacy as a political act, albeit a negative or inversed political act. There is a moment of sovereignty involved in the *decision* to withdraw from politics, one that may well be markedly more disdainful of the 'enemy' than the decision to engage with him or her in battle.

This is the politics of avoiding politics, the politics of avoiding the political exposure to the other. It certainly qualifies as one of the major modes of resistance to the politics of reconciliation in South Africa. Although this mode of resistance would appear less destructive than the acts of hostility that may ultimately mark Schmittian sovereignty, it can certainly be argued to contribute most insidiously to the fact that South Africa is still a racially divided country; not that is, to the fact that reconciliation has largely remained a matter of clerical or moralistic rhetoric that can hardly be backed up with hard social facts. But even if this materialist pursuit of private wealth had not been marked with a reactionary deliberation, even if it had been a simple continuation of a 'purely' mercantile life style, one would still have had to be as wary of equating it with the grateful and gracious whiling or lingering with things and fellow mortals invoked above as a precondition for the restoration of sociality. The apparent whiling or lingering with things of the apolitical mercantilist all too often regresses into the self-centered consumerism of the wealthy. It all too often regresses into a lack of real respect for and concern with anyone who does not match their formidable buying power.

However, it is not the subjective morality or 'lack of morality' of the apolitical mercantilist that is of concern as far as the question of reconciliation is concerned. A serious concern with reconciliation would want all people involved in the restoration of a regular sociality in the wake of social trauma to do as they themselves see fit. It will become even clearer below that reconciliation had best not be approached by means of some or other prescriptive blueprint. The problem is nevertheless that the lack of social care and concern, concomitant with apolitical mercantilism, all too tangibly translates into a solidification of existing socio-economic divisions. This is especially the case when apolitical mercantilism features prominently in the wake of traumatic disruptions of sociality. Such a solidification of existing socio-economic divisions may well latently thwart the reconciliation process in ways that may come to light only many years down the line. This solidification can be said to constitute a slow version of intensification that simply takes a longer time to come to a head. Recent events in Zimbabwe cannot, for instance, not be reduced to the undeniable political opportunism of a reckless dictator running amok. They also reveal to what extent the socio-economic divisions of colonial Zimbabwe have managed to survive the transition to majority rule and keep Zimbabwe a racially, deeply divided country.[41] When a liberation struggle turned into civil war, as in the case of Zimbabwe, or barely avoided doing so, as in the case of South Africa, every life spared should all the more be aware of an impossible extra time granted for the time being. This radical and thankful sense of mortality should bring home the insight that one does not play around with a second chance as if nothing is, or ever was, at stake. This does not apply only to the former oppressors. It applies also, as will become clear below, to the liberators. Another outbreak of hostilities is bound to claim more lives and limbs on both sides. Both sides should therefore share in an acute sense of having been spared thus far and be wary of unnecessarily running the risk of further hostilities. But as far as the entrenchment of pre-liberation socio-economic divisions is concerned, it is mostly the former oppressors and the beneficiaries of oppression who run the risk of inviting another round of traumatic social unrest and upheaval and possibly even civil war.[42]

1.5.2 Religious or clerical moralism

The clerical and moralistic response to the social trauma of apartheid and to the question as to what would be required to restore sociality in post-apartheid South Africa, constitutes the second mode of resistance to reconciliation that I wish to examine. Clerical and moralistic rhetoric has indeed been a major resort among white South Africans in trying to come to terms with a sense of guilt regarding the role they played in the history of apartheid.[43] The guilt at issue here relates to the fact that the National Party (NP) government, which institutionalised apartheid, enjoyed consistent support from the majority of the exclusively white electorate over more than four decades, and

---

41 The tension between 'symbolic reconciliation' and 'socio-economic reconstruction' is further explored by Karin van Marle in chapter two of this collection. Henk Botha also takes up this distinction in chapter five, where he introduces a contrast between 'moral' and 'political' (or material) concepts of equality.

42 See in this regard the arguments regarding the role of 'free market economies' and ethnic strife in formerly oppressed societies, in Amy Chua 'The privatization-nationalization cycle: The link between markets and ethnicity in developing countries' (1995) 95 *Columbia LR* 223–303; and Amy Chua *World on fire:: How exporting free market democracy breeds ethnic hatred and global instability* (2004), especially 127–175.

43 Epitomised by Charles Villa-Vicencio publicly bursting into tears during the Conference on Racism in Sandton in 2000.

to the fact that even those who were opposed to apartheid and did not support the NP, did far too little to resist apartheid effectively. Clerical and moralistic rhetoric has, unfortunately, also been a salient feature of the proceedings of the TRC. To the extent that this rhetoric invoked and still invokes the necessity of some deep and specifically Christian moral catharsis for the restoration of a normal society in post-apartheid South Africa, it too seems to insist on some *exceptional moment* or *moment of truth* in the history of South Africa with regard to which some or other specific action, response or even decision needs to be taken. Something specific, something expressly moral and markedly religious must be done to eradicate and absolve South Africans from the scourge of apartheid. The end of apartheid would come about through an exceptional moment of political theology or theological politics. A Christian doctrine of repentance and forgiveness would *unite* black and white South Africa against the enemy of racism. All the elements of a Schmittian doctrine of sovereignty are evident here. Derrida writes in this regard:

> [W]hen Desmond Tutu was named president of the Truth and Reconciliation Commission, he christianised the language of an institution uniquely destined to treat 'politically' motivated crimes ... With as much good will as confusion, it seems to me, Tutu, an Anglican archbishop, introduced the vocabulary of repentance and forgiveness. He was reproached for this, amongst other things, by a non-Christian segment of the black community.[44]

The confusion to which Derrida refers here, relates to his strict analysis of what pure forgiveness would mean. Tutu, argues Derrida, brought the notion of forgiveness to bear in the context of an institutional project of national reconciliation in South Africa. This is precisely what forgiveness cannot be. Reconciliation may be a laudable and indispensable goal to pursue for purposes of peace and stability, but it must not be confused with forgiveness. Forgiveness cannot be aimed at the achievement of some goal. It is not part of an instrumental economy. One does not forgive in order to achieve something. One simply forgives. This forgiveness, moreover, constitutes an aporia, since strictly speaking, one can only forgive the absolutely unforgivable. If one only forgives what can be forgiven, one does not forgive and is not even required to forgive. If one would only forgive those who repent, those who through repentance transform themselves into forgivable persons, there would be nothing and no one to forgive.[45] Tutu's confusion relates not only to the instrumentalisation of forgiveness. It relates also to the Christian linking of forgiveness to the condition of repentance.

Now, it is hardly possible, if not simply impossible, to imagine a victim of a serious and intentional human rights violation or any other significant wrong, *personally forgiving* the perpetrator without the latter repenting and asking for forgiveness. Anyone who has experienced having been wronged knows all too well the hard or tight knot or nut of resistance to forgiveness and reconciliation that besieges the traumatised mind. This nut may very well be almond shaped. It may well relate to the *amygdala*, the

---

44 Derrida (n 35) 42. Further substantiation for this christianisation: Piet Meiring 'The Baruti vs the lawyers', in Charles Villa-Vicencio and Wilhelm Verwoerd (eds) *Looking back, reaching forward* (2000); TRC Report I 108; Desmond Tutu *No future without forgiveness* (1999); Donald Shriver *Forgiveness in politics: An ethics for enemies* (1995).

45 Derrida (n 35) 38–39.

little crude control room responsible for processing our fears at the basis of the cortex of the brain.[46] It appears that this nut will simply not crack without the assistance of a recognition and acknowledgment by the perpetrator of the wrong that he or she has inflicted. One might say that the acknowledgment of the wrong pulls its teeth. The acknowledgement of the wrong would seem to make it less repeatable and therefore less fearful. The acknowledgement of the wrong somehow helps to loosen the knot, somehow helps to crack the nut. The relation between fear and the inability to forgive in the absence of a degree of repentance, needs to be examined more fully than can be done here. But if this relation concerns an economy, as Derrida would seem to insist, it is an economy so incircumventible and inevitable that it would be pointless to dismiss it simply as irreconcilable with real forgiveness. Derrida's acute analysis of the concept of forgiveness may therefore simply be too strict to allow for a significant ethical point regarding forgiveness on a personal level. But it embodies a most significant suggestion regarding the nature of social or national reconciliation and 'forgiveness', and it is this suggestion that I wish to elaborate on in what follows. The suggestion at issue speaks most clearly from a contemplation of hospitality in *Voyous*. At issue in the contemplation is the gift of forgiveness, the *don* of the *pardon*. The gift of forgiveness takes place beyond the exacting demand for a transforming repentance. It also takes place beyond the demand for amnesia; the demand that the past simply be forgotten. It does not turn on the economic contractual terms of amnesty. Derrida writes:

> Similar [to the gift], it is only beyond calculation that forgiveness would know how to arrive at and from the other, beyond any excuse, amnesia, amnesty, acquitment or prescription, beyond even the demand to be pardoned and thus beyond transformative repentance, which is most often made the condition for forgiveness, at least in that which dominates the tradition of the abrahamic religions.[47]

The passage states that the gift of forgiveness would not require a transforming repentance. I shall stress the adjective 'transforming' or 'transformative' (*transformateur*) as we proceed. Let one, nevertheless, begin to reflect on this passage by inferring that forgiveness would involve a certain graciousness. One could also say that it would involve a certain magnanimity. It would thus perhaps simply consist in the opposite of a smallness or small mindedness. One could say, going very fast, that forgiveness would consist in the small almond-shaped and fearful part of the brain *not taking control* in the wake of trauma as it is bound to do. Forgiveness would consist in a larger, more extensive (remember Nancy's Psyche?) and courageous consideration of the issues at stake when forgiveness becomes a question. It would courageously consider a plurality of factors, if not simply the factor of plurality, the factor of more than one still needing or hoping to coexist. It would consist in opening up again *to* the Arendtian moment of the political after an unforgivable and fearfully unforgiving withdrawal from it.

---

46 William Connolly *Why I am not a secularist* (1999) 28–29. I am indebted to Peter Fitzpatrick for this reference. See also Michael Ondaatje *Anil's ghost* (2001) 134–135.

47 Translated from Derrida (n 37) 205: 'De même un pardon ne saurait arriver à l'autre ou *de* l'autre qu'au-delà du calcul, au- delà de l'excuse, de l'amnésie, de l'amnistie, de l'acquittement ou de la prescription, au-delà même de la demande de pardon, donc au-delà du repentir transformateur, don't on fait le plus souvent la condition, du moins dans ce qui *domine* la tradition des religions abrahamatiques.'

The failure to forgive would consist in the persistence of the withdrawal from the concern with plurality. It would consist in the insistent nut- or knot-like tightening around the self of the Schmittian move towards sovereign unity. It would reflect an *essential* return to unity or the closing-in of and on the self at the expense of otherness and plurality. The insistence that the other repentantly transform himself or herself would at most be a slightly more oblique version of the same movement. This insistence cannot but betray the pluralist concern with an other that is truly an other, an other that is not required to transform in accordance with requirements of forgiveness imposed on the other by the self.[48]

There is thus a clear Schmittian moment of political intensification evident in the clerical and moralistic reaction to apartheid, a Schmittian moment that can easily be seen to detach itself from the Arendtian concern with plurality. This detachment from plurality consists in two things. It consists, firstly, in the insistence on the Christian mode of forgiveness as the one and only recipe for reconciliation, the insistence that everyone in post-apartheid South Africa unite in a Christian understanding of reconciliation. The dynamics of this unity would consist in a 'transforming repentance and forgiveness' that reduces everyone involved to sameness or oneness. Intent as this Christian understanding of reconciliation is on considerations of personal salvation and personal absolution from guilt, it, secondly, all too readily also offers an exit from the political as an encounter and engagement with others. It opens the door for a reduction of social reconciliation to the simplistic missionary spreading of the elementary good news that South African society could be healed if only whites would repent and blacks would forgive, good news that all too easily gives rise to the complacent attitude that one has done one's bit of repentance and can now carry on with one's own life.

The clerical and moralist resistance to reconciliation can predictably provoke further resistances to reconciliation. Two forms of resistance are especially foreseeable: resistance from blacks to the substantive emptiness of clerical and moralist discourses as far as social justice is concerned, and resistance from whites to the clerical and moralist call to accept and acknowledge guilt that they do not experience. The good news of repentance and forgiveness cannot but soon appear to be rather shallow or empty, when it becomes evident that repenting whites otherwise get to carry on with their affluent lifestyles and forgiving blacks continue to live in relative poverty if not outright squalor – as if transition and reconciliation required no more than the good emotions or *intentions* concomitant to repenting and forgiving. One would simply be naive to believe that the proceedings of the TRC made a significant difference to the way South Africans live in post-apartheid South Africa. It could not have made a huge difference to millions of blacks (many of them non-Christians at that) as regards their frustrations with the crippling poverty from which they simply cannot escape on their own strengths alone. It certainly did not make a huge difference to the lack of active engagement among whites as regards socio-economic reconstruction, a lack of engagement that can only aggravate

48 Compare the brilliant engagement with this question of the sameness required for understanding, forgiveness and reconciliation in Bernard Schlink's short story '*Die Beschneidung*' in *Liebesfluchten* (2000).

black resistance to the 'good news' that black and white South Africa have been, or can become, reconciled through repentance and forgiveness.

The insistence of moralist discourses on confessionary admissions of guilt and repentance as a precondition for reconciliation, is, on the other hand, bound to provoke resistance to reconciliation from whites who committed crimes and violated rights in the name of an ideology that they served in good, albeit disastrously shortsighted, faith. It is bound to invite even more resistance from those whites who benefited from, but never actively or personally committed, the crimes and violations of rights of the erstwhile system of oppression.

All these predictable reactions to the clerical or moralist discourse of reconciliation – the exit from the political through quick and easy repentance, negativity regarding the demand for moral repentance when no guilt is experienced, and the resistance to the substantive emptiness of moralist discourses as far as social justice is concerned – reflect withdrawals from the engagement with others and otherness, withdrawals from the engagement with those with whom peaceful co-existence must be pursued in the wake of social trauma. One should therefore be extremely wary of moralist discourses that induce or provoke these withdrawals. One should be extremely careful not to confuse reconciliation with articulations of a new moral order that exact repentance and forgiveness. Doing this runs the significant risk of simply repeating or perpetuating existing social tensions and divisions, either through all too easy compliance with, or through resistance to, the new moral order. Reconciliation should much rather be understood in terms of cultivating a *sense of responsibility* on the side of both the former oppressors and the former oppressed, a *sense of responding to the other* from both sides of the social divide. This is, I believe, the suggestion regarding social or national reconciliation that one can draw from Derrida's notion of a hospitality that would require neither transformative repentance from former oppressors, nor amnesia from the former oppressed. Transformative repentance and amnesia both aim at an erasure of the tensions and differences between the oppressor and the oppressed, tensions and differences without which a sense of responsibility experienced as a sense of responding to an other is no longer conceivable. Transformative repentance and amnesia aim at unity, and false unity at that. They destroy in advance the plurality which reconciliation should aim to restore.

The sense of responsibility that is experienced as a response to otherness need not sever the link between forgiving and repentance and the link between forgiving and reconciliation as absolutely as Derrida would seem to require. Reflected in the magnanimous consideration of the factor of plurality and the plurality of factors that constitute forgiveness (according to the reading of the passage on hospitality in *Voyous* elaborated above), would also be a regard for the irreducible need of wronged persons that wrongdoing be acknowledged. But the magnanimous consideration of plurality would also include a regard for the necessity for a courageous decision to let go of the need for such acknowledgment. The magnanimous concern with plurality would thus involve a double regard, a regard for the inevitability of a certain economy of forgiveness and a regard for forgiveness as the very suppression of this economy. This double regard could translate into an allowance for softer or even implicit acknowledgments of guilt and wrongdoing and softer or implicit gestures of forgiveness. This softer or magnanimous approach to reconciliation may well not be appropriate or possible as regards instances of personal reconciliation, but one can easily imagine it to facilitating the bilateral or multilateral relaxations of sovereign resistances to reconciliation needed for national or social reconciliation. The Arendtian moment of the plurality of the political stands a much better chance between the more vague parameters of implicit acknowledgment of wrong and implicit forgiveness. At issue here would be the crucial hospitable move from an exclusive and simplistic social contract to complex and multiple social contractions elaborated above, the crucial hospitable shift from the banality of an explicit and exclusivist patriarchal sexualisation of the social, to the subtlety of a shared social eroticism. Unlike Derrida's pure forgiveness, reconciliation thus conceived would not be devoid of economy, but it would also consist in a conscious and quite feasible suppression of this economy.

The suppression of the economic exchange of repentance and forgiveness at issue in the magnanimous consideration of plurality elaborated above, would imply that the implicit repentance and forgiveness on which it turns, cannot be demanded. Such a demand would again make repentance and forgiveness *explicit* or *exacted* requirements for reconciliation and would thus again reduce reconciliation to the economy that Derrida distinguishes from forgiveness. The responsibility for reconciliation at issue in the magnanimous consideration of plurality, can therefore not be demanded. At issue in the magnanimous consideration of plurality would therefore not be a demand for responsibility, only an *allowance for* responsibility. The implicitness of repentance and forgiveness in the magnanimous consideration of plurality is the very scope of the magnanimity that allows for responsibility.

Allowing for the chance of responsibility or *giving* responsibility a chance certainly risks the chance that responsibility may not materialise. This goes without saying. But the notion of *demanding responsibility* is a contradiction in terms. Responsibility cannot be demanded without destroying the condition of *freedom to respond* on which it turns. The demand for responsibility thus patently poses the greater risk to responsibility and the reconciliation that may ensue from it. This is the aporia of reconciliation. It *requires* but cannot *demand* responsibility.[49]

1.5.3 Cultural politics

Towards the beginning of 2000 a group of Afrikaans-speaking intellectuals and some less intellectual fellow travellers initiated a political movement in South Africa, aimed at the preservation of Afrikaans in the face of what they perceived to be the increasing

49 However, the freedom of responsibility and the freedom to respond to responsibility does not allow for an escape *from* responsibility. One can fail to live up to one's responsibility, but one cannot really deny one's responsibility. Existence as such exposes us to responsibility. I am particularly indebted to Drucilla Cornell for emphasising this Heideggerian and Derridean point in her comments on this chapter. Years ago, to come to terms with this enigmatic dynamics of responsibility, I referred to the *paradox* of responsibility (Johan van der Walt *Twilight of legal subjectivity: Towards a deconstructive republican theory of law* LLD (RAU) (1995)): 'The notion of responding to a responsibility confronts us with a paradox. It clearly involves an element of choice and a complete absence of choice. Responding to a responsibility to which one is called to respond is not the act of a subject. But neither is it simply a matter of being "subject to" a responsibility. To be responsible is a mode of existence that cannot be reduced to either the passive or the active voice.'

marginalisation, if not victimisation, of Afrikaans by the ANC government. The group calls itself and is generally referred to, as the Group of 63. The movement has not yet gained the momentum that would make it a significant role player in the spectrum of South African politics. It is doubtful whether this is bound to happen soon in view of the poor performance of Afrikaner politics in the 2004 elections. The recently established Freedom Front Plus (a consolidation of old-order conservative parties, such as the Conservative Party and the Freedom Front, which resisted the gradual dismantling of apartheid by the NP government), the only party that represented Afrikaner interests as such in the 2004 elections, attracted a negligible percentage of the national vote.[50] The electoral future of the kind of politics pursued by the Group of 63 must therefore be considered to be rather bleak.[51]

It is for reason of their bleak electoral future that the Group of 63's *relation to,* if not *relationship with,* a radical reactionary organisation called the Boeremag must be subjected to scrutiny. Increasing frustration with the electoral process may well eventually give rise to an increase of non-democratic and ultimately unlawful endeavours to achieve political goals, something that can come to have a negative effect on the process of inter-racial reconciliation in South Africa. The goal of the Boeremag is to overthrow the government violently. Towards the end of 2002 members of this movement were responsible for a spate of bomb explosions in the course of which one person, a black woman, was killed. Most of the individuals responsible for the explosions were subse-

---

50 The Freedom Front, to be sure, only presented itself as a political alternative to the National Party in the 1994 elections. It was founded only right at the end of the National Party government by General Constand Viljoen, a former chief of the South African Defence Force. So strictly speaking it was founded too late to actually resist the dismantling of apartheid, but its members can surely be presumed to have formerly belonged predominantly to political groups that resisted the dismantling of apartheid.

51 This leaves one of the arguments that I develop below with a considerable predicament. I take the African National Congress to task in what follows for what I argue to be a simplistic understanding of its laudable and consistent subscription to non-ethnicity and non-racialism in post-apartheid South Africa. The argument is, in short, that the new phase of post-apartheid politics at which we have arrived ten years after the transition, may well require a new understanding of the principles of non-ethnicity and non-racialism, one that would allow for ethnic minorities to enjoy some or other form of self-determination at a local level. But what is the point of this argument, especially as far as Afrikaner politics is concerned, if there is no real political desire evident for such self-determination? The quest for Afrikaner self-determination would at present seem to be hardly more than the pipe dream of a small handful of intellectuals, a dream styled on the examples of minority identity politics in Europe and elsewhere in the world (I leave out of consideration thousands of diehard racists whose resistance to reconciliation in post-apartheid South Africa I consider to be a private and not a political matter – I do not think this private racist resistance has any political potential left). So again, why bother to pay so much attention to this dream in this chapter? For this reason: I believe the dream of Afrikaner sovereignty to be a good example of the ultimately simply existential, and for that reason often a-rational, origins of the political that Schmitt explains so well (Schmitt refers to the 'irrational' in this regard (*Der Begriff des Politischen* (n 6) 39), but I differ from him on this point since the irrational is most often drenched with all sorts of rationalities or rationalisations), such a good example of the psychological resistances that mark the political at its roots, as Derrida might put it. An incisive regard for and understanding of these existential, a-rational and psychological origins of the political is crucial for the process of national reconciliation in post-apartheid South Africa, hence my engagement in what follows with what may well be little more than the last remnants of this existential, a-rational and psychological quest for political sovereignty among Afrikaners in post-apartheid South Africa. The Afrikaners may well be giving up their dark dreams of sovereignty, but the dark dreams of sovereignty are bound to return in unforeseen ways in times to come, perhaps from most 'enlightened' quarters. Sovereignty is after all, as Derrida points out so well (n 60), a matter of an eternal turning and thus of an eternal returning. It is the eternal returns of existential quests for sovereignty that national reconciliation on the basis of a constitutional democracy, in South Africa, but also elsewhere in the world, will always have to contend with.

quently arrested and are currently standing trial on charges of treason. Shortly after the explosions, the Group of 63 organised a march to the government buildings in Pretoria and presented the government with a memorandum that referred to the explosions. In the memorandum the Group of 63 clearly dissociated itself from the unlawful activities of the Boeremag, but nevertheless ventured to proclaim the explosions as indicative of the level of discontent among the Afrikaner people.[52] This stance is evidently not completely devoid of some sympathy with or some understanding of the decision to resort to unlawful means to pursue Afrikaner interests.[53]

The Group of 63 nevertheless takes care not to present itself as a reactionary movement. Many of its members were formerly members of, or closely associated with, political parties that resisted the gradual dismantling of apartheid by the National Party government. The group nevertheless now expressly rejects apartheid and the racist politics that underpinned apartheid. It clearly aims to present itself as *constructively* engaged in the new political dispensation and has expressed sharp criticism of the withdrawal into private and apolitical pursuits of wealth and materialistic domestic bliss so pervasively evident among Afrikaans-speaking South Africans today. The group seem to want to take part actively in the politics of reconciliation in post-apartheid South Africa. The political stance it takes in this regard clearly features markedly communitarian characteristics. The notion of a language community is taken as its point of departure in its communitarian politics. It is this notion of a language community that I wish to examine in what follows. The specific question that I wish to pose in this regard is whether or to what extent this communitarian politics, aimed at promoting and safeguarding the concerns and interests of a specific language community, constitutes another mode of resistance to the restoration of sociality, in the wake of the racist disruption of South African sociality in the course of more than four decades of NP government.

The Derridean stance as regards hospitality beyond amnesia, amnesty and the demand for a transforming repentance elaborated above precludes one from confronting the Group of 63 with facile accusations of forgetfulness. One could so easily ask whether the members have forgotten that Afrikaans and the promotion of Afrikaans were significantly involved and instrumental in the racist politics of apartheid. The Soweto uprisings of 1976, an event that marked the beginning of the critical last phase of the resistance to apartheid, specifically singled out the imposition of Afrikaans as a medium of instruction in schools as the immediate point of grievance. One could so easily ask whether they are unaware that blacks pervasively shared the sentiments of singer Miriam Makeba expressed in the following passage from her biography:

---

52 The Group had the good timing to hand over their letter to the government on the very day that the mother of Mary Mokone, the black woman killed by the bomb explosions, was buried (*The Sowetan* (2002-11-15)). See also the remarkable comment of Andries Bezuidenhout in a letter to *Rapport* (2002-11-17) 26.

53 One must acknowledge the fact that some Afrikaners, to their credit, rejected the lawless acts of the Boeremag unconditionally. See in this regard the report on the press statements of Francois Venter, the chairman of the Afrikaner Bond, by Willem Jordaan in 'Afrikaner-leiers looi groep van 63' *Beeld* (2002-11-15) 5. Some members of the Group itself also criticised the leaders for their actions in this regard. See the letter of Johann Lodewyk Marais to *Beeld* (2002-11-22) 20.

> [T]he Afrikaners spoke Afrikaans, which is a mongrel Dutch with some German. Afrikaans has a guttural and ugly sound. It would later be very effective to use when the authorities ordered native families from our homes or commanded soldiers to fire into unarmed crowds. It is the language of genocide, and, in fact, it sounds like the German the Nazis speak in Hollywood movies.[54]

Again, the Derridean hospitality elaborated above precludes one from asking these questions. Any response to the politics of the Group of 63 that would today voice the sentiments of Makeba expressed above, would fall dismally short of a Derridean hospitality, if such a hospitality were possible. Any insistence that Afrikaans-speaking South Africans articulate a *transforming repentance* would fall dismally short of a Derridean hospitality, if such a hospitality were possible. The facile tearful confession of involvement in, or failure to oppose, sufficiently, the abuses of apartheid on a public platform à la Charles Villa-Vicencio[55] is not what reconciliation requires from Afrikaans-speaking people. I would want to insist, as Frank Michelman in a different but not entirely unrelated context does, that there is no cause for tears here. Reconciliation requires one to think deeper. It requires a contemplation of the tearless thoughts of the more tender heart.[56] A serious concern with reconciliation would not demand from Afrikaans-speaking people to simply and repentantly to transform or suspend their concerns with their own language and culture in order to become equal citizens in post-apartheid South Africa. Reconciliation would not even demand responsibility from Afrikaans-speaking South Africans *vis-à-vis* the political concerns of others, the political concerns of the broader South Africa. As noted above, responsibility cannot be demanded, it can only be granted. A serious concern with reconciliation can only allow for, or give, responsibility in the hope that it will be accepted. It must simply live non-vindictively with the real risk that responsibility may never be accepted.

There are, however, already a number of indications of reluctance or failure on the part of the cultural politics of the Group of 63 to take on a responsibility that exceeds the exclusive concerns with its own affairs. Shortly after its formation the group called on the South African government to impose a moratorium on affirmative action.[57] This was done against the background of an employment market still hugely skewed in favour of whites as a result of more than 40 years of apartheid economics. Shortly after its formation the group announced social-upliftment projects for poor Afrikaners.[58] Never, as far

54 Miriam Makeba *Makeba – my story* (1988) 5.

55 See footnote 43 above.

56 Frank Michelman '*Modus vivendi postmodernus*? On just interpretations and the thinning of justice' (2000) 21 *Cardozo* LR 1945 at 1953; Wiliam Wordsworth: 'Thanks to the human heart by which we live, thanks to its tenderness, its joys and its fears we receive thoughts that do often lie too deep for tears'. From: *Intimations of immortality from recollections of early childhood*, in Harold Bloom and Lionel Trilling (eds) *The Oxford anthology of English literature: Romantic poetry and prose* (1973) 181. See also my comments on Michelman in Johan van der Walt 'Frankly befriending the fundamental contradiction: Frank Michelman and critical legal thought', in Henk Botha et al. (eds) *Rights and democracy in a transformative Constitution* (2004) 213 at 215; 230.

57 'Groep van 63 vra "sonsakklousule" teen diskriminasie' *Beeld* (2000-07-28) 11. Working documents of the group refer simplistically to affirmative action as a new forms of racial discrimination in post-apartheid South Africa. 'Die vraagstuk van die Afrikaanse minderheid. Situasie-dokument van die Groep van 63, November 2000' 7. I am indebted to Etienne van Zyl for the references to this document.

58 Danie Goosen 'Groep wil "tweede fase" van SA se demokratiseringsproses begin' *Beeld* (2000-05-16) 9.

as I can recall, has there been a pronounced call from the circle of Afrikaner politics to use the considerable economic power of Afrikaners towards a reconstruction of South Africa as such and therefore to imaginatively co-operate and compete with, and thus even pressurise government, as far as this reconstruction is concerned.

Once again, those concerned with reconciliation, those consciously mortal South Africans who are aware that the time has already been up, and will for ever have been up for everyone in South Africa, cannot risk jeopardising the impossible or miraculous rest of time left to them by being vindictive with regard to these signs of a failure to come to terms with the responsibility towards, and for, others required by reconciliation. It is much rather the concern with reconciliation itself that has to come to terms with a certain lack of reconciliation. This lack of reconciliation may well be irreducible, hence the thought expressed in 'Psyche and sacrifice': nothing will be reconciled in the time of reconciliation.[59]

The concern with reconciliation nevertheless requires a close examination of the rhetoric of the Afrikaner politics of the Group of 63. The first important point to consider in this regard is the fact that it pursues its concerns with the preservation of the language and culture of Afrikaners against the background of well-entrenched constitutional guarantees relating to the linguistic and cultural concerns of minority groups in South Africa. However, thus far the group has been reluctant to attach much significance to this constitutional protection. One reason for this could well be a rather crude conviction that the Constitutional Court and the juridical system will simply toe the executive and legislative line of the ANC when it comes to the constitutional review of acts of parliament and government that affect Afrikaner interests negatively.[60] However, probably much more significant in this regard is the sentiment that a concern with the merely juridical safeguards of cultural concerns already evinces a co-optation into a liberal political order that leaves little room for, or at least does not really address, the communitarian concerns of the groups' politics. The constitutional protection of cultural and language rights would reduce these concerns to the incidental interests of

59 Van der Walt 'Psyche and sacrifice' (n 1) 651.

60 See Buys 'Omskep grondregtelike regte in praktyk' *Rapport* (2003-08-17) 16 for one of the crudest articulations one can read in this regard: 'Die Grondwet regeer immers nie die land nie, maar die ANC as politieke party, wat ná die reuse-politieke magsverskuiwing in die praktyk feitlik eiehandig nasionale wetgewing maak om só inhoud aan die grondwetlike raamwerk te gee – wetgewing wat die politieke magsverhouding weerspieël. Daarna pas die getransformeerde staatsadministrasie die wetgewing toe en bestuur die land volgens die regerende party se beleidsrigtings en -vertolking. *Dit word gerugsteun deur 'n konstitusionele hof wat, hoewel onafhanklik, hoogs waarskynlik die ANC se vertolking van sleutelwette sal steun*.' (The Constitution does after all not govern the country, but the ANC as political party, which after the gigantic shift of power in practice drafts and enacts national legislation virtually unilaterally and thus gives contents to the constitutional framework – legislation that reflects the political power relations [in South Africa]. Thereafter the transformed state administration applies the legislation and manages the country according to the governing party's policy frameworks and interpretation. *This process is then supported by a constitutional court that, although independent, will very probably support the ANC's interpretation of key legislation*.') [Emphasis added]. Buys is the executive head of the labour union Solidariteit. See my attempt to counteract this simplistic view of the Constitutional Court's jurisprudence in Johan van der Walt 'Afrikaners moenie wonderwerke van konstitusionele hof verwag' *Rapport* (2003-08-24) 16 (arguing that Buys's view appears to be oblivious to at least two cases recently decided at the time of Buys's comments, in which the Constitutional Court held government policy to be unconstitutional). In response to my article several letters to Rapport reiterated the view that the Constitutional Court would not adjudicate matters of Afrikaner interest fairly and neutrally. See the letters of Buys himself and of DA Cilliers in *Rapport* (2003-08-31) 25 and of Dan Roodt in *Rapport* (2003-09-14) 21.

dispersed individuals who have no distinct political identity, irrespective of whether a group of individuals would be involved in the pursuit of these rights. The communitarian concern with cultural and linguistic rights would for this reason have to express and found itself through political action that exceeds the mere protection of rights through juridical means. At issue, in other words, would thus have to be localised political action that resists the reduction of cultural differences to the legal interests of some individuals in the quaint aesthetic remnants of erstwhile communities. At issue would have to be a return to some political identity that exceeds the merely incidental cultural concerns of some individuals in the ultimately cosmopolitan melting pot of a centralised state.

At issue then, if the above analysis of the reluctance of the Group of 63 simply to pursue its concerns through available juridical means is correct, would be a concern with a cultural foundation that would found a politics that would, in turn, found or re-found its own cultural foundation. Following Derrida and Nancy, one could say that this turning or returning to itself or turning around itself, this turning around its own foundations and origin, constitutes the essence of sovereignty.[61] But this could well be moving too fast. At issue is nevertheless at least a Schmittian political intensification that moves towards the brink of sovereignty. The shadow of a dark dream is certainly raising its head here. However, this shadow should not as such be dismissed as irreconcilable with the reconciliation that one might hope for in post-apartheid South Africa. Depriving the political of its shadowy moments may well reduce it to an overly illuminated, overly enlightened, or overly rationalistic technocracy. According to the argument elaborated above, the Schmittian moment of intensification that gives rise to the moment of the political and to the sovereignty of the political unit must be understood as part and parcel of the political contractions that mark sociality. It thus contributes to, or takes part in, sociality as long as it does not become severed or severs itself from the Arendtian concern with plurality. When the latter happens, asserts the argument above, the political contraction becomes reduced to a social contract and the breach of contract or breach *by* contract that cannot but disrupt sociality and/or frustrate reconciliation in the wake of an already disrupted sociality.

What is the status of the sovereign return to the linguistic and/or cultural origin of the self that characterises the cultural politics of the Group of 63? Is it just part and parcel of the political contractions of sociality in post-apartheid South Africa, or does it already risk the decisive breach by social contract that comes to pass whenever the Schmittian political moment is severed from the Arendtian, that is, from the concern with plurality that necessarily involves a concern with an other, others and otherness?

In vernacular phrases as fine as one can hope to expect from the most eloquent of philosophers in any other language of the world, Danie Goosen, a prominent spokesperson of the Group of 63, articulates a notion of the political that would indeed seem to turn on the interplay between the Schmittian and Arendtian conceptions of the political

---

61 Jean-Luc Nancy *La création du monde ou la mondialisation* (2002) 152: 'Le souverain est rapport à soi (à soi comme à la loi, et il n'est que cela…'; Derrida (n 36) 33: '[La] souveraineté est une circularité, voir une sphericité. La souveraineté est ronde, elle est arrondissement'.

elaborated above. He conceives of the political in terms of an interplay between exclusion and inclusion of otherness, in terms of a need to lay down boundaries and then take leave of them again as would seem necessary in view of the historical exigencies of changing times.[62] The only consistency that he insists upon as far as this play of inclusion and exclusion is concerned is language, the language of a particular linguistic community. The language of a particular linguistic community would seem to warrant and not frustrate for him the play between inclusion and exclusion in a way that culturally and historically more fixed phenomena such as race and ethnicity cannot hope to do. The open historicity of language would seem to be the key to this play of exclusion and inclusion. Language, he argues, can indefinitely articulate and accommodate the new and the different without transgressing the fundamental principles and boundaries of its own linguisticity. Language thus constructs a familiar world that the members of the language community have in common. The familiarity of this common world nevertheless remains irreducibly exposed to difference and the encounter with otherness.[63] Goosen would seem to be contemplating something along the lines of Nancy's notion of an inoperative community that would exist *en commun* and thus exceed any reduction to *communion* or the common, *le commun*.

These fine thoughts must not only be confronted with the elements of the predominantly self-concerned politics of the Group of 63 outlined above, and with the fact that the *language community* in the name of which this linguistic politics is articulated is and will remain, especially in view of the predominant concern with the own affairs of this linguistic community, also an *ethnic and racial community* that is unlikely eventually to shed its current ethnic or racial character.[64] It must also be confronted with the more fundamental question whether the language of this inclusive and exclusive play of the political *can ever be named* without reducing it to a fixed identity or presence that ultimately cannot but predominantly, if not exclusively, exclude, at least at a certain level of depth, otherness and difference. At issue is not only the privileging of presence that Derrida detected in Saussure's containment of *parole* through *langue*.[65] At issue is also Agamben's insight that the naming faculty of language through which the singular and the different *comes* to language cannot itself be named without reducing it to a name, without reducing it to what is already *actually* and no longer *potentially* available in language.[66] One can also say in Heideggerian terms that a language community that

---

62 Danie Goosen 'Só sterf "nuwe" taalbeweging 'n vroeë dood' Beeld (2000-10-26) 11.

63 *Ibid.*

64 There are of course people other than white people who speak Afrikaans as a first or good second language, but they are certainly not significantly taken by the language politics of the Group of 63. Robert Kirby, an Afrikaans writer and poet, refers to the new cultural or language politics of the Afrikaners (white Afrikaans-speaking South Africans) as a useful trick aimed at pursuing the old nationalist and racist goals of the Afrikaners in a politically correct or acceptable manner. Kirby 'Ek sal nie meedoen aan die dodedans rondom Afrikaans' *Rapport* (2004-01-18).

65 Jacques Derrida *Positions* (1981) 27-28.

66 Giorgio Agamben *Potentialities* (1999) 52-56. Compare also Giorgio Agamben *The coming community* (1993) 'Linguistic being is a class that both belongs and does not belong to itself, and the class of all classes that do not belong to themselves is language'. Goosen, however, would probably not be impressed by these arguments. He is expressly dismissive of what he calls 'the borderless word' of Agamben's 'hypermoralistic postmodernism'. Danie Goosen 'Nuwe dekade van politieke energie wag dalk op Afrikaner' *Rapport* (2003-11-16) 26.

would suppress the events of naming and renaming itself in order to adopt a name would no longer be *unterwegs zur Sprache*. It would simply be calculating with the commonplace terminology of an already existing language. It would be speaking in code.

Can a linguistic community and a linguistic politics that is incisively concerned with the *naming of the new*, the *naming of the different and the other*, that linguistically distinguishes all *naming* from *names*, afford for itself the luxurious certainty and fixity of an existing name? Can a linguistic community ever be named with reference to existing names such as Afrikaans or English or any other language without suppressing the faculty and event of naming and thus of the irreducible plurality on which its very linguisticity turns? Does this adoption of a name for the language community, on which the politics of the Group of 63 turns, not ultimately explain its exclusive concern with own affairs, its patent lack of an imaginative charity that would exceed the concern with own affairs? And does this adoption not ultimately reduce its 'cultural politics' to a rather mercantile withdrawal from South African politics? Does the exclusive or predominant concern with an ultimately exclusively *Afrikaans* language community, however inclusively conceived, not constitute a contractual withdrawal from the ever *unterwegs* community of languages of South African politics? To invoke Heidegger again: one falls into commerce and calculation when one is no longer on the way to language. One would hope that there is more of a response to otherness afoot in the apparently rather self-centred language politics of the Group of 63 than mere calculation and commerce.

1.5.4 Non-racialism in a unitary state

Again, these questions are asked not in order to demand responsibility, but to allow for, or give, responsibility. They are not asked *in the name of a demand for* but in the naming of a *potentially new* and therefore as yet always *still lacking* responsibility, as Emilios Christodoulidis avers so finely with reference to Agamben.[67] This allowing for, and giving of, responsibility may well amount to the question whether one should not allow the boundaries or borders on which the cultural politics of the Afrikaner people seems to turn at present. Why not go so far as to allow them, in principle, the political and territorial boundaries that would ultimately seem to energise the political intensification behind their rather transparent cultural concerns? Why not allow them a chance – as unconditional as logistically, geographically and legally possible – independently to articulate and invent new ways of existing *with* the other peoples of South Africa, of coexistence or existence *en commun* that could eventually come to redeem their racist past? Why not grant them the *volkstaat* (people's state) that section 235 of the South African Constitution allows them in principle?[68]

---

67 Agamben *The coming community* (n 66) 42.

68 S 235 reads: 'The right of the South African people as a whole to self-determination, as manifested in this Constitution, does not preclude, within the framework of this right, recognition of the notion of the right of self-determination of any community sharing a common cultural and language heritage, within a territorial entity in the Republic or in any other way, determined by national legislation.'

One of the fundamental reasons for thus far not granting the Afrikaner people the substantially independent *volkstaat* for which General Viljoen and the Freedom Front bargained so gallantly during the transition period (this may well be the high-water mark among the rare occasions of truly gentlemanly and civilised political action in the history of resistant Afrikaner politics) is of course the principled non-ethnicity of the ANC and their insistence that the whole of South Africa was to be liberated from apartheid, something that could not allow for any form of continued racial or ethnic separation.[69] General Viljoen later retired from politics, rather disillusioned with the way the ANC government ultimately never took the promise of a *volkstaat* in section 235 seriously.[70]

Now, the principled non-ethnicity of the ANC is a laudable democratic principle that must be understood to have played a significant role in the surprisingly smooth negotiations that paved the way for a peaceful transition to democracy in South Africa. Had the Africanism of the Pan African Congress (PAC), which left the ANC in 1957 for reasons of the latter's non-ethnicity, been a more formidable factor to contend with during the negotiations for a democratic South Africa, the whole process might well have been fraught with insurmountable multilateral resistances to a peaceful transition. However, when the very non-ethnicity that must be hailed to have been a decisive factor in the peaceful transition to democracy hardens into a principle that no longer includes, but begins to exclude, differences, it risks frustrating and ultimately even undoing the peaceful democratisation that it facilitated during the negotiation process. The insistence on non-ethnicity in a unitary state itself then turns into a mode of resistance to real reconciliation. It itself then comes to represent an exclusively or predominantly Schmittian return to unitary political sovereignty. It thus takes leave of the Arendtian concern with plurality that initially appeared to mark it so clearly. It thus turns into a form of inverse ethnicity that certainly does not bode well for the future of the reconciliation process in South Africa.

There may well be formidable logistic, geographic and even moral obstacles to granting substantial independence to the Afrikaner or any other ethnic or cultural minority in South Africa. However, the principled refusal to consider the possibilities of surmounting these obstacles seriously can well be said to constitute a resistance as threatening to the indispensable continuation of the process of reconciliation in South Africa as any of the resistances outlined above. The insistence on non-ethnicity in a unitary state no longer translates unproblematically into a time of reconciliation in which mortals live on thankfully in the extra time impossibly granted to them in the wake of a moment of disrupted sociality, a moment of disrupted sociality that has always signified and will always have signified that their time has, in fact, always already been up.

---

69 Another fundamental reason is of course the already mentioned lack of manifest political desire for an Afrikaner Volkstaat among Afrikaners. Compare (n 51) above.

70 Sawyer 'Disillusioned Viljoen tells why he is leaving politics' *The Star* (2001-03-16) 1.

1.6 The time of a fourfold engagement

Who will remain hospitable to whom, who will be responsible for, and towards, whom in post-apartheid South Africa? Who will be the host and who will be the guest?[71] When it comes to reconciliation and the responsibility for reconciliation, the tables seem to turn all the time. The ANC's insistence on non-ethnicity may well be said to have been crucial for the early phases of reconciliation in post-apartheid South Africa. However, a continued concern with a by now rather simplistic and unthinking non-ethnicity may well come to threaten the very reconciliation it facilitated earlier on. It may come to provoke resistances to the process of reconciliation for the sake of what may plausibly be called the intensified sovereignty of a political unit that considers itself to be the one and only subject of the triumph over apartheid. In the meantime, the continued ability of the Afrikaner people to suspend their dark desire for cultural and ethnic sovereignty, without which the transition process might never have begun without outright civil war, may well have become an even more crucial factor in the continued process of peace and reconciliation in post-apartheid South Africa.[72] More crucial than any other factor, may well be the impossible tolerance of the millions of people who still live in squalor ten years after the transition to democracy in 1994.

Where does reconciliation ultimately come from? From whom? When does it begin and who can lay claim to its origins? My aim is to examine the time of reconciliation. But one should perhaps flip another genitive and simply refer to the reconciliation of time, the reconciliation granted by time. At issue is perhaps simply the fourfold engagement of heaven and earth, and mortals and gods that still happens to open up time and space, still happens to open up also quieter times and spaces in the wake of traumatic disruptions of sociality.[73] Indeed, as Derrida suggests towards the end of *Voyous*, not even the gods or a god can lay a sovereign claim to this miracle.[74]

Neither could a bishop or priest or TRC. Piet Meiring writes the following with reference to the various approaches to reconciliation among the members of the TRC:

> On the one hand there were the lawyers and jurists and politicians who, their feet firmly planted on *terra firma*, warned that we should not be too starry eyed when we speak about reconciliation. When the dust settles in the streets, when the shooting stops, when people let go of one another's throats, be grateful. That is enough! That is, in our context, as far as reconciliation goes. Archbishop [Tutu] and the *baruti* (priests), on the other hand, favoured a far more lofty definition. When they spoke about reconciliation they clothed it in religious terminology ... it was often said that only because God had reconciled us to him by sacrificing his Son Jesus Christ on the cross, did true and lasting reconciliation between humans become possible.[75]

---

71 Jacques Derrida 'Responsabilité et hospitalité' in *Manifeste pour l'hospitalité* (1999) 117-120.

72 In fact, continued calls for a *volkstaat* or a Zulu Kingdom may indeed be a crucial factor as regards our responsibility to continue to question false notions of reconciliation, false notions of reconciliation that may also go by the name of an unthinking non-ethnicity, irrespective of the question whether the actual institution of a *volkstaat* is a feasible and desirable goal in a post-apartheid South Africa.

73 Heidegger (n 38) 165–166. The Heideggerian reflections on this engagement are also taken up in chapter three of this collection by Wessel le Roux, who translates them into Lyotard's understanding of the ethics (and constitutionalism) of paganism.

74 Derrida (n 37) 160–161.

75 Jean-Luc Nancy *Le Sens du monde* (1993) 141.

This vertiginous passage hardly allows for the notion of *terra firma* that it alleges lawyers and politicians occupy. So many questions arise from it. The first would have to be whether the notion of a sacrifice that would facilitate true and lasting reconciliation between humans does not constitute the darkest of sovereign dreams that humanity dreams. Does this dream of sacrifice and of true and everlasting reconciliation between human beings not nourish the seemingly interminable re-enactments of sacrifice evident in all sovereign disruptions of sociality? Nancy draws attention to the intimate connection between the history of sovereignty and the history of sacrifice.[76] It is the threat that all sovereign claims to true reconciliation and to the grounds of such true reconciliation pose to the very ideal of reconciliation that this chapter aims to highlight. It is the threat that all lofty discourses about reconciliation or *all lofty discourses as such* pose to reconciliation that this chapter hopes to stress. Another instance of lofty language: 'Against a flood crashing with the weight of a brutalising past on to new usurping politics, the [small boat of the] Commission kept alive the idea of a common humanity.'[77]

Antjie Krog can be pardoned for this moment of self-absorption at the end of *Country of my skull*. It features, after all, in a paragraph that also refers to many shortcomings of the commission. It must nevertheless be stressed that the commission can at most be said to have contributed, along with many other things, to keeping the idea of a common humanity alive in post-apartheid South Africa. And like all the other things, that may have contributed to keeping the idea of a common humanity alive in post-apartheid South Africa, the commission may also have contributed to the innumerous threats that always render the idea of a common humanity irreducibly precarious, hence the critical engagement above with the moralistic, clerical or 'lofty' language adopted by some of the commission's members.

This chapter would, in view of the critical engagement with the lofty discourse of the commission, seem to take the lawyerly or political stance on reconciliation mentioned in the passage above. 'When people let go of one another's throats, [simply] be grateful.' This would seem to be confirmed by the remark above that reconciliation is simply a gift of time that a particular time affords a particular people. But this simple gift of time is not as simple as to allow simply for a fatalism regarding reconciliation. The platitude of fatalism may well constitute a simple inversion and therefore another repetition of our lofty languages regarding reconciliation. The gift of time cannot be contemplated without paying attention to the timely and untimely gifts of a responsibility that exceeds own concerns. Indeed, responsibility often comes too late, but one must be thankful when it comes at all. Reconciliation cannot be contemplated without reference to this timely, and all too often untimely, responsibility. But does this not just shift the level of fatalism to the occurrence or non-occurrence of responsibility?

How exactly responsibility relates to time and the gift of time remains an unfathomable mystery. Language regarding responsibility can so easily lapse into either simplistic notions of fate or simplistic notions of subjectivist or sovereign interventions

---

76 Piet Meiring (n 44) 129–130, as quoted by Wilhelm Verwoerd *Equity, mercy, forgiveness: Interpreting amnesty within the South African Truth and Reconciliation Commission* PhD (RAU) (2003) 123.

77 Derrida (n 37) 160–161: 'That is why, that is about which we speak'.

that force the hand of time. The ingenious Martin Heidegger spent a lifetime pondering the question on the relation between care (*Sorge*) and time, only to leave one with but a few rather frail insights into it. But the frailty of Heidegger's insights may well be crucial for any insight into responsibility. At issue in this frailty is the precarious undertaking that steers clear of both *terrae firmae* invoked in the passage above, the *terra firma* of an 'anonymous fate' and that of subjectivist or sovereign interventions that can force fate. Responsibility would always relate to a *terra infirma*. That is indeed why one talk's about responsibility, to modify slightly a remark by Derrida in *Voyous*: 'Rien n'est moins sûr, bien sûr … Voilà pourquoi, voilà de quoi nous parlons …'[78] Why would one talk about that which is certain and firm?

So one can only begin to talk about a responsibility that ties into, or relates to, a destiny that is neither a matter of fate nor a matter of subjectively forcing fate. Responsibility can be said to take part in the destination or destining of one's destiny in ways that one cannot fathom. However, without responsibility one's destiny indeed turns into the all too fathomable matter of fate and fateful attempts to force fate. Responsibility can be said to be the name for the circumspect and careful participation of mortals in the fourfold engagement between gods and mortals and heaven and earth that opens up time and space. And sometimes this fourfold engagement opens up the quieter time and space of reconciliation.

This Heideggerian articulation of reconciliation must not be understood or allowed to introduce a new loftiness into the examination of the time of reconciliation that is at issue here. At issue in the Heideggerian language invoked here is the simplest and most minimalist of abstractions regarding the fundamentals of reconciliation.[79] So indeed, one must simply be grateful or be grateful in a simple fashion when the shooting stops and when people let go of one another's throats. But one also has a responsibility regarding the possible cessation of such hostilities. There is always a chance to make and/or prolong peace. Again, the responsibility to make use of this chance cannot be demanded. Responsibility can only be given. It is also not we who give responsibility. *You and I* can only (but I also think *we* must) talk about responsibility in a way that makes possible the experience that responsibility is given to us, the experience that responsibility can be assumed, the experience that constitutes the very chance for the assumption of responsibility.[80]

---

78 Krog (n 39) 278.

79 The poetic quality of Heidegger's thought should not be confused with loftiness. He may have succumbed to loftiness occasionally (and at a certain point disastrously so), but the thrust of his thinking was on the contrary much rather marked by a destruction or deconstruction of the lofty or grand ideas of Western metaphysics and by a hermeneutics of facticity; that is, an explication or *Auslegung* of the fundamental conditions of existence, hence also the notion of the fourfold, the simple understanding of existence in terms of the engagement of earth, sky, mortals and gods. One could of course have invoked more abstract or even simpler terminology here, such as Derrida's *différance* or Nancy's *partage*.

80 My use of the first personal plural in Van der Walt (n 1) was questioned by Bert von Roermond during the second workshop in Tilburg (see again n 3 above) and this led to an insightful discussion that contributed much to my understanding of the crisis of reconciliation. Von Roermond subsequently also made available to the participants writing of his on the impossibility of using the first person plural coherently in any linguistic statement. I also benefitted much from these writings. For earlier attempts on my side to come to terms with this problem, see Van der Walt 'The (im)possibility of two together when it matters' (n 16) and *Tangible mais intouchable, la loi du tact, la loi de la loi. The future and futurity of the public-private divide in view of the horizontal application of fundamental rights* (2002).

We can only, but also must, talk about responsibility in a way that minimises the always already too vast potential for resistance or resistances to responsibility, hence the talking about responsibility and various instances of possible responsibility and irresponsibility in post-apartheid South Africa above.[81] Talking about responsibility is the first step towards reconciliation. It is the first step that mortals can take as regards the time of reconciliation. However, ultimately, the time of reconciliation does remain the reconciliation of time, the reconciliation that belongs to time. Reconciliation is the gift of time that mortals cannot force, claim, dictate or appropriate. Too much is always still up to the other players in the fourfold, the earth, the sky, the gods (especially the darker ones among them, the ones who induce resistances). Reconciliation is a gift mortals can only receive – receive through their participation in the fourfold, receive by accepting responsibility for reconciliation.

BIBLIOGRAPHY: CHAPTER ONE

Agamben, G. *Potentialities.* Stanford: Stanford University Press, 1999.

___. *The Coming Community*. Minneapolis: University of Minnesota Press, 1993.

Arendt, H. *The Human Condition.* Chicago: University of Chicago Press, 1989.

Bakhtin, M. *Rabelais and his World.* Bloomington: Indiana University Press, 1968.

Chua, A. 'The Privatization–Nationalization Cycle: The Link Between Markets and Ethnicity in Developing Countries'. *Columbia Law Review* 95 (1995):223.

___. *World on Fire: How Exporting Free Market Democracy Breeds Ethnic Hatred and Global Instability*. New York: Doubleday, 2004.

Connolly, W. *Why I Am Not a Secularist*. Minneapolis: University of Minnesota Press, 1999.

Derrida, J. *Donner Le Temps 1. La Fausse Monnaie.* Paris: Galilée, 1991.

___. *Voyous.* Paris: Galilée, 2003.

___. *Manifeste Pour L'hospitalité.* Paris: Éditions Paroles D'Aube, 1999.

___. *Cosmopolitanism and Forgiveness.* London: Routledge, 2001.

___. *États d'âme de la Psychoanalyse*. Paris: Galilée, 2000.

___. *L'autre Cap.* Paris: Les Editions de Minuit, 1991.

___. *Le Toucher, Jean-Luc Nancy.* Paris : Galilée, 2000.

___. *Politiques De L'amitie.* Paris: Galilée, 1994.

___. *Positions*. Chicago: University of Chicago Press, 1981.

___. *Résistances de la Psychanalyse*. Paris: Galilée, 1996.

81 There may well be something psychoanalytic at issue in talking about responsibility that would minimise resistance to responsibility. Psychoanalysis is often referred to as the 'talking cure'. However, more strictly speaking it should rather be referred to as 'talking therapy in the absence of cures'.

Fitzpatrick, P. *Modernism and the Grounds of Law.* Cambridge: Cambridge University Press, 2001.

Freud, S. *Gesammelte Werke.* Frankfurt: Fischer Taschenbuch Verlag, 1999.

Goosen, D. 'Groep wil "Tweede Fase" van SA se Demokratiseringsproses Begin'. *Beeld* (16 May 2000).

Goosen, D. 'Só Sterf "Nuwe" Taalbeweging 'n Vroeë Dood'. *Beeld* (26 October 2000).

Goosen, D. 'Nuwe Dekade van Politieke Energie wag Dalk op Afrikaner'. *Rapport* (16 November 2003).

Heidegger, M. *Vorträge und Aufsätze.* Pfullingen:Neske, 1985.

Jordaan, W. 'Afrikaner-Leiers Looi Groep van 63'. *Beeld* (15 November 2002).

Kant, I. *Werke in 10 Bänden*. Darmstadt: Wissenschaftliche Buchgesellschaft, 1983.

Kirby, R. 'Ek sal nie Meedoen aan die Dodedans Rondom Afrikaans'. *Rapport* (18 January 2004).

Krog, A. *Country of My Skull*. Johannesburg: Random House, 1998.

Lefort, C. *L'invention Démocratique.* Paris: Fayard, 1994.

Makeba, M. *Makeba: My Story,* Johannesburg: Skotaville, 1988.

Meiring, P. 'The Baruti vs The Lawyers'. In *Looking Back, Reaching Forward*, edited by C. Villa-Vicencio and W. Verwoerd. Cape Town: University of Cape Town Press, 2000.

Michelman, F. 'Constitutional Authorship, "Solomonic Solutions" and the Unoriginalist Mode of Constitutional Interpretation'. In *'Meaning' in Legal Interpretation*, edited by G. Bradfield, and D. van der Merwe. Cape Town: Juta, 1998.

Michelman, F. 'Law's Republic'. *Yale LJ* 97 1988:1496.

Michelman, F. '*Modus Vivendi Postmodernus*? On Just Interpretations and the Thinning of Justice'. *Cardozo LR* 21 (2000): 1945.

Mouffe, C. *The Return of the Political.* London: Verso, 1993.

Nancy, J. L. *Être Singulier Pluriel.* Paris: Galilée, 1996.

___. *La Communauté Désoeuvrée.* Paris: Christian Bourgeois, 1999.

___. *Le Sens Du Monde.* Paris: Galilée, 1993.

___. *Corpus*. Paris: Métailié, 2000.

___. *La Création Du Monde Ou La Mondialisation.* Paris: Galilée, 2002.

Ondaatje, M. *Anil's Ghost.* New York: Alfred A. Knopf, 2000.

Sawyer. 'Disillusioned Viljoen Tells Why He is Leaving Politics'. *The Star* (16 March 2001).

Schlink, B. *Die Beschneidung in Liebesfluchten*. Zurich: Diogenes, 2000.

Schmitt, C. *Der Begriff des Politischen*. Berlin: Duncker und Humblot, 1996.

Shriver, D. *Forgiveness in Politics: An Ethics for Enemies.* Oxford: Oxford University Press, 1995.

Tutu, D. *No Future Without Forgiveness.* London: Rider, 1999.

Van der Walt, J. 'Horizontal Application of Fundamental Rights and the Threshold of The Law in View of the *Carmichele* Saga'. *SAJHR* 19 (2003):521.

___. 'Psyche and Sacrifice'. *Journal of SA Law* (2003):635.

___. 'Frankly Befriending the Fundamental Contradiction: Frank Michelman and Critical Legal Thought'. In *Rights and Democracy in a Transformative Constitution*, edited by H. Botha, A.J. van der Walt and J.W.G. van der Walt Stellenbosch: SUN Press, 2003.

Van der Walt, J. 'The (Im)Possibility of two Together when it Matters'. *Journal of SA Law* (2002): 462.

___. 'Afrikaners Moenie Wonderwerke van Konstitusionele Hof Verwag'. *Rapport* (24 August 2003).

Wordsworth, W. *Ode: Intimations of Immortality from Recollections of Early Childhood*. In *The Oxford Anthology of English Literature: Romantic Poetry and Prose*, edited by Bloom and Trilling. New York: Oxford University Press, 1973.

TWO

Lives of Action, Thinking and Revolt: A Feminist Call for Politics and Becoming in Post-Apartheid South Africa

Karin van Marle

2.1 Introduction

Action, thinking and revolt – or maybe the absence thereof within apartheid and post-apartheid law, politics and critique in general and human rights discourse in particular – provide the impetus for this chapter.[1] Significant background for the contemplation of a post-apartheid politics is provided by the work of two theorists responsible for much reflection on action, thought and revolt, Hannah Arendt and Julia Kristeva.[2] In Arendt's work, action, as an essential part of the human condition, is significant. However, thinking, or the life of the mind, plays as big a part as action in her life and theory. The tension between a life of action and the life of the mind provides multiple ways and angles from which to contemplate politics, theory and critique. It is mainly the notion of life in Arendt, as emphasised by Kristeva, that is central to my tentative reflections here. I also focus on moments in Kristeva's work that continue Arendt's devotion to action and thought, particularly her notion of 'revolt' and her call for eternal questioning and contestation. I further draw on the notion of becoming as developed by Gilles Deleuze and Félix Guattari.[3] These notions supplement my own concern for more and continuous critical reflection. Writing from within a post-apartheid context, I am haunted by the seeming absence of action, thinking and revolt, and ultimately a politics of becoming in South African

---

1 I would like to thank the following colleagues who were part of a weekly reading group during the late 1990s and who also recently participated in a panel at the 2004 Law & Society Conference in Chicago, where I presented an earlier version of this chapter, for their continuous engagement and discussions: André van der Walt; Henk Botha; Johan van der Walt and Wessel le Roux. I also want to thank Jonathan Klaaren, who chaired our panel in Chicago; Stewart Motha for his interest in the project and Drucilla Cornell, who participated in another seminar as critical commentator on our papers, as well as Danie Brand for many discussions.

2 See in general Hannah Arendt *The origins of totalitarianism* (1966), *The human condition* (1958) and *On revolution* (1963); and Julia Kristeva *Hannah Arendt: Life is a narrative* (2001) (hereinafter Kristeva (2001a); *Hannah Arendt* (2001) (hereinafter Kristeva (2001b); *Revolt she said* (2002); and *The sense and non-sense of revolt: The powers and limits of psychoanalysis Vol 1* (2000). The work of Arendt also plays an important role in Johan van der Walt's reflections on reconciliation in chapter one of this collection. The same applies to André van der Walt's discussion of the public dimension of property in chapter four.

3 See Ian Buchanan and Claire Colebrook *Deleuze and feminist theory* (2000). See also Gilles Deleuze and Félix Guattari *A thousand plateaus: Capitalism and schizophrenia* (1987) and Gilles Deleuze *Negotiations 1972–1990* (1995).

life. It urges me to ask, following Drucilla Cornell, to what extent, if at all, transformation, in the sense of a radical restructuring of not only the system but of subjects themselves, has been put into motion over the past decade?[4] Did mere evolution occur? Is the product of our negotiated revolution another hegemonic system where dissent will not be allowed to challenge the new order? Would, what Lourens du Plessis refers to as the 'monumental' moments in the South African transition, turn out to be pervasive?[5] Could a politics of action, thought and revolt be contemplated within the present context, nationally and internationally?

I tentatively argue that the enthusiastic embrace of human rights and the new Constitution,[6] in other words, the shift from politics to law, the political to the legal, at the very least contributes to what I perceive as an absence of action, thinking and revolt. I turn to two South African perspectives: one on the Constitution, the other on human rights in particular. I start with Lourens du Plessis's discussion of the monumental and memorial moments in South African constitutional discourse.[7] Thereafter I put forward Christof Heyn's 'struggle theory of human rights'.[8] The struggle theory of human rights attempts to provide both an explanation of the origin of and a justification for the existence of human rights. I argue that the struggle theory could be seen as an example of the monumentalism that Du Plessis describes. By employing Arendt and Kristeva (but also Spivak and Cornell)[9] I question the struggle theory's equation of human rights with legitimate struggle. I find the equation of *human* with *legitimate* and *rights* with *struggle* reductive. My tentative argument rests on the notion that the translation of struggle into rights, humanity into legitimacy, and politics, thinking and narrative into an economy of the private, puts a damper on action, thinking, revolt and a politics of becoming. The memorial constitution might provide a better space from whence to think a politics of becoming.

Central to the South African transition from apartheid to post-apartheid stands the political compromise that was reached between the former regime and the new. The South African TRC, which was provided for in the postamble of the interim Constitution,[10] was the manifestation of this compromise. I argue that, like the Constitution, the Truth and Reconciliation Commission also had its monumental and memorial moments. Like monumental approaches to the Constitution and human rights, the monumental moments in the commission do not provide a space for a critical questioning, for what Mamdani calls social reconciliation and for a politics of becoming.[11] I argue that this embrace of law and human rights similarly influenced

---

4 Drucilla Cornell *Transformations* (1993).

5 Lourens du Plessis 'The South African constitution as memory and promise', in Charles Villa-Vicencio (ed.) *Transcending a century of injustice* (2000) 63.

6 Constitution of the Republic of South Africa, 1996 (hereinafter 'the constitution').

7 Du Plessis (n 5).

8 Christof Heyns 'A struggle approach to human rights', in Arend Soeteman (ed.) *Pluralism and law* (2001) 171.

9 Drucilla Cornell 'Unlicensed lunacy: Spivaks' feminism and human rights', unpublished paper presented at Spivak Conference. Copy on file with author.

10 Constitution of the Republic of South Africa Act 108 of 1993 (hereinafter 'the interim Constitution').

11 Mahmood Mamdani 'When does reconciliation turn into a denial of justice?', in Sam Nolutshungu (ed.) *Memorial lectures* (1998) 1.

feminist politics and struggle after apartheid. The notion of gender mainstreaming is a good example of the way human (or women's) rights and their implementation reduce action, thought and revolt to the language and strategies of policy, machinery and co-option. I end by asking if 'bits and pieces' (or what Verne Harris in another context refers to as the 'archival sliver')[12] of a politics of action, thought and revolt can be (re)created in present (and absent) South African lives, actions, thoughts and revolts. The content, meaning and understanding of the notion of action and revolt that I subscribe to is not one of violence or militancy, but rather one of continuous contestation and questioning.[13] I question the use of struggle as an explanation for the origin of human rights, not because I am arguing for a situation of disorder and violence, but because I do not want to see struggle coupled with and reduced to that which could be contained by the concept of what is legitimate. In a way I further pursue the reflection on attention that I (following Simone Weil) have previously described, with much caution and hesitation, as an approach of slowness.[14] Just as an approach of slowness does not mean succumbing to the limits of the law and legal politics or to a naïve belief in law's capacity (if anything such an approach would sharpen law's failure), action and revolt also do not mean succumbing to haste or to struggle that amounts to violence. The argument is much more tentative – a reflection on absences, possibilities, breaks and continuances.

2.2 Monumental and memorial constitutionalism

> Tell me a story, Pew.
> What kind of story child?
> A story with a happy ending.
> There's no such thing in all the world.
> As a happy ending?
> As an ending.
> — Jeanette Winterson[15]

Commentators have employed various metaphors to describe the constitution. The image of the constitution as bridge, as used in the postamble of the interim Constitution and as further developed by the late Etienne Mureinik[16] and the late Justice Mahomed,[17] has frequently been recalled to stand in service of constitutional claims to reconciliation, healing and unity.[18] Lourens du Plessis chooses three other images in his reflection

12 Verne Harris 'The archival sliver: A perspective on the construction of social memory in archives and the transition from apartheid to democracy', in Carolyn Hamilton et al. (eds) *Refiguring the archive* (2002)136.

13 Henk Botha argues in chapter five of this collection for a conception of equality (he calls it complex equality), which seeks doctrinally to re-open the possibility of political action and revolt in these terms.

14 Karin van Marle 'Law's time, particularity and slowness' (2003) 19 SAJHR 245.

15 Jeanette Winterson *Lighthousekeeping* (2004) 49.

16 Etienne Mureinik 'A bridge to where? Introducing the interim Bill of Rights' (1994) 10 *SAJHR* 31. For a critique of the bridge metaphor see for example André van der Walt 'Dancing with codes: Protecting developing and deconstructing property rights in a constitutional state' (2001) 118 *SALJ* 258.

17 *AZAPO v President of the Republic of South Africa* 1996 (8) BCLR 1015 (CC).

18 The way in which the metaphor of the bridge has architecturally framed post-apartheid constitutionalism is critically discussed by Wessel le Roux in chapter three of this collection.

on the constitution in the context of reconciliation, memory and justice, namely the constitution as promise, as monument and as memorial.[19] My focus will fall mainly on the last two of these images. For Du Plessis a constitution serves the dual function of narration and authorship of a nation's history. He relates what he calls, 'the potency with which [a constitution] can mould a politics of memory' to 'the authority with which it can shape the politics of the day'.[20] However, he concedes that the constitution is but one of many participants in telling a nation's history and accordingly also one of many determinants of a nation's future. He explains that the possibility of the constitution's promise is dependent on how the constitution deals with memory, thereby drawing a connection between past and future, and one could say reasserting the point that future events should also influence constitutional memory. Du Plessis, like others,[21] focuses on the tensions within the constitution as a form of redemption. Following the work of Johan Snyman, he describes the constitution as simultaneously monumental and memorial.[22] Although monuments and memorials share a concern with memory, they differ significantly in the way they remember. Monuments celebrate and memorials commemorate. For example, after a war has been won a monument will be created, celebrating the heroes and achievements of war. Memorials are created to commemorate the dead.

In discussing the constitution as monument, Du Plessis refers to the constitution as 'hardly a modest text'.[23] Both interim and final constitutions make reference and lay claim to the achievement of a 'peaceful transition' to a non-racial democracy; to the recognition of the 'injustices of our past'; and the honouring of 'those who suffered for justice and freedom in our land'; to the need for healing the 'divisions of the past' and for building a 'united and democratic South Africa'.[24] Du Plessis also refers to the entrenchment of the values of democracy, human dignity, equality and freedom as 'monumental flair'.[25] As a final point of the constitution as monument he refers to some of the Constitutional Court's decisions, most notably *S v Makwanyane*[26] in which capital punishment was declared unconstitutional. He describes the various decisions as 'imbued with value statements' that focused on constitutionalism not only nationally but also internationally. Du Plessis goes on to argue that, although no one should be cynical about the 'monumental achievements' of the South African Constitution, one should also embrace the 'restrained constitution'. For du Plessis, the restrained constitution is the constitution as memorial, namely the idea that a written constitutional text cannot alone provide justice, but rather reminds one to strive for justice.[27] He uses the

---

19 Du Plessis (n 5) 63.

20 *Ibid.*

21 See for example Henk Botha 'Democracy and rights: Constitutional interpretation in a postrealist world' (2000) *THRHR* 563; Karl Klare 'Legal culture and transformative constitutionalism' (1998) 14 *SAJHR* 146.

22 Johan Snyman 'Interpretation and the politics of memory'(1998) *Acta Juridica* 312.

23 Du Plessis (n 5) 64.

24 *Ibid.*

25 *Ibid.*

26 *S v Makwanyane* 1995 (3) SA 391 (CC).

27 Du Plessis (n 5) 65.

notion of subsidiarity (or constitutional restraint) as an example of how the constitution can operate as memorial. He further relies on 'the open community of interpreters' to take part in the fulfilment of the constitution as a promise that is as much reliant on the memorial constitution as on the monumental constitution.[28]

In another context I have employed Du Plessis's metaphorical description of the constitution in a tentative refiguring of the constitution as yet another image: the constitution as archive.[29] With reference to the meaning of archive as the place where things commence, the place from which order is given and the place that contains memory, an analogy can be made between archive and constitution. As the archive traces only particular aspects of the past, the Constitution similarly traces only particular aspects of the South African past and nation. What is contained in the Constitution is already interpretations of a past and a nation's aspirations. The archive cannot contain memory: nor can the constitution. The archive simultaneously urges to remember and to forget; the constitution does the same. The constitution as monument is the 'death drive' of the constitution, the drive to destroy all traces without any reminder. The constitution, like the archive, also works against itself. The Truth and Reconciliation Commission, as a creation of the monumental constitution, similarly worked against itself. As many commentators have shown, the commission failed to fulfil the task of nation building, reconciliation and healing.[30] I have previously argued that this failure could paradoxically be seen as a success,[31] and I want to connect this with Du Plessis's memorial constitution. The memorial moments (moments of failure) in the TRC process are those that could serve as what Verne Harris calls the 'archival sliver',[32] the possibility of a politics of becoming, to which I return below.

Mahmood Mamdani describes the South African transition as an example of where 'reconciliation turned into a denial of justice'.[33] His critique of the South African approach to reconciliation is similar to the critique of the constitution and the Truth and Reconciliation Commission as monumental, described above. Jacques Derrida's contemplations on reconciliation, justice and forgiveness are also significant in this respect.[34] In contrast to the struggle approach discussed below, Mamdani takes seriously not only reconciliation and justice, but also post-apartheid politics. Mamdani recalls South Africa's conscious search for an alternative paradigm in its rejection of Nuremberg trials and its embrace of a 'negotiated revolution', which entailed an embrace of the Latin American ways of dealing with the past. However, he asks, 'how does one go

---

28 *Idem* 66.

29 Karin van Marle 'Constitution as archive', in Scott Veitch (ed) *Law and the politics of reconciliation* (2006) 215.

30 See for example Emilios Christodoulidis 'Truth and reconciliation as risks' (2000) 9 *Social and Legal Studies* 179–204; Verne Harris 'The archive, public history and the essential truth: The Truth and Reconciliation Commission reading the past' in Hamilton et al. (n 12) 161.

31 Van Marle (n 14).

32 Harris (n 12).

33 Mamdani (n 11).

34 Jacques Derrida *Archive fever* (1996); *On cosmopolitanism and forgiveness* (2001).

beyond the compromise of 1994? … How can reconciliation be made durable?'[35] He raises two questions about South Africa's option of truth telling: is reconciliation an inevitable outcome of truth telling; and whose truth was told? Mamdani critiques the way in which the difference between perpetrator and beneficiary has been obscured, and argues that a focus on the former would lead to a focus on criminal justice, while a focus on the latter would lead to a focus on social justice. Taking this further, he argues that the distinction between perpetrator and beneficiary encompasses another distinction, one between *narrow, political* reconciliation and *broad, social* reconciliation. (I read Mamdani's use of *political* here to mean a mere instrumental politics that negates plurality and critique. His use of *social* is closer to the understanding of politics which I argue for.)[36] He contends that as social reconciliation is not possible without political reconciliation, political reconciliation will not prove durable without social reconciliation. Beneficiary and victim must be reconciled as the majority in order to deepen and broaden political reconciliation to social reconciliation.[37] He suggests that the degrees of reconciliation to justice should be recognised; to view justice merely as criminal justice is limiting and not necessarily to the benefit of victims. He argues for a shift of focus 'from agents and activists to that of winners and losers, from those whose victimhood was more anonymous and circumstantial, from gross human rights abuses – murder, torture, rape – to gross systemic outcomes like pass laws and forced removals, abuses which racialised both poverty and affluence'.[38]

He explains that this shift would relocate agency in a historicised structure, but that it would also entail a shift in logic, that although perpetrators are personally and individually liable, beneficiaries might not be. However, beneficiaries should join victims in their outrage and not shirk responsibility for the ongoing consequences of unequal distribution of socio-economic power. Mamdani is asking for more than a mere moral burden on beneficiaries. He is asking for the state as 'upholder of the public good' to carry that burden and address it in an executive and legislative manner. To make reconciliation durable, Mamdani argues for a move from a *narrow recognition of rights to a broad recognition that underlies the need to right historical wrongs*.[39] He argues that one should move beyond an absolute emphasis on either social justice or individual rights so that both can be contextualised and revitalised.[40] He explains South Africa's negotiated reconciliation as follows: in the first instance the security of the minority was protected by breaching the rights of the majority. The next instance should entail the breach of the economic individual rights of the minority. If this is not envisioned,

35 Mamdani (n 11) 12.

36 I thank Stewart Motha for drawing my attention to this.

37 The tension between political reconciliation (as it is understood here) and the politics of reconciliation is highlighted by Johan van der Walt in chapter one of this collection. Henk Botha also incorporates the distinction between political and social reconciliation (as the terms are used here) into his critique of dignity-based conceptions of equality in chapter five of this collection.

38 Mamdani (n 11) 15.

39 *Idem* 16.

40 *Ibid*.

reconciliation will not be durable because future social justice will have to give way to 'a sort of a pragmatic, day-to-day accommodation'.[41] Following on this, Mamdani describes the constitution as a 'Hobbesian pact' in which the minority traded political rights for security of privilege. Although he concedes that political reconciliation might have been a 'momentary necessity', he argues that it should not turn into a 'permanent condition'.[42] He also questions the Truth and Reconciliation Commission's ideological claim to truth – in his view the commission did not address the truth of the majority of South Africans. By focusing only on the experience of agents and activists, the commission negated the ordinary people, with the result that many of the evils of apartheid, socio-economic inequality and social injustice, are presently seen as part of normal life. It is here that reconciliation, for Mamdani, turns into an 'embrace of evil'.[43] Recalling the distinction between the constitution as monument and as memorial, one can argue that political reconciliation would be reflective of the monumental and social reconciliation of the memorial. The monumental constitution shares the 'death drive' with the archive; political reconciliation does too. It aims to destroy traces of past inequalities by normalising these inequalities in the present, thereby negating possibilities of social justice in the future.

Derrida's view that there is no necessary link between reconciliation and justice connects with Mamdani's. To reconcile by 'reconstituting a community', to make a 'practical compromise' in order 'to go on doing business and surviving' can occur without any justice being involved.[44] Derrida distinguishes 'authentic reconciliation' from reconciliation, in order to describe a way of thinking about reconciliation that could be closer to justice. Authentic reconciliation would entail a 'promise of perpetual peace', of 'indefinite friendship and peace'.[45] A similar and obvious point could be made in relation to the entrenchment of human rights in a constitution – as such they do not provide for justice and are part of the practical compromise that ensures business as usual. Commenting on the impossibility of closure of the archive, Derrida explains that the archive will always be open to new readings, interpretations and contestations. In this way the archive's attempt to forget (its death drive?) will be unsuccessful, because there is no final way in which to know or to measure if something has been forgotten. He refers to 'the coming back of the forgotten' in modern times[46] – 'because the context remains open, there is a future for the archive'.[47] If one relates this to the Constitution and human rights, there might be a possibility of preventing total closure: reinterpretation and invention of new meaning could be possible in the future. Tentatively, my argument is that this would only be possible in an approach that regards the Constitution

41 *Idem* 16–17.

42 *Idem* 18.

43 *Ibid.*

44 Jacques Derrida 'Archive fever in South Africa' in Hamilton et al. (n 12) 38 at 76. See also Derrida *On cosmopolitanism and forgiveness* (n 34).

45 Jacques Derrida (n 44) 76.

46 *Idem* 78.

47 *Ibid.*

and human rights as memorial and not monumental, in a space that is opened to a politics of action, thought and revolt, a politics of becoming.

A notable example of South African writing that treats not only the Constitution, but also the Roman law tradition in a way that resembles the notion of memorial rather than monument, is that of André van der Walt. In an article entitled 'Roman law, fundamental rights, and land reform in southern Africa', Van der Walt argues that Roman law should be approached with a concern for creating a 'historical sensitivity, with reference to the crisis and the traumas of Roman law, rather than concentrate on the golden thread of continuity [the monumental] in the life of Roman law'.[48] He contends that Roman law's value lies in its experience of crisis, traumas, change and transformation – not in how it survived these, but in how it was changed and transformed by 'leaving the well-trodden paths and venturing into new and unknown territory'.[49] In contrast to the traditional and monumental approach to teaching Roman law, in which its 'higher, more universal and more equitable values' are emphasised Van der Walt suggests a narrative approach that focuses on the 'breakdown point and discontinuities'.[50] Similar to his reflection on Roman law is his approach to the Constitution, in which he calls for tentativeness and sensitivity to the paradoxes of the new order and a resistance of orthodoxy (monumentalism).[51]

2.3 Monumental struggle

For Christof Heyns, 'human rights is the flipside of the coin of legitimate resistance'.[52] He describes his understanding of human rights as the 'struggle approach' to human rights and captures it in the equation 'human rights = legitimate resistance', an equation that according to him can be read from both sides – in other words legitimate resistance (also) = human rights.[53] For Heyns the 'force' of human rights can be explained by this link between human rights and resistance. No matter how one explains human rights, in other words, which political, philosophical or theoretical approach or perspective one follows, Heyns argues that the concept of human rights itself serves as a 'countervailing force' to the power of the state as well as society. This belief in the force of human rights brings him to state that human rights are 'guides to action and triggers of resistance', and further that 'as such, human rights is a potentially revolutionary concept'. His proof for this is, for example, 'the clampdown worldwide by authoritarian regimes on human rights organisations'. However, in haste Heyns adds that 'it should be noted

48 André van der Walt 'Roman law, fundamental rights, and land reform in southern Africa' in J.E. Spruit (ed.) *Roman law at the crossroads* (2000) 162.

49 *Idem* 163.

50 *Idem* 165.

51 André van der Walt (2001) (n 16); 'Tentative urgency: sensitivity for the paradoxes of stability and change in social transformation decisions of the Constitutional Court' (2001) 16 *SAPR/PL* 1; 'Resisting orthodoxy – again: Thoughts on the development of post-apartheid South African law' (2002) 17 *SAPR/PL* 258. See also chapter four in this collection.

52 Heyns (n 8).

53 *Ibid*.

that human rights doctrines do not operate within the context of the anarchist tradition – human rights proceed from the (often unspoken) assumption that there is a general duty to political obedience, to which human rights norms constitute exceptions'.[54] Human rights do not oppose or challenge the existence of the state as an institution but, in fact, endorse it. Only the 'illegitimate use of such power' may be challenged. Disobedience can be allowed only in 'extreme cases if it is justified, because of a general obligation to obedience'. Heyns follows the traditional view of constitutions as social contracts and adds to this that human rights should be regarded as the 'escape clauses'. For him the concept of human rights is the 'ultimate guarantor of popular sovereignty' and the 'foundation for intervention by the international community' in the domestic affairs of other states.[55]

The above discussion is the crux of the struggle theory and Heyn's argument. He elaborates further on this with reference to what he calls the history of the link between human rights and legitimate resistance,[56] as well as an application of the struggle approach to specific human rights issues.[57] I refer only to some aspects of these discussions. Heyns stresses that the link between human rights and legitimate resistance is not only conceptual, and proceeds to provide *proof* of this with reference to historical events and human rights documents that contain the right to resistance. His examples encompass the Magna Carta of 1215, John Locke's defence of the 'Glorious Revolution' of 1688, the American Declaration of Independence of 1776 and Jean-Jacques Rousseau's thoughts, which were echoed in the French Revolution of 1789. Although these are the well-known examples of the Western experience, Heyns contends that there is a *general* practice that after a period of strife and revolution, bills of rights and human rights instruments are written in order to prevent future recurrences. Human rights, he argues, are to a large extent retrospective in nature. Because of the link between human rights and legitimate resistance, Heyns regards human rights instruments as 'the closest approximation available today of a codified list of possible grounds for illegal resistance'.[58] He explains the foundation of, or the reason for, human rights as the 'common sense realisation' that 'the causes of dysfunction in all its forms must be removed', which leads him to say that the morality of human rights is nothing but 'an attempt at long term rationality'.[59] He identifies South Africa as a primary example of a country where human rights emerged from struggle and explains that Nelson Mandela's famous words, 'the struggle is my life' served as inspiration for the struggle approach to human rights. I want to express a slight uneasiness here and ask: does Heyns mean that Mandela's words can also be translated as 'human rights is my life', or as '*legitimate* struggle is my life'? Heyns regards the Freedom Charter of 1955 as 'the document that

---

54 *Idem* 172.

55 *Ibid*. In chapter one of this collection Johan van der Walt powerfully criticises the idea that the protection or restoration of the social contract lies at the heart of politics and reconciliation after apartheid.

56 *Idem* 172–178.

57 *Idem* 78–187.

58 *Idem* 173.

59 *Ibid*.

more than any other serves as a codification' of the struggle. Similarly, according to him, the 1996 Constitution of South Africa should be regarded as 'the culmination of the struggle'.[60]

According to Heyns, the struggle approach to human rights – to regard legitimate struggle as the conceptual counterpart of human rights – affects one's approach to a variety of human rights issues. He refers to the identification of human rights claims; the understanding of different generations of rights; approaches to the counter-majoritarian dilemma; and the universalist/relativist debate. In fact, for Heyns the struggle approach to human rights can serve as the *ultimate explanation*/narrative for human rights because it provides a more reliable foundation for human rights than natural law and theories about morality. Heyns even reinterprets Marx and contends that, although Marx rejected the language and concept of rights, he might have agreed with the concept if he had realised that human rights could be understood in terms of struggle and that they included economic and social rights. In Heyns' formulation, Marx was all along asking for the 'recognition of what would later come to be called the second generation of human rights'.[61] For Heyns a 'more solid basis' for the concept of human rights can be found by following the struggle theory and by then looking at history, and in particular, the history of struggles. He notes that the question of 'whose history' must be asked, but continues to argue that in respect of certain issues there is in actual fact *agreement*. In other words, there is some sort of *general consensus* on what could be perceived as legitimate resistance. For Heyns, where there is a 'lower level of agreement about the legitimacy of resistance' there will automatically also be a lower level of agreement on whether one is dealing with an issue of human rights. Again he places emphasis on the fact that the struggle theory of human rights is not a 'blanket endorsement of all actions that call themselves struggle' because 'struggles could also be misplaced or excessive'.[62] A struggle must be legitimate and to evaluate such legitimacy one has to find historical evidence that the issue at stake is of 'central importance to the human species'. Related to this is the requirement that illegal resistance should only be invoked as 'a last resort' or if 'all else fails'.[63] A further requirement is one of proportionality between the infringement of a right and the acts of resistance. For an interest to achieve the status of something that it is legitimate to fight for is, according to Heyns, a gradual process that is not a response to the 'passions of the moment', but rather to what, through history, has been seen as a feature of human nature. He accordingly argues that human rights are not grounded in natural law, but in human nature. History and the history of human struggle serve for Heyns as the 'true foundation and validation of human rights'.[64] The origin of some rights can be traced directly to instances of struggle. The origin of others is more indirect. Apparently following Dworkin, without explicitly referring to him, Heyns explains the origin of indirect struggles with reference to the notions of *fit* and *coherence*: the specific human rights claims must fit according to

60 *Idem* 176.
61 *Idem* 180.
62 *Idem* 181.
63 *Ibid*.
64 *Idem* 182.

the underlying principles and ultimately the foundation of human rights will depend on the coherence with historically accepted grounds of resistance.[65] According to Heyns the struggle theory can resolve/mediate the tension between various generations of human rights and the counter-majoritarian dilemma, by illuminating the relationship between human rights and democracy. Similarly, the universalist/relativist issue can be solved by the struggle approach. Heyns concedes that one cannot tell one single unified history of the world – *not yet*. He refers in this regard to the forces of globalisation that would increase universalisation and the contribution of human rights in this process.

In his conclusion he addresses the notion of history and time, responsibility and passion. History for him is closely tied to the concept of legitimacy. In his view, the normative aspect of the struggle approach can be captured in the word *legitimate*, and what is legitimate is to be found in history: 'history reflects beliefs that have stood the test of time'.[66] His understanding of responsibility is closely tied to the concept of human rights; the struggle approach to human rights is for him a call for responsibility to give direction to new struggles and also to protect existing norms. He describes passion, the foundation of human rights, as 'passion tempered by history'.[67]

I shall turn to Arendt, Kristeva and Deleuze later as a way of critically engaging with the struggle approach to human rights, but before that I hazard a few preliminary and tentative thoughts. An obvious problem that one could have with the struggle theory is its 'grand narrative' (monumental) style of argumentation. The struggle theory does not claim only to provide the *ultimate foundation* and *explanation* for human rights; it claims also to *solve all possible tensions, debates and struggles (!) on human rights*. It relies on a modernist acceptance of rationality and human reason, follows an abstract form of agency and supports the notion of the all-and-ever-present subject. The theory, although it recognises with some reluctance the problematic consequences of asserting a single history, ultimately assumes the possibility and preferability of one universal truth. Andrew Norris, in a discussion of Jean-Luc Nancy's vision of what community should entail, draws attention to Nancy's reliance on Arendt's critique, in *The origins of totalitarianism*,[68] of political theories that centre on rights.[69] Arendt argues that one should recognise a basis of civil rights, 'the right to have rights' through political action. Human rights should be seen as a form of action, not a set of moral truths. To concentrate on rights that are attached to politically passive and invisible legal subjects could lead to misdirection in one's resistance to totalitarianism.[70] Heyns might argue that this is what he envisioned in the formulation

---

65 *Idem* 183.

66 *Idem* 187.

67 *Idem* 188.

68 Arendt (1966) (n 2).

69 Andrew Norris 'Jean-Luc Nancy and the myth of the common' (2000) 7 *Constellations* 272. See also Jean-Luc Nancy 'Of being singular plural', in *Being singular plural* (2000); *The experience of freedom* (1993).

70 Norris (n 69) 276. Simone Weil's objection to rights must also be recalled: 'The notion of rights is linked with the notion of sharing out, of exchange, of measured quantity. It has a commercial flavour, essentially evocative of legal claims and arguments. Rights are always asserted in a tone of contention; and when this tone is adopted, it must rely upon force in the background, or else it will be laughed at.' Simone Weil 'Human personality' *Selected essays 1934–43* (1962) 18; see also Steven Burns 'Justice and impersonality: Simone Weil on rights and obligations' (1993) 49 *Laval théologique et philosophique* 477–486 at 481.

of the struggle approach to human rights. However, the strong requirement of legitimacy and the reliance on mostly Western history as yardstick is not true to the Arendtian tradition of active politics and the centrality of life and narrative. Later, I shall explore, via Arendt and Kristeva, the reductions that occur when coupling *politics* with *law* (struggle with rights) and *humanity* and human life with *legitimacy* (human with legitimate). Closely linked with the above is also the ethical notion of responsibility that is reduced to a mere instrumental responsibility that corresponds with rights. Ultimately, I lament that passion and the passion of the moment is limited and reduced to a tempered passion

Another reason why, in my view, the struggle approach fails to address post-apartheid politics is because it aims to provide a reason and justification for the existence of human rights, without showing concern for politics.[71] Also, for the struggle approach, the eventual entrenchment of human rights in international treaties and conventions is the end of political struggle rather than its beginning. The struggle theory is not only celebratory and monumental but, in a sense, despite Heyns' claim to the contrary, is not all that different from natural law explanations of the origins of, and justification for, human rights. The struggle here is reduced to the level of explanation and justification, and is not taken to be part of an active and continuous politics. Encompassed in this approach are the limits of institutional politics that could function only within the sphere of what is perceived as legitimate. Struggle is monumentalised and with it human rights as the outcome of struggle. Human rights are put up as the instrument that could bring light to the world, with international human rights documents as lighthouses to spread the word.[72]

An example in which the possibility of political struggle in a 'new' South Africa was refuted by a judicial argument based on the notion of a monumental approach to rights and constitutionalism is the dissenting judgment of Sachs J in the Constitutional Court case of *Pretoria City Council v Walker*.[73] In this case Walker, a white resident of the formerly exclusively white ('old') Pretoria, faced with a court order to pay arrear charges for services rendered by the Pretoria City Council, challenged the council's policy of charging different service rates for the inhabitants of old Pretoria and the inhabitants of formerly black townships outside old Pretoria (a policy that resulted in residents of old Pretoria cross-subsidising service provision to residents of former townships). He also challenged the council's practice of enforcing debts for services rendered only against residents of old Pretoria and not against residents of former townships. Walker's complaint was one

---

71 In chapter five of this collection Henk Botha shows, with reference to the right to equality, why any justification of rights should also be informed by a concern with politics.

72 I borrow this image from Heyns himself – on the front cover of his latest book on African human rights law (consisting of analyses of the human rights law of different domestic African jurisdictions and the applicable regional human rights law, coupled with a compilation of relevant human rights documents) is a drawing of a lighthouse (one of Nelson Mandela's prison drawings) (Christof Heyns (ed.) *Human rights in Africa* (2004)). Above (see text accompanying n 56), I refer to Heyns's assertion that Mandela's words 'The struggle is my life' served as an inspiration for the struggle approach to human rights. The uneasiness that I express above at this use of Mandela's famous words, perhaps also applies to the use of his drawing.

73 *Pretoria City Council v Walker* 1998 (3) BCLR 257 (CC). Sachs J's dissent appears at paras 100–141 of the decision.

of indirect, unfair racial discrimination in violation of s 8(2) of the interim Constitution, premised on the fact that residents of 'old' Pretoria (who paid higher rates – according to consumption – and against whom debt was enforced) were still almost exclusively white, whereas residents of the former townships (who paid a lower, flat rate for services, whose services were cross-subsidised by residents of old Pretoria and against whom debt was not enforced) were still mostly black.[74] The majority of the court (per Langa J) held that the council's policy of charging different rates for different areas and of cross-subsidising services in former townships with revenue raised in old Pretoria was not unfair discrimination, but that its practice of selective debt enforcement did discriminate unfairly on grounds of race and was as a result unconstitutional.[75]

Sachs J, in his dissent, disagreed with the conclusion of the majority that the practice of selective debt enforcement was discriminatory at all, arguing that in order to constitute indirect discrimination a practice had to have an adverse impact on a complainant – something that, according to him, was absent in this case.[76] His argument could have stopped there, but Sachs J nevertheless continued to consider whether, had he deemed the practice to be discriminatory, it would in addition have been unfair.[77] It is in his consideration of the fairness of the practice of selective debt enforcement that Sachs J's monumentalising understanding of the advent of constitutionalism and rights in South Africa emerges. To show that the practice of debt enforcement, even if discriminatory, is nevertheless fair, Sachs J focuses on the purpose of the practice, which justifies any discriminatory impact that it might have. For him the important task with which the council was faced and to which it tried to give effect, partly through its practice of selective debt enforcement, was 'the need to re-establish the *rule of law*' and to achieve 'acceptance by all inhabitants of the city of the entitlements and responsibilities that went with municipal citizenship'.[78] He sees the task of the city council as one of *integration* and of creating a *united* city.[79] This leads him to the conclusion that the case was actually 'not really about money but about the spirit of *civic responsibility*' and about 'the rights and *responsibilities of citizenship*',[80] about a process of drawing people who had previously been excluded from full citizenship and the benefits of membership of a municipal community into the dos and don'ts, the normative framework of proper, constitutionally mandated political life. Sachs J's argument comes down to the following: even though the people of the two townships in question, Atteridgeville and Mamelodi, had in an earlier period used non-payment as a 'weapon to secure full citizenship rights for themselves',[81] these methods should not be tolerated in a new South Africa. The promulgation of the new Constitution was the beginning of an era in which everyone

74 The background to the case and the complainant's arguments are set out at paras 17–24 of the majority judgment.

75 *Pretoria City Council v Walker* supra (n 73) at paras 68, 81 and 87.

76 *Idem* paras 105–118.

77 *Idem* paras 119–136.

78 *Idem* para 134.

79 *Ibid*.

80 *Idem* para 133.

81 *Ibid*.

could enjoy citizenship rights. Pretoria had to be reconstructed – and civil disobedience was not part of this reconstruction. The view of community articulated by the justice is one of unity and harmony in which there can be no place for political struggle and dissent. Such unity and harmony can be achieved because the foundation of this community is the rule of law, and the normative expectations of rights and responsibilities. In other words, as a result of the constitution and entrenched bill of rights there is no space for activist politics, revolt and contestation in a new, reconstituted South Africa. No wonder activists of the Soweto Electricity Crisis Committee quite often end up in jail, or protestors at the World Summit on Sustainable Development were tear-gassed and jailed. The space of what is regarded as 'legitimate' or within the ambit of the 'rule of law' seems to be very small

2.4 Memorial life

> Tell me a story, Pew.
> What story, child?
> One that begins again.
> That's the story of life.
> But is it the story of my life?
> Only if you tell it.
> — Jeanette Winterson [82]

Julia Kristeva places much emphasis on the centrality of the notion of *life* in Arendt.[83] Life was central to Arendt's work not only because of her own circumstances, which forced her to leave Nazi Germany and flee first to Paris and later New York, but also because she always believed that life and thought cannot and should not be separated. Her work entails life placed at the centre of thought and thought put into action. Kristeva interprets this as follows:

> [I]n this specifically Arendtian trait, we might be tempted also to see something unique to women, since human rights 'repression' (in the Freudian sense) is said to be 'problematic' for women and thus they are prevented from isolating themselves in the obsessive fortresses of pure thought, where men compete so successfully, and are anchored instead in the reality of their bodies and in relationships with others.[84]

However, she notes that Arendt takes this further in the sense that her political writings focus on the theme of life. In *The origins of totalitarianism*, Arendt equates Nazism and Stalinism, on the grounds that both of these movements denied human life. She feared that modern times were haunted by a 'radical evil' which denounced human life as 'superfluous'.[85] Totalitarianism and its destruction of human life are continued by 'automation' – by consumerism and technology. In *The human condition*, Arendt

---

82 (n 15) 109.

83 Kristeva (2001a) (n 2) and (2001b) (n 2). See also Jerome Kohn (ed.) *Responsibility and judgment: Hannah Arendt* (2003).

84 Kristeva (2001a) (n 2) 4.

85 *Ibid.* See also Arendt *The origins of totalitarianism* (n 2) 459.

redresses this destruction of human life by a 'vehement defence of life'.[86] Arendt places emphasis on the uniqueness of each and every human life, which she describes as 'the miracle' that could save the world from its normal routine.[87] The fact of natality (new beginning) can provide faith and hope. Kristeva mentions Arendt's critique of the metaphysical tradition that grants privileged status to the contemplative life. In contrast to this tradition's privileging of the contemplative life, Arendt argues that 'activity means life'.[88] However, Kristeva also notes Arendt's strong rejection of life for life itself, which for her meant a kind of calculated way of living without thinking. 'Vitalist activism', which amounts to consumerism, the cult of individual life, as well as the life of the species, leads to an emphasis on the vital process without any aspiration for immortality.[89] Kristeva reminds of Arendt's critique of Marx's assumption that 'the process of thought is itself a natural process'.[90] Arendt praises the life that is 'specifically human': that is, a life that can be told as a narrative and shared with other humans. By contending that the possibility of telling a story is what makes a life truly human, Arendt revives what Kristeva refers to as the 'praxis of the narrative', thereby connecting life, narrative and politics. Narrative has a twofold meaning – it refers to the duration and immortality of the work of art but also includes a historical narrative, the life of the polis.[91]

Kristeva identifies another stage in Arendt's thought, in which her meditation on the active life links with her thinking on the life of the mind in its three components: thought, will and judgement. Significant is Kristeva's insight that Arendt had already started to work on this in *The human condition*. Kristeva explains that Arendt's understanding of life amounted to the 'ongoing exploration of the various forms it takes, its manner of becoming other, and the complex figures that result from all of this'.[92] Arendt always took the 'interlacing' of life and thought seriously and therefore denounced the value of life for life itself: 'Life does not fullfill itself unless it never ceases to inquire into both meaning and action.'[93] It is important to note that Arendt's focus on life is not an uncritically optimistic celebration of a beautiful and simple life. Similarly, the possibility of new beginning does not necessarily entail something good, but something that 'cannot be expected from whatever may have happened before', something of 'startling unexpectedness'.[94] I read Arendt's notion of life to be similar to Laurie Anderson's notion of 'life on a string', when she sings: 'Some people know exactly where they're going. The pilgrims to Mecca, the climbers to a mountain top. But me I'm looking for just a single moment so I can slip through time.'[95]

---

86 *Idem* 5. See also Arendt *The human condition* (n 2).

87 *Ibid*. See also Arendt *The human condition* (n 2) 247.

88 *Idem* 7. See also Arendt *The human condition* (n 2) 96–101.

89 Kristeva (2002a) (n 2) 7..

90 *Ibid*. See also Arendt *The human condition* (n 2) 321.

91 *Idem* 8.

92 *Idem* 9.

93 *Idem*. See also Arendt *The human condition* (n 2) 324.

94 Arendt *On revolution* (n 2) 177-178. See also Emilios Christodoulidis 'Constitutional irresolution: law and the framing of civil society' (2003) 9 *European Law Journal* 401.

95 Laurie Anderson 'Life on a string' *Life on a string* (2001).

Kristeva defines the 1968 social revolution's understanding of freedom as 'not freedom to change or to succeed, but freedom to revolt, to call things into question'.[96] She argues that contemporary liberalism regards freedom merely as free enterprise, with the result that the understanding of freedom to revolt no longer exists in people's minds. For her, liberty as revolt is not just 'an available option, it's fundamental'.[97] Following Arendt, she states that without this notion of freedom, neither the life of the mind nor social life is possible. By life she does not mean mere maintenance, repetition and management. She states: 'The telling moment in an individual's psychic life, as in the life of societies at large, is when you call into question laws, norms and values'.[98] By calling things into question, by eternal contestation one prevents values from becoming frozen, and by questioning one gives them new life. Kristeva interprets revolt beyond its pure political meaning; to say that revolt is purely political is reductive. She gives meaning to the word revolt by turning to its philosophical and etymological meanings. Going back to its Sanskrit roots, she defines revolt as 'to discover, open, turn and return'. Philosophically, it relates to the idea that truth can be acquired by retrospective turn, by memory.[99] She contends that the events of the twentieth century have shown that political revolts (revolutions) betray revolt in the psychic sense. Revolt in a psychic sense 'refers to a state of permanent questioning, of transformation change, an endless probing of appearances'.[100] Recalling the etymological relation between revolt and return, patience, distance and repetition, Kristeva understands revolt as not simply rejection and destruction, but also as starting over.[101] Commenting on thinking, she wants to consider it as 'revelation, an exploration, an opening, a place of freedom'.[102] She argues against the 'robotization of humanity' and follows Arendt's call to 'rehabilitate anxious thinking against calculated thinking that is just computerizing'.[103] With reference to Arendt, Klein and Colette, Kristeva argues that women, like men, have a significant role to play in revolt.[104]

As Arendt's approach to human life and humanity (her belief that political action and thought are what distinguish human life from other forms of being) is critical of the notion of a society, or life captured by human rights and of the equalisation of *human* with *legitimate*, so Kristeva's call for eternal revolt disrupts the coupling of *rights* with *struggle*. Following Arendt and Kristeva, one finds that the dangers of a society overtaken by human rights discourse become clear – the results being a complacent society where political action, thought, eternal questioning and contestation are absent and replaced by an understanding of freedom as mere commercial/economic freedom and

96 Kristeva (2002) (n 2) 12. See also, in general, Kristeva (2000) (n 2).
97 Kristeva (2002) (n 2) 12.
98 *Ibid.*
99 *Idem* 100.
100 *Idem* 120.
101 *Idem* 122.
102 *Idem* 114.
103 *Ibid.*
104 *Idem* 95.

of thought as calculated and instrumental. I later argue that the emphasis on human rights had a similar effect on feminist politics.

2.5 Gender mainstreaming – continuing the reduction

As already alluded to above, in my view, gender mainstreaming as a continuation of human/women's rights could have a reductive and limiting effect on feminist theory and politics. This is because mainstreaming negates difference for strategic or pragmatic purposes and assumes unity. Mainstreaming is also politically problematic because it creates a danger of co-option. It is useful to recall here Bonnie Honig's description of 'agonistic' feminism.[105] Honig describes Arendt as neither a 'theorist of gender' nor a 'woman theorist', but as a 'theorist of an agonistic and performative politics'. Agonistic feminism does not presuppose an already known and unifying identity of woman, but 'differentiated, multiple beings that are always becoming, always calling out for amendment'. Honig draws on 'resistibility' as a precondition of Arendt's politics and on her view of identity as the 'performative production' and not the 'expressive condition or essence of action'.[106] For her the value of Arendt's theory for feminist politics lies in her rejection of an expressive, identity-based politics. Honig bases the notion of agonistic feminism on Arendt's reflections on the American Declaration of Independence.[107] For Arendt the real source of the authority of the American constitution was not the 'constative'[108] moment but the 'performative'. Arendt opposed all attempts to conceive of politics as the expression of shared identities such as gender, race, ethnicity or nationality (or human rights). The self, accordingly, is a 'complex site of multiple identities that are always performatively produced'.[109] From Arendt's perspective, a political community that constitutes itself on the basis of a prior, shared, and stable identity threatens to close the spaces of politics, to homogenize or repress the plurality and multiplicity that political action postulates.[110]

Spivak's critical feminist engagement with human rights must also be recalled. Cornell, commenting on her work on human rights, highlights the political and ethical significance of Spivak's focus on 'the limit of representation'.[111] Spivak calls us to a 'radical revision' of what humanity entails and emphasises the question of representation. Cornell phrases this question as: Who is entitled to be the representer in human rights

---

105 Bonnie Honig 'Towards an agonistic feminism: Hannah Arendt and the politics of identity', in Bonnie Honig (ed.) *Feminist interpretations of Hannah Arendt* (1995) 135. See also, in the same volume, Honig 'Introduction: The Arendt question in feminism' 1; Mary Dietz 'Feminist receptions of Hannah Arendt' 17; Patchen Markell 'Annotated bibliography on Hannah Arendt and feminism' 357.

106 See also Honig's discussion of Arendt's and Derrida's readings of the American Declaration of Independence in her 'Declarations of independence: Arendt and Derrida on the problem of founding a republic' (1991) 15 *American Political Science Review* 97.

107 *Ibid*.

108 The constative refers to the fixed, unchangeable phrases.

109 Honig *Feminist interpretations of Hannah Arendt* (n 105) 148.

110 *Ibid*.

111 Cornell (n 9).

discourse? She also asks who is positioned to act as the enforcer of human rights.[112] Following her own reading of the ethical moment in deconstruction, Cornell argues that Spivak is calling us to this ethical moment by showing how 'precisely our representation of ourselves as subjects of rights … is inseparable from the way in which the question of human nature is often "begged" in human rights discourse'.[113] She explains this as follows: human rights advocates seemingly respond to the call of others by acting responsibly, by doing the right thing, without noticing that by doing this, they might be acting in a harmful way, by wrongfully representing those whom they seek to help. Cornell recalls Spivak's warnings to be cautious in defining what it means to help, as well as who is in need of help. In translating human rights into women's rights, questions of human nature and responsibility must be recalled. Irreducible asymmetry must be taken as guide in the investigation of the difficult question of representation and responsibility.[114] Cornell's focus on Spivak highlights the danger that human rights discourse poses, not only for politics but also for ethics. In human rights discourse – including women's rights and gender mainstreaming – politics and ethics are consumed by optimist grand narrative style statements and policies.

Without going into Deleuze and Guattari's multiple and layered works in any depth, I want to refer briefly to their reliance on Virginia Woolf's stream of consciousness writing in their call for becoming.[115] Differentiating between a molar and molecular politics, they argue that the former would be the politics by which a female subjectivity is claimed. Although this could have a certain strategic value, it could lead to 'slavish subordination of action to some high ideal'.[116] They define molecular politics as a politics of questioning and activation through which 'those tiny events that make such foundations possible' are questioned.[117] Deleuze and Guattari thus identify a double politics that produces two dynamic senses of movement: a molar politics as the organisation of a subjectivity and a molecular movement as the continuous challenge of becoming.[118] For them woman's subjectivity must not function as a ground but as a 'molar confrontation' that is part of a 'molecular women's politics'.[119] Woman's subjectivity must not be a mirroring of man, but 'must affirm itself as an event in the process of becoming'.[120] For Deleuze and Guattari all becomings 'begin with and pass through becoming woman'.[121] Because man is the universal ground of reason, becoming will always begin with his opposite. Man and woman can be seen as events within a field of singularities. Virginia Woolf is recalled as a good example of living in the 'between', 'never ceasing to

112 *Idem* 4.
113 *Ibid*.
114 *Idem* 5.
115 Buchanan and Colebrook (n 3) 2; Deleuze and Guattari (n 3) 277. See also, in general, Deleuze (n 3).
116 Buchanan and Colebrook (n 3) 1. See also Gilles Deleuze *Nietzsche and philosophy* (1983) 123.
117 Buchanan and Colebrook (n 3) 1.
118 *Ibid*. See also Deleuze and Guattari (n 3) 276.
119 Buchanan and Colebrook (n 3) 1.
120 *Ibid*.
121 *Idem* 2.

become'. Woolf's writing does not represent an already expressed female identity, but a continuous exploration of woman – Woolf 'writes woman'.[122] Through her stream of consciousness writing 'identity is seen as the effect of a flow of speech'.[123] Buchanan and Colebrook, applying Deleuze to feminist theory, remark that feminism never aimed merely to challenge certain wrongs but also wanted to think differently.[124] They identify sexual difference as 'the question of our epoch – as the opening of a possibility for thinking beyond subjectivity and identity'.[125]

Human rights and also women's rights would be closer to molar politics, a politics of grounding. Unfortunately, a molecular politics is absent in these discourses, where rights are monumentalised and not opened to a continuous questioning. Any sense of becoming remains impossible. Human is reduced to immanence, albeit legitimate, with rights as the light and documents as lighthouses to keep one on the straight and narrow.

2.6 These must be the bones of a fallen angel[126] – the possibility of the archival sliver

> Tell me a story, Silver.
> What story?
> The story of what happened next.
> That depends.
> On what?
> On how I tell it.
> — Jeanette Winterson[127]

If the law, the constitution and human rights are, and will always be, caught up in their own limits, monumentalism and immanence, where does one turn to for a politics of action, revolt and becoming, in particular in a society where law, constitutionalism and human rights are seemingly all-pervasive? When invoking Derrida's comments on the impossibility of closure of the archive above, I tentatively referred to a similar

---

122 *Ibid.*

123 *Ibid.*

124 *Ibid.*

125 *Idem* 2–3. However, they also critically ask if Deleuze and Guattari's invocation of Woolf and the women's movement might be another domestication and subordination.

126 Laurie Anderson 'Pieces and parts' *Life on a string* (2001). Laurie Anderson tells the following story: 'They say that in 1842 on a plantation in Alabama the slaves unearthed a huge skeleton, the bones of a giant whale, a leviathan, from the time when all the world was covered with water from the Andes to the Himalayas and even Alabama was deep down under. And the slaves looked at the huge bones and they said: These must be the bones of a fallen angel. These must be the bones of a fallen angel. Out on the ocean out on the water, we look for signs of him. He looks like a giant snow hill, a fountain. Then he disappears. He's a speck on the horizon. We see him only in parts. The flash of a tail, his beating heart, He's in pieces and parts.' The same album also includes the song 'Statute of Liberty': 'Statue of Liberty stands in the harbor. Holding her torch. Hello, goodbye to all the men and women who pass through her port into the ocean. Now you're just another speck on the horizon, just another speck on the sea. Cool water, cool me. Freedom is a scary thing, not many people want it.'

127 Winterson (n 15) 129.

impossibility of the closure of law. Derrida argues that the archive will always be open to new readings, interpretations and contestations. The archive's attempt to forget will, as a result, always be unsuccessful. Could the same be said about the law? I am hesitant to make this argument. If one proclaims the limits of the law, should one not be consistent? Could I give in to the tension, to the opening of another paradox, law's potential within its impotence? But perhaps, in order to prevent another monumental reading, it is exactly the exploration of this paradox that could keep alive the memorial constitution and, ultimately, a political and ethical engagement with the limits of the law. I suppose with this I fall into the trap (again) of what my colleague Wessel le Roux has so succinctly described as another attempt at redeeming modernity,[128] or what Emilios Christodoulidis calls 'constitutional optimism'.[129] But I would like to recall Peter Fitzpatrick: 'Here we no longer find simple assurance. But assurance despite; not a clear correspondence or a nice subordination between things but rather what is isomorphic and mutually prehensive; not what is either compatible or contrary but compatible and contrary. Above all, in a sense, these lines of resolution and irresolution assume the lineaments of law'.[130]

Verne Harris describes the potential of the archive as offering nothing more than 'a sliver of a window'.[131] He rejects the common notion that archives reflect a glimpse on reality and argues that even if there was 'a reality' it is 'unknowable': with reference to Derrida, he explains that the event in its uniqueness is irrecoverable. Even that which could be recovered is fundamentally shaped by 'the act of recording' and thus always already interpreted. The reality reflected by archives is a complicit and deeply fractured and shifting reality.[132] Harris focuses on what he sees as the connections between 'the archival sliver and social memory'.[133] The archive, instead of closing down meanings, should strive for a releasing of meanings. The prevailing positivist paradigm would not allow a space for even 'the sliver of a window'.[134] Four features of this positivist paradigm are: (1) a pre-occupation with 'packaged information', excluding most, if not all, competing narratives; (2) a lack of understanding of the problematic of oral history; (3) a belief that one true version of reality can be represented without any interpretation; and (4) a neglect to expose the multiple layers of any text.[135] These four features are also applicable to traditional approaches to the constitution. The main concern of legal formalism and positivism has always been with ready-made, 'packaged' solutions. Traditional approaches to law share the insensitivity to oral history, thereby excluding

---

128 Wessel le Roux 'The aesthetic turn in the post-apartheid constitutional rights discourse' (2006) *Journal of SA law* 101–112. See also his comments about the redemptive nature of imaginative politics and jurisprudence in chapter three of this volume.

129 Christodoulidis (n 94) 401.

130 Peter Fitzpatrick *Modernism and the ground of law* (2001) 4.

131 Harris (n 12) 136.

132 *Ibid.*

133 *Ibid.*

134 *Idem* 149.

135 *Idem* 150-151.

many voices. The law can only acknowledge one version of reality/truth and, accordingly, fails to see multiple layers of texts and contexts. According to Harris, viewing the archive as 'a sliver of a sliver of a sliver of a window' would help the archive to be recognised as an 'enchanted thing, defined not by its connections to 'reality', but by its open-ended layerings of construction and reconstruction'.[136]

Could an approach of openness towards the archive, and for our purposes here also to the constitution, ultimately respond successfully to the inherent 'death-drives' of both? Could a reading and an application of the constitution as memorial, rather than a monument, contribute to a future where, to use Mamdani's terms, political reconciliation is durable and social reconciliation is taken seriously? As suggested above, this may seem a little optimistic. Christodoulidis reminds us that even 'constitutional optimism' ('constitutional pluralism' and 'constitutional agonistics') in arguments for inclusive constitutionalism creates 'constitutional irresolutions'.[137] He warns against the co-option of 'resistance as affirmation' by constitutional optimism. It is this kind of co-option that I think is also taking place in many human rights and gender mainstreaming discourses, in particular when it claims a connection with struggle. Christodoulidis calls for a refusal 'to settle for a political rationality that finds opportunity where the possibilities of radically reshaping the political landscape are already undercut'.[138] Should one in other words be cautious not only of the monumental constitution, but also of the memorial constitution, of not only political reconciliation, but also of social reconciliation? Could the archival sliver, in its interaction with a past and future and memory and imagination, for a moment reflect reconciliatory politics in a 'pure' sense? Christodoulidis could be regarded as having some optimism for politics: 'I think, that a radical rethinking of politics is under way in the mobilization of the anti-globalisation movements and with it comes an "epistemological break" with this "inclusive" pattern and frame of reference'.[139] In South Africa there are also examples of anti-globalisation movements, and every now and then one finds that they successfully rely on rights claims and constitutional politics in their challenge to neo-liberal capitalist policies. I am not arguing that they are successfully challenging what representation misses, nor the inevitable reductions of law, but I am hesitant to say that these civil actions are merely always already 'framed, called into line and belied'.[140] This calls for further research and investigation. For the present I tentatively frame the approach to law by these activists as memorial, and inquire into the potential of the memorial, the non-celebratory, the failed.

In a recent decision, *Khosa v The Minister of Social Development*,[141] the Constitutional Court had to decide whether certain sections of the Social Assistance Act[142] and the

136 *Idem* 151.

137 Christodoulidis (n 94).

138 *Ibid*.

139 *Idem* 432.

140 *Ibid*.

141 *Khosa v Minister of Social Development; Mahlaule v Minister of Social Development* 2004 (6) BCLR 569 (CC).

142 Act 52 of 1992.

Welfare Laws Amendment Act,[143] which limited access to certain social assistance benefits to South African citizens and their children, were constitutionally valid. Khosa and others were permanent residents who were in need of old-age pensions, child support and care-dependency grants, but who did not qualify to receive these benefits as they were not citizens. They challenged the respective statutory provisions as inconsistent with the s 9(3) prohibition on unfair discrimination and the s 27(1) right of everyone to have access to social security and assistance. The fate of these people recalled for me the words of Simone Weil, quoted by Christodoulidis in another context: '"You do not interest me." No man can say these words to another without committing a cruelty and offending against justice.'[144] The *Khosa* case presents a clear example in which the state, through parliamentary legislation, confirmed that claim. The message was that, if you are not a citizen of this country, 'you do not interest me', or at least do not interest me enough to care for your well-being.[145] The Constitutional Court decided that the legislation was constitutionally invalid, rejecting the arguments of the state in justification thereof. Although Mokgoro J wrote a long and detailed judgment in which she explained why the legislation was inconsistent with two constitutional rights,[146] I sense something else at play in her decision that is more important here than the legal discussion – something beyond law and legal language, something beyond rights that Simone Weil captured as follows:

> At the bottom of the heart of every human being, from earliest infancy until the tomb, there is something that goes on indomitably expecting, in the teeth of all experience of crimes committed, suffered, and witnessed, that good and not evil will be done to him. It is this above all that is sacred in every human being [...] This profound and childlike and unchanging expectation of good in the heart is not what is involved when we agitate for our rights. The motive which prompts a little boy to watch jealously to see if his brother has a slightly larger piece of cake arises from a much more superficial level of the soul. The word justice means two very different things according to whether it refers to the one or the other level. It is only the former one that matters.[147]

I sense a certain politics and ethics at play, a concern with protecting and enhancing lives, striving for a society where no one, but least of all the state, is allowed to say: 'You do not interest me.' This politics or ethics is at least hinted at in the following excerpt from Mokgoro J's judgment: 'Sharing responsibility for the problems and consequences of poverty equally as a community represents the extent to which wealthier members of the community view the minimal well-being of the poor as connected with their

143 Act 106 of 1997.

144 Emilios Christodoulidis 'Reconciliation as potentiality', unpublished paper read at a conference on 'Time, Reconciliation and the Law', Glasgow, May 2004. The Weil quote is from Simone Weil 'On human personality' in David McLellan (ed.) *Utopian pessimist: The life and thought of Simone Weil* (1990).

145 *Ibid.*

146 The exclusionary statutory provisions were found to be both unfairly discriminatory in violation of s 9(3) of the constitution and inconsistent with the right of everyone to have access to social security and assistance (s 27(1)). See *Khosa v Minister of Social Development* supra (n 141) at paras 40–85 for Mokgoro J's reasoning and conclusions in this respect.

147 Weil (n 70) 10; Burns (n 70) 480.

personal well-being and the well-being of the community as a whole'.[148] Could this decision be seen as an example of Harris's 'sliver of a sliver of a sliver of a window'? Of course, if one wants to recall the claims of law's violence and exclusion, this can also be done here – permanent residents have been granted social security and, accordingly, a chance to survive, but others who do not fall within either of the categories of 'permanent resident' or 'citizen' still are of no interest.[149]

In this chapter I have lamented the seeming absence of action, politics and revolt in present South Africa. I have put a great deal of the blame on the pervasiveness of law, constitutional law and human rights. I have relied on the distinction between monument and memorial, and between monumental and memorial approaches to the constitution and human rights. I used Arendt's concern with life, action and politics, Kristeva's call for continuous questioning and contestation, and Deleuze and Guattari's eternal becoming to counter the monumentalism of the struggle approach to human rights. I also referred to Cornell's elaboration of Spivak's critique on rights, in particular the ethics of representation concerning human rights. I argue for the monumental constitution, like Laurie Anderson's whale or Statue of Liberty, to remain as nothing but 'a speck on the horizon' and in 'bits and pieces', as memorial, its claim to light refuted.[150] Maybe in some very tentative way, having at our disposal nothing but 'the bones of a fallen angel',[151] we could hope for and dream for another law, another reconciliation and another life:

'Will that be done one day? It is not around the corner, as is said. But since the hypothesis of this unpresentable task announces itself, as a dream for thought, this madness is perhaps not so mad …'[152]

BIBLIOGRAPHY: CHAPTER 2

Books and articles

Arendt, H. *On Revolution.* New York: Penguin Books, 1977.

___. *The Human Condition.* Chicago: University of Press, 1958.

___. *The Origins of Totalitarianism.* New York: Harcourt Brace, 1966.

Botha, H. 'Democracy and Rights: Constitutional Interpretation in a Postrealist World'. *THRHR* 63 (2000):563.

148 *Khosa v Minister of Social Development* supra (n 141) at para 74.

149 The judgment explicitly declines to address the position of other excluded groups, such as temporary residents, asylum seekers and illegal immigrants, hinting instead that such groups can legitimately be excluded from social assistance benefits. See *Khosa v Minister of Social Development* supra (n 141) at para 59.

150 Anderson 'Pieces' (n 126) and 'String' (n 95). See footnote 126 for a brief description of Anderson's preference for the 'whale' or the 'Statue of Liberty' to be seen and thought of as no more than a speck on the horizson, as bits and pieces rather than a coherent whole.

151 Anderson 'Pieces' (n 126).

152 Derrida (2001) (n 34) 60. See also Fitzpatrick (n 130) 6: 'There is always "in" the legal judgment a "secret", a mystery, a "madness"'.

Buchanan, I. and C. Colebrook. *Deleuze and Feminist Theory.* Edinburgh: Edinburgh University Press, 2000.

Burns, S. 'Justice and Impersonality: Simone Weil on Rights and Obligations'. *Laval théologique et philosophique* 49 (1993): 477–486.

Christodoulidis, E. 'Constitutional Irresolution: Law and the Framing of Civil Society'. *European Law Journal* 9 (2003): 401.

___. 'Truth and Reconciliation as Risks'. *Social and Legal Studies* 9 (2000): 179–204.

Cornell, D. *Transformations.* New York: Routledge, 1993.

Deleuze, G. *Nietzsche and Philosophy.* Translated by H. Tomlinson. New York: Columbia University Press, 1983.

___. *Negotiations 1972–1990.* New York: Columbia University Press, 1995.

Deleuze, G. and F. Guattari. *A Thousand Plateaus: Capitalism and Schizophrenia.* Minneaoplis: University of Minnesota Press, 1987.

Derrida, J. *Archive Fever: a Freudian Impression.* Chicago: University of Chicago Press, 1996.

___. *On Cosmopolitanism and Forgiveness.* New York: Routledge, 2001.

Dietz, M. 'Feminist Receptions of Hannah Arendt'. In *Feminist interpretation of Hannah Arendt*, edited by B. Honig. University Park: Pennsylvania State University Press, 1995.

Du Plessis, L. 'The South African Constitution as Memory and Promise'. In *Transcending a Century of Injustice,* edited by C. Villa-Vicencio. Cape Town: IJR, 2000.

Fitzpatrick, P. *Modernism and the Ground of Law.* Cambridge: Cambridge University Press, 2001.

Harris, V. 'The Archival Sliver: A Perspective on the Construction of Social Memory in Archives and the Transition from Apartheid to Democracy'. In *Refiguring the Archive,* edited by C. Hamilton et al. Cape Town: David Philip, 2002.

Harris, V. 'The Archive, Public History and the Essential Truth: the Truth and Reconciliation Commission Reading the Past'. In *Refiguring the Archive,* edited by C. Hamilton, V. Harris, J. Taylor, M. Pickover, G. Reid and R. Saleb. Cape Town: David Philip, 2002.

Heyns, C. 'A Struggle Approach to Human Rights'. In *Pluralism and Law*, edited by A. Soeteman. Dordrecht: Kluwer Academic, 2001.

___. *Human Rights Law in Africa.* The Hague: Kluwer Law International, 2004.

Honig, B. 'Declarations of Independence: Arendt and Derrida on the Problem of Founding a Republic'. *American Political Science* 15 (1991):97.

___. 'Introduction: The Arendt Question in Feminism'. In *Feminist interpretations of Hannah Arendt*, edited by B. Honig. University Park: Pennsylvania State University Press, 1995.

___. 'Towards an Agonistic Feminism: Hannah Arendt and the Politics of identity'. In *Feminist interpretations of Hannah Arendt*, edited by B. Honig. University Park: Pennsylvania State University Press, 1995.

Klare, K. 'Legal Culture and Transformative Constitutionalism'. *SAJHR* 14 (1998):146.

Kohn, J. *Responsibility and Judgment: Hannah Arendt.* New York: Random House, 2003.

Kristeva, J. *Hannah Arendt: Life is a Narrative.* Toronto: University of Toronto Press, 2001.

___. *Revolt she Said*. New York: MIT Press, 2002.

___. *The Sense and Non-Sense of Revolt: The Powers and Limits of Psychoanalysis Vol 1.* New York: Columbia University Press, 2000.

Le Roux, W. 'The Aesthetic Turn in The Post-Apartheid Constitutional Rights Discourse'. *Journal of SA law* (2006):101.

Mamdani, M. 'When Does Reconciliation turn into a Denial of Justice?'. In *Memorial Lectures,* edited by S. Nolutshungu. Pretoria: HSRC, 1998.

Mureinik, E. 'A Bridge to Where? Introducing the Interim Bill of Rights'. *SAJHR* 10 (1994): 31.

Nancy, J. *Being Singular Plural.* Stanford: Stanford University Press, 2000.

___. *The Experience of Freedom*. Stanford: Stanford University Press, 1993.

Norris, A. 'Jean-Luc Nancy and the Myth of the Common'. *Constellations* (2000):7.

Snyman, J. 'Interpretation and the Politics of Memory'. *Acta Juridica* (1998):312.

Van der Walt, A. 'Dancing with Codes: Protecting, Developing and Deconstructing Property Rights in a Constitutional State'. *SALJ* 118 (2001):258.

___. 'Resisting Orthodoxy yet Again: Thoughts on the Development of Post-Apartheid South African Law'. *SAPR/PL* 17 (2002):258.

___. 'Roman Law, Fundamental Rights, and Land Reform in Southern Africa'. In *Roman Law at the Crossroads*, edited by J. Spruit, W. Komba, and M. Hinz. Kenwyn: Juta, 2000.

___. 'Tentative Urgency: Sensitivity for the Paradoxes of Stability and Change in Social Transformation Decisions of the Constitutional Court'. *SAPR/PL* 16 (2001):1.

Van Marle, K. 'Law's Time, Particularity and Slowness'. *SAJHR* 19 (2003):245.

Weil, S. 'Human Personality'. In *Selected Essays, 1934–43.* London, Oxford, 1962.

___. 'On Human Personality'. In *Utopian Pessimist: The Life and Thought of Simone Weil,* edited by McLellan. New York: Poseidon Press, 1990.

Winterson, J. *Lighthousekeeping.* London: Fourth Estate, 2004.

Case law

AZAPO v President of the Republic of South Africa 1996 (8) BCLR 1015 (CC).

Khosa v Minister of Social Development; Mahlaule v Minister of Social Development 2004 (6) BCLR 569 (CC).

Pretoria City Council v Walker 1998 (3) BCLR 257 (CC).

S v Makwanyane 1995 (3) SA 391 (CC).

THREE

Bridges, Clearings and Labyrinths: The Architectural Framing of Post-Apartheid Constitutionalism

Wessel le Roux

3.1 Introduction

Peter Goodrich writes that in virtually all its pre-classical definitions 'the word "law" – as, for example, *halachah, shari'a, Dike or dharma* – refers either directly or incidentally to the path, the way or the road: the law is the order of our going; it is the map, the compass, the route taken across a landscape, the direction by which we find the next

The law as path: The Great African Steps flanked by the old prison wall to the right, and the new Constitutional Court building to the left.

encampment'.[1] If not the word itself, then at least the dominant metaphors associated with it have, to the present day, remained tied to spatial images related to the crossing and mapping of a territory. Take post-apartheid law and constitutionalism, for example. The postamble of the interim Constitution of 1993,[2] which came into operation on 27 April 1994, described South African law as a path that lead across a definite topographical break in the political landscape. Closer investigation of the text revealed that the topographical break was more like a deep chasm, the path of the law more like a 'historical bridge' that had to make possible the safe crossing of a treacherous divide.

Almost a decade later, on 21 March 2004, President Thabo Mbeki officially opened the new Constitutional Court building on Constitution Hill in Braamfontein.[3] It was immediately claimed that this building, much like the constitutional bridge that preceded it on the path of the law, was a physical dramatisation of the democratic legal transformation that was unfolding in South Africa.[4]

From bridge to court building, the first decade of post-apartheid constitutionalism is marked by two significant architectural structures and events. Each of these events can be interpreted as a powerful statement about the nature of legal transformation in South Africa. The meanings that have become attached to these two events in South African legal writing, or what could be called the *architectural framing of post-apartheid constitutionalism*, form the topic of this chapter.

The chapter begins with an exploration of the different assumptions that constitutional writers have (by implication) made about the architectural design of the constitutional bridge between past and future. These interpretations range from the brutalism of a solid highway bridge to the eco-architecture of a narrow and windswept suspension bridge. Each of these interpretations rests upon, and at the same time inscribes, post-apartheid law into a particular understanding of space. The spatial aesthetics associated with each of these two bridges are, in turn, directly linked to a different understanding of the path or aesthetics of post-apartheid law.[5] I have in mind not so much where the path of the law might lead, but the manner in which it cuts or inscribes itself into the normative landscape (as open highway or as winding footpath). In order to explore these links, the discussion borrows heavily from the critique of Cartesian conceptions of abstract space and the hegemony of vision that have been

---

1 Peter Goodrich *Languages of law: from logics of memory to nomadic masks* (1989) 213.

2 Act 108 of 1993.

3 For a coffee-table introduction to the history of the building project which culminated in this historic moment, see Lauren Segal et al. (eds) *Number Four: the making of Constitution Hill* (2006).

4 Albie Sachs 'Judge and jury' (1998) *South African Architect* 27 at 29.

5 I use the term 'aesthetics' here in the same sense in which it is employed by Pierre Schlag 'The aesthetics of American law' (2002) 115 *Harvard LR* 1049. Schlag uses the term to suggest a more comprehensive approach to what is usually called the form (as opposed to the substance or content) of the law. The aesthetics of law is a coalescence of images and schemas, rhetorical forms, metaphors and other tropes, perceptual modes and sensibilities, dramatic tensions, sensory impressions and emotions and feelings (1052–1053). It refers to the specific patterns of thought or the way in which legal concepts and categories, like rights, are employed in the process of legal argumentation. My argument rests strongly on the discussions of the aesthetics of post-apartheid constitutionalism recently undertaken by André van der Walt 'Dancing with codes – protecting, developing and deconstructing property rights in a constitutional state' (2001) 118 *SALJ* 258; and Henk Botha 'Metaphoric reasoning and transformative constitutionalism' (2002) *TSAR* 612 (part 1) and (2003) *TSAR* 20 (part 2); 'Freedom and constraint in constitutional interpretation' (2004) 20 *SAJHR* 249.

implicit in recent critical theory. The design of the new Constitutional Court building is read in the light of this critique. The design reflects a deliberate attempt to instil a new (post-Cartesian) philosophy of space into South African architecture and thus to introduce a new (post-formalist) aesthetic into South African law. This alternative aesthetic centres on the architectural depiction of law as a clearing under a tree. This is the topic of the second part of the chapter.

From walking over a bridge to stepping into a clearing. This metaphoric shift has been celebrated by some as a powerful vindication of the repeated calls for a republican conception of transformative constitutionalism, for a shift in law from instrumental rationality (the highway) to communicative or deliberative rationality (the clearing).[6] In this vision, legal meaning is constantly subjected to an open process of dialogical contestation. Rights are accordingly not conceived of as rigid boundaries that require bridges and bridging, but as clearings that facilitate gatherings and the deepening of relationships through dialogue. However, a series of recent judgments by the Constitutional Court, most notoriously that delivered in *S v Jordan*,[7] have exposed the limits of this dialogical approach to post-apartheid constitutionalism. By focusing on the nature of the heterotopian urban spaces marked by marginal figures such as prostitutes, I hope in the third part of this chapter to draw attention to a gothic or labyrinthian constitutionalism in which the constitutional community is marked, not by its constant dialogical self-modulation, but by its constant deconstruction or dislocation. This chapter thus explores the path(s) of post-apartheid constitutionalism through the architectural metaphors of the bridge (crossing), the clearing (gathering) and the labyrinth (dislocating) respectively.

3.2 Bridges

The postamble to the interim Constitution of 1993 described the Constitution as a 'historic bridge' that would at the same time form the 'secure foundation' for a post-apartheid society.[8] The foundationalist language that accompanied the introduction of the bridge metaphor suggested from the outset that this constitution was to be understood as a concrete bridge; of the type most frequently found in South Africa along major

6 See for example Jacques de Ville *Constitutional and statutory interpretation* (2000); Henk Botha 'Civic republicanism and legal education' (2000) 41 *Codicillus* 23.

7 *S v Jordan* 2002 (6) SA 642 (CC). See also the discussion of the case by Henk Botha in chapter 5 of this collection.

8 The postamble stated that the interim Constitution 'provides a *historic bridge* between the past of a deeply divided society characterised by strife, conflict, untold suffering and injustice, and a future founded on the recognition of human rights, democracy and peaceful coexistence and development opportunities for all South Africans, irrespective of colour, race, class, belief or sex'. A few lines down in the same postamble we read that the 'adoption of this Constitution *lays the secure foundation* for the people of South Africa to transcend the divisions and strife of the past' (emphasis added).

highways. This image of the Constitution immediately caught the imagination of the South African legal community. The solidity of the concrete structure and the neatness with which it separated the world into opposing sides brought welcome conceptual relief amidst the uncertainties and anxieties of the times. The image promised that transformation in post-apartheid South Africa could be managed as the linear progression from one side of a conceptual dualism to the other. Transformation was essentially a process of *reversal* within an established normative hierarchy (as opposed to an unsettling *displacement* of the normative foundations of the hierarchy itself). The interim Constitution already neatly and helpfully defined that hierarchy in its postamble. It was not long before constitutional writers began substituting their own versions of the opposites between which legal transformation was to occur.[9]

The bridge metaphor was soon seized upon by the justices of the Constitutional Court in an attempt to capture the spirit of transformation after the fall of apartheid. In *Azapo v The President of the Republic of South Africa*,[10] the late Justice Didcott held that the bridge metaphor in the postamble to the interim Constitution implied an absolute break between the old and the new. The Truth and Reconciliation Commission (TRC) was designed precisely in order to achieve this absolute break. It implied that 'once the truth about the iniquities of the past has been established and made known, the book should be closed on them'.[11] For this reason the commission was preferable to a series of criminal and civil trials that would keep the wounds of the past open for an indefinite period. With this judgment, transformative constitutionalism was doubly inscribed into a linear conception of time: transformation meant moving forward from one side of a bridge to the other; and would as such soon be a thing of the past. As the book on the past would be closed, so the bridge from the past would be crossed.

It was not long before constitutional writers expressed concern about the linear conception of transformation, which the metaphor of the bridge seemingly implied. Pierre de Vos, for example, explains how the bridge metaphor was latched onto in order to restore an objective foundation for constitutional interpretation after the debunking of textualism.[12] The bridge metaphor held out the promise that the meaning of the constitutional text could be objectively determined with reference to the ills of the past. It implied that the history of South Africa could be neatly divided from some neutral vantage point into the apartheid past and the democratic future. The elevated vantage point in question could presumably be obtained from a look-out point on top of the concrete structure of the newly constructed constitutional bridge. From here a constitutional interpreter would be able to command the whole of the surrounding historical

---

9 Etienne Mureinik 'A bridge to where? Introducing the Interim Bill of Rights'(1994) 10 *SAJHR* 31 described the interim Constitution as a bridge from a deterministic 'culture of authority' to an open-ended dialogical 'culture of justification' (32).

10 *Azapo v The President of the Republic of South Africa* 1996 (4) SA 671 (CC).

11 *Idem* 701G–H.

12 Pierre De Vos 'A bridge too far? History as context in the interpretation of the South African constitution' (2001) 17 *SAJHR* 1.

landscape and settle the meaning of the constitutional text with reference to the evils of a fixed and completely knowable past.[13]

As attractive as the historical vistas from the top of the constitutional bridge might seem to be, De Vos was not won over by this disembodied look-out on the world. The idea of a concrete bridge with a commanding panoramic view, he argued, skewed one's understanding of history because it denied that history is always a political construction from a position within history itself. It also skewed one's understanding of constitutional interpretation because it claimed that the meaning of a legal text could be discovered with reference to the historical context in which it is read. Lastly, it skewed one's understanding of legal transformation because it presented transformation as the linear progression from the evils of the past (as we now understand them) to the cures of the future (as we now understand them), thus blinding us to new forms of marginalisation and oppression that might arise.[14]

André van der Walt sounded a similar warning about the dangers that the bridge metaphor held for what he took to be a proper understanding of transformative constitutionalism.[15] Like De Vos, he argued that the bridge metaphor threatened to reduce legal transformation to the linear and instrumental movement from one fixed position to another fixed position (the two sides of the bridge). This understanding of transformation is especially problematic where the two positions in question tend to lock legal thought into the same pattern of thinking. According to Van der Walt, this is precisely the case with the transformation of South African property law. The opposition to the apartheid property regime has by and large taken for granted the spatial conception of property developed in the Roman-Dutch tradition. In terms of this conception, rights are subjective freedoms individually exercised by the legal subject within fixed boundaries set by the law.[16] On the basis of this spatial conception of rights, the transformation of property has largely been approached as the redistribution of rights in property as understood within this paradigm. In fact, Van der Walt goes so far as to suggest that the bridge metaphor, tied as it is to the idea of rigid boundaries, lacks transformative potential because it merely amounts to a restatement of the basic analytical or spatial aesthetic

---

13 In chapter two of this collection, Karin van Marle draws a distinction between monumental and memorial engagements with the past, law and life in general, in order to problematise this assumption and law's claims of formal closure in general.

14 De Vos (n 12) 20–21.

15 Van der Walt (n 5).

16 André van der Walt (n 5) discusses this spatial aesthetic, its possible origins in German Pandectism and its correlative in the homelands policy of grand apartheid in detail. He summarises the conception of rights as bounded spaces as follows: 'Rights and the relationships between them are literally seen as clearly demarcated and separated spaces, basically in the same way that pieces of land and the boundaries between them are portrayed on a map. The underlying presupposition is that this is the only or the best or at least a suitable or morally, socially, politically and legally defensible way of enjoying and exercising rights. Rights are held and exercised individually, in clearly and strongly demarcated zones of exclusive autonomy, where the emphasis falls on the ability of the holder of the right to exclude others, to enforce his will on them, and to develop and assert his individual autonomy and personal well-being in the process. The function of the law is to define, patrol and enforce respect for the boundaries and to punish transgressions' (275). These same themes are further explored by van der Walt in chapter four of this collection.

of the Roman-Dutch private law paradigm.[17] In terms of this aesthetic, as described by Pierre Schlag, law operates in geometric fashion, like the straight lines of a grid drawn over a two-dimensional plane.[18] Legal conclusions are reached by placing the conceptual grid of the law over the facts at hand and noting the resulting legal coordinates. Factual particularities merely provide an opportunity to refine the comprehensiveness of the abstract conceptual grid.

In an attempt to break the hold of grid-like conceptions of space and law, André van der Walt suggests two alternative metaphors for the path of law through space. These alternatives both stem from his conviction that a 'more complex [understanding of] movement through time and space' is needed as a precondition for a truly transformative constitutionalism.[19] Van der Walt's first alternative is a more relational and less linear conception of the bridge metaphor itself.[20] A bridge, he reminds us, is not simply an instrument for getting from one place to another, but is brought into being by the abyss between the two points that it spans. Bridging is thus essentially a state of being suspended in the in-between. If the Constitution is not read as a bridge, but as an act of bridging in this sense, the greatest danger to transformation would be to stay on either side of the bridge, content in the apparent security of the conceptual ground under one's feet. Van der Walt invites post-apartheid legal scholars to risk the suspension of fixed legal positions and concepts, thus opening the possibility of more imaginative responses to the plight of the most vulnerable members of the political community.

Van der Walt's second alternative to the static and grid-like spatial aesthetic of the common law is the metaphor of the 'long walk' suggested by the title of Nelson Mandela's autobiography.[21] In spite of its equally linear overtones, says Van der Walt, the metaphor of 'the long walk' does allow for a more complex understanding of the legal journey through time and space. For one, it does not reduce every legal decision along the way to a stark choice between two abstract conceptual positions. The idea of transformative constitutional law as a 'long walk' at least leaves open the possibility of a more embodied and contextually rich traversal of space and time.

Van der Walt does not explore this suggestion any further, but perhaps Karin van Marle's discussion of the way in which a captured member of the San tribe from the nineteenth century experienced the long walk between his rural home and Cape Town, might help

---

17 *Idem* (n 5) 295.

18 Schlag (n 5) 1058. The relationship between modern Cartesian conceptions of absolute but empty space and the spatial aesthetics of classical legal thought is carefully explored by Schlag. Schlag identifies four aesthetics within which American law is cast: the grid, energy, perspectivist and dissociative aesthetics respectively. The grid aesthetic dominated American legal history in the classical scientific jurisprudence of roughly 1879–1920. Writing from an American perspective, Schlag suggests that this mode of legal thought is architecturally supported by the office towers of the modernist grid-like city and the 'fancy corporate law office on the thirty-eighth floor, where the ethereal, perfectly typed words of impeccably dressed attorneys produced highly mediated, largely unseen effects on the messy flesh of humanity below' (1061). Van der Walt's corresponding argument is that in the South African context this mode of legal thought is architecturally underscored by the bridge metaphor as it is usually understood.

19 Van der Walt (n 5) 259, n 10.

20 *Idem* 295–296.

21 *Idem* 259. Nelson Mandela *The long walk to freedom: The autobiography of Nelson Mandela* (1994).

to unpack the metaphor of constitutionalism as the manner of walking that Van der Walt has in mind.[22] Van Marle explains how the prisoner, known simply as //Kabbo, did not remember his homeland and his journey to Cape Town in terms of the spatial coordinates of mapped space or the universal flow of calendar time. The links between his past and the present were simply not mapped. His memories were materially tied to concrete objects and events that could not even be captured in the abstract conceptual network of language (let alone that of law or colonial maps). The attempt to reduce //Kabbo's memories to language is typical of the monumental culture of Bleek, the European philologist in whose custody //Kabbo eventually found himself.[23] The contrast between the embodied materiality of //Kabbo's indigenous African culture and the disembodied abstractness of Bleek's European culture, as it is encapsulated in the phenomena of philology, map making and neo-classical architecture, is decisive for van Marle's critique of modern law. She regards legal formalism and the static grid aesthetic it implies, as an essential part of the same culture that gave rise to uniform concepts of abstract time and homogeneous concepts of abstract space. At the same time, she presents //Kabbo's indigenous culture as the starting point for an alternative conception of post-apartheid law. Because of the radical materiality or embodiedness which marks //Kabbo's movement through time and space, he is more aware of, and attentive to, the complexity and polyvalence of objects and events. Van Marle calls for an introduction of this kind of attentiveness into constitutionalism, or what she calls the 'ethical interpretation' of rights.[24] Might this be what André van der Walt has in mind when he invites one to practise constitutionalism as a long or slow walk to freedom?

Van Marle suggests a second way in which the aesthetics of walking can be employed as a disruption of the jurisprudence of liberal legalism. In addition to the repressed materiality of traditional San culture, she also suggests the world of the novel (Milan Kundera's genre of *slowness*) as a second possible starting point for an alternative post-apartheid constitutionalism.[25] Van Marle specifically points out that Kundera draws a distinction between the spirit of the novel and the spirit of our age, by juxtaposing two

---

22 Karin van Marle 'Law's time, particularity and slowness' (2003) 19 *SAJHR* 239 at 246–247.

23 The relationship between //Kabbo and Bleek is powerfully reconstructed by MartinHall 'Earth and stone; archeology as memory' in Sarah Nuttall and Carli Coetzee (eds) *Negotiating the past: the making of memory in South Africa* (1998) 180–200. According to Hall, the 'Miscast' exhibition, which opened in 1996 in Cape Town, was an attempt to employ the materiality of San culture as a means of subverting the colonial project of symbolic domination (196). Hall significantly traces the roots of this colonial project back to the Renaissance and the mathematical principles and Albertinian rules of perspective (194). Even more significantly, he regards both the neo-classical civic architecture in the Cape Town Gardens (which today includes the post-apartheid Parliament building) and the leather-bound books in the public library, as extensions of that same undertaking in abstract visuality (188). Like Van Marle, Hall presents the culture of //Kabbo as radically subversive to this monumentalisation of space, culture and law.

24 Karin van Marle 'In support of a revival of utopian thinking, the imaginary domain and ethical interpretation' (2002) *TSAR* 501. The ethical interpretation of equality is an alternative to both formal and substantive concepts of equality. An ethical concept of equality does not try to define or describe the true reality of the gendered relationships between the sexes and thus to define the essential differences between men and women. Ethical interpretation responds to the utopian promise of the 'not yet' contained in the very idea of human rights. Because it does not accept any reality as given or final, it is always open to multiple interpretations of reality.

25 She further develops this jurisprudence of *slowness* in chapter two of this collection.

stock characters: the speeding motorcyclist and the ambling pedestrian.[26] Each of these figures captures a different way of moving through space and time (thus also through life). This contrast sheds new light on the aesthetics of walking and the constitutional implications that Van der Walt seeks to derive from that aesthetics.

The motorcyclist (who is depicted by Van Marle as the counterpart to the common law scientist) perceives space in abstract terms as a homogeneous plane, carved open and neatly divided by the straight lanes of the concrete highway. The ambler (who is freed from linear connotations of the long walk) perceives space in embodied terms as a rich and concrete interweaving of particular sights, sounds, smells and other tactile impressions. Given the European origin of Kundera's distinction, it seems sensible to associate Kundera's ambling pedestrians with the pedestrianised remnants of the old gothic towns of medieval Europe. On this basis, Van Marle could be read as presenting the street network of the gothic city (in its own way erotically dedicated to a celebration of the materiality, richness, messiness, particularity and plurality of life) as a second alternative to the hegemony of grid-like conceptions of space and grid-like conceptions of law. If legal formalism metaphorically conceives of the path of the law 'as a long, straight line, as a steady linear progression which proceeds on the basis of general principles', as was recently suggested by Henk Botha,[27] then legal formalism could be regarded as a close approximation to the straight lines which Haussman sought to impose with his baroque boulevards on the still largely medieval and gothic urban landscape of nineteenth century Paris. The rise of legal formalism would be nothing less than the total Haussmanisation of the law. Legal formalism could, from this perspective, be understood as an integral part of the hegemonic displacement of a gothic *sense of place* (the mediaeval street) with a modernist or Cartesian *concept of space* (the baroque boulevard and later the modernist bypass).[28]

---

26 Van Marle (n 22) 238.

27 Henk Botha 'Freedom and constraint' (n 5) 252. Botha contrasts the metaphoric depiction of the law as the straight lines of a grid with Duncan Kennedy's idea of the 'legal field' as an alternative spatial aesthetics for constitutional adjudication (260-264). Like André van der Walt, Botha claims that the traditional common law understanding of rules as clear boundaries frustrates the transformative aspirations of post-apartheid constitutionalism: 'There is a danger that constitutional guarantees may be reduced to common law-rules, or that common-law rules may be insulated from constitutional scrutiny, or that the adjudicative habits and assumptions which made certain outcomes appear inevitable under the apartheid legal order, will continue to go unchallenged' (276). Botha claims that constitutional guarantees should not be reduced to determinate norms with clear, solid boundaries but should rather be approached as broad flexible standards which allow for contextual, case-by-case analysis (277). It might be appropriate in this context to point out that the idea of law as a spatial field was originally developed by Felix Cohen 'Field theory and judicial logic' (1950) 59 *Yale LJ* 238 as a reaction against the hold of Cartesian conceptions of abstract and uniform space neatly divided in a grid-like fashion by legal boundaries (250). The 'field' introduced the ideas of relativity and curvature or perspective into conceptions of space and law. See also Laurence Tribe 'The curvature of constitutional space: What lawyers can learn from modern physics' (1989) 103 *Harvard LR* 1.

28 The transition from *place to space* is the central theme of two important studies by Edward Casey: *Getting back into place: Toward a renewed understanding of the place-world* (1993) and *The fate of place: A philosophical history* (1997).

The history of this displacement has been told many times and can easily be recalled to underscore Van der Walt's and Van Marle's attempts to break the hold of abstract conceptions of space and law on post-apartheid constitutionalism. Scott Lash, for example, describes the shift from the gothic labyrinth to the baroque grid as the essence of modernity.[29] The new grid of boulevards and avenues overran the old gothic city with abstract images of the city as a whole, and equally abstract ideas of absolutism and state power.[30] Closed and shadowy gothic squares were opened up and replaced with public spaces and vistas dominated by monuments, symmetrically flanked by public buildings. A regime of visuality came to dominate a more bodily, lateral, labyrinthine, uterine and feminine production of space.[31]

The production of public space in the baroque city was closely tied to the rise to public prominence of the allegory of a blindfolded Justitia, the goddess of justice. Martin Jay explains that it was only at the end of the fifteenth century that a blindfold suddenly appeared over the eyes of the goddess.[32] Initially a satirical addition, by the mid-sixteenth century it had become fully incorporated into the official legal discourse of the time. This curious incorporation coincided with other changes that occurred in the representation of law: artworks were removed from courtrooms and illustrations from law books, colourful seals on legal documents were replaced with simple signatures and judges became robed in neutral black and white colours. Jay relates these changes in legal culture to the rapid rise of science and abstract Cartesian versions of visuality in early modernity (at the cost of the more concrete versions of visuality that reigned during the Middle Ages). In this regard the blindfold of Justitia is interpreted by Jay as an attempt to veil the embodied perceptiveness associated with the feminine and the gothic, precisely to ensure that the hegemony of the new Cartesian conception of space was also extended to law. These changes all sought to purge law of any tactile or sensual attachments, a process that set law firmly on the road to what Jay calls 'the modern cult of the abstract and determinant norm of legal formalism'.[33] The new paradigm of impartial and formal justice resonated closely with the rise of the new urban, secular and bourgeois culture of the early modern period. It is therefore not surprising that an explosion of statues and fountains depicting a blindfolded Justitia can suddenly

29 Scott Lash *Another modernity, a different rationality* (1999) 17–88.

30 Walter Benjamin *The arcades project* (2002) 11–12 explains that the true aim of Haussman's projects was to secure the bourgeois city against civil war. The widening of the old streets was intended to make the erection of barricades impossible, the construction of the new avenues was to furnish the shortest route between the barracks and the workers' districts. This was thus a thoroughly military aesthetic, in which the speed of movement so abhorred by Van Marle and Kundera was the operative term.

31 Lash (n 29) 64.

32 Martin Jay 'Must justice be blind? The challenge of images to the law' in Costas Douzinas and Lynn Nead (eds) *Law and the image: The authority of art and the aesthetics of law* (1999) 19–35.

33 *Idem* 23–24.

be found next to the newly erected public buildings on the town squares of the baroque cities described by Lash.

David Harvey's comprehensive study of postmodernity provides further detail about the intimate relationship between modern law and the abstract Cartesian conception of space and the hegemony of vision.[34] Harvey claims that the history of capitalism, from medieval times to globalisation, has always been a 'geographical affair' closely linked to the manipulation of conceptions of space and place.[35] Relying on the work of Henri Lefebvre, Harvey explores various ways in which the struggle for power has taken the form of a struggle for space.[36] Harvey's argument centres around the way in which Renaissance conceptions of space supported the rise of individualism, subjective rights of ownership, nationalism and parliamentary democracy at the expense of feudal and dynastic privileges.

The argument is best illustrated by means of the history of map-making. Medieval maps told spatial stories. These spatial stories mapped practical space as a series of meaningful places along a path. Medieval map-making followed the paths between these places from the inside, as it were, and depicted changes in the embodied perspectives involved. These maps lacked a single, all-inclusive vantage point, and therefore typically emphasised the sensuous rather than the rational and objective qualities of a spatial order. The Renaissance brought about a radical transformation of this embodied approach to the depiction of space. Alberti introduced rules of perspective in mid-fifteenth-century Florence. Maps could now be drawn from a fixed disembodied or abstract point or single perspective. This perspective was elevated and distant, completely out of sensory reach, and resulted in a coldly geometric and systematic sense of space. Maps, like the courtrooms and books described by Jay, were, as a result, stripped of all signs of experience, and became abstract and purely functional systems for the grid-like ordering of the world.[37]

Harvey claims that the new map making was essential to the establishment of a new regime of subjective property rights.[38] In this regard he argues that the importation of the Ptolemaic map from Alexandria to Florence around 1400 was a decisive moment. The Ptolemaic grid allowed places to be located as mere positions or coordinates on a plane, as if the world were viewed from the outside. The result was the idea that space as a whole was knowable, quantifiable, conquerable and containable for purposes of private human ownership and action. This view was finally consolidated in the institution of private property in land, and the buying and selling of space as a commodity.

---

34 David Harvey *The condition of postmodernity: An enquiry into the origins of cultural change* (1989) 201–307.

35 *Idem* 234.

36 The basic assumption is that 'the class struggle is inscribed in space. Indeed it is the struggle alone which prevents abstract space from taking over the whole planet and papering over all differences' (quoted in Harvey (n 34) 237).

37 Harvey (n 34) 242–257 .

38 *Idem* 247.

There was, as Lefebvre has argued, no better way of achieving the complete homogeneity of space than through its total pulverisation and fragmentation into freely alienable parcels of private property to be bought and sold on the market.[39]

The complexity of the movement through time and space that Van der Walt and Van Marle wish to bring to law through the metaphor of the long or slow walk would resemble something of the embodiedness of medieval conceptions of urban space and the spatial stories of medieval map-making (as it would resemble the materiality of indigenous African cultures). Their argument, as I have tried to develop it over the last few pages, is that this type of embodiedness is not only precluded but actively suppressed by the grid-like aesthetic of private law science and the dominant interpretation of the bridge metaphor in post-apartheid constitutional discourse. For this reason, André van der Walt suggests that the idea of a long walk, rather than the idea of a single crossing, should direct thinking about post-apartheid legal transformation. He also suggests that the activity of walking and the experience of being suspended between two fixed points, are closely related (the house that I have left and the destination that I approach). Lastly, Van der Walt suggests that the architecture of bridges should respond to the aesthetics of walking (being on the way), rather to that of crossing (getting home). In this his tentative remarks show a remarkable similarity to Martin Heidegger's understanding of the architecture of bridges.

On 5 August 1951 Heidegger presented an influential discussion of bridges and bridging, informed by a critique of abstract, grid-like conceptions of space. The lecture dealt with the post-war housing shortage in Germany.[40] In the lecture Heidegger introduced a distinction between 'buildings' and 'dwellings'. Amongst buildings he counted highways and highway bridges (presumably, then, where Kundera's motorcyclist would be found). Heidegger's list of dwellings included an eighteenth century farmhouse nestled in the Black Forest, but more importantly, the river bridge in the *Altstadt* of Heidelberg (presumably in the vicinity where Kundera's amblers would be found). Heidegger introduced the distinction between the highway bridge and the Heidelberg bridge in order to clarify certain reservations he harboured about the post-war housing schemes. The real plight to be addressed, he said, lay not in the lack of houses but in the homelessness or nihilism dominating the current precarious age. Standardised mass housing could reduce the housing shortage, but it could not in any way counter the homelessness or nihilism enveloping modern subjectivity. The reason was simply that mass-produced housing, like all 'buildings', remained trapped in the abstract conception of Cartesian space and the technocratic revolution it engendered in the Western world. What was needed to counter this homelessness was a different understanding of the way human beings moved through space and time, an understanding Heidegger called 'dwelling'.

39 *Idem* 254.

40 Martin Heidegger *Basic writings* (1977) 320–339.

Heidegger explained that human beings existed as mortal dwellers on the earth, under the sky and before the gods. These elements constituted the fourfold dimensions of ethical human existence.[41] Dwelling meant caring for, or preserving, the fourfold in its rich particularity. To 'dwell' meant to save the earth (not to exploit and master it), to receive the sky (not to resist the natural flow and rhythms of the world), to await the gods (not to worship false idols), and to initiate human beings into their mortality (not to kill or otherwise eliminate the possibility of a good death). However, this ethical care-taking of things and fellow mortals does not and cannot take place in the abstract. Heidegger insisted that '[d]welling preserves the fourfold by bringing the essence of the fourfold into things'.[42] The essence of the fourfold can be brought into things in two ways: (1) by cultivating nature or (2) by constructing things. Dwelling is therefore never a purely passive letting-be of the fourfold. To dwell ethically means to build ethically. Building ethically, in turn, means to gather the fourfold together and thus to charge abstract space with a sense of place; to create an opening in the world where events can occur. It is in order to illustrate this ethics of building that Heidegger turns to the old river bridge in Heidelberg. The bridge gathers the fourfold together, says Heidegger, because it saves the earth by gathering it together in a landscape around the stream, it receives the sky by allowing the water to rise and fall without hindrance according to the rhythms of the seasons, and it initiates humans into their mortality before the gods by stimulating and providing meditative spaces where reflection about the ultimate crossing in life can occur.[43]

The old bridge creates a location – or a sense of bounded space – that differs radically from mathematical or abstract conceptions of boundless space. As such the bridge creates a possibility or opening for human dwelling. The design of the bridge is significant because the ontological (or ethical) dimension of the architecture is dominated neither by instrumental concerns about the function of the bridge (as is modernist highway architecture), nor by aesthetic concerns about its image (as is neo-classical civic architecture).[44]

Heidegger's understanding of the ethical dimension of architecture and his discussion of the old bridge in Heidelberg has inspired a number of attempts to formulate a

---

41 The Heideggerian fourfold is also explored in chapter one of this collection, where Johan van der Walt uses it as a way of approaching the ethics of responsibility and reconciliation in post-apartheid South Africa.

42 Heidegger (n 40) 329.

43 *Idem* 330.

44 Heidegger's conception of the ethical dimension of building and buildings has not appealed to everyone. Karsten Harries (*The ethical function of architecture* (1998) 152–166), for example, agrees on the one hand with Heidegger that our experience of space is an experience of bounded spaces, mediated by our encounter with things and the places or locations they constitute. This experience can thus not be captured in Cartesian conceptions of abstract, mathematical and boundless space. In this sense nihilism rests on a false and overly reductive understanding of our being in space. However, Harries takes the need for an ontological or ethical architecture seriously enough to raise concerns about the relevance of Heidegger's conception of such an architecture for modern metropolitan living. Harries questions whether Heidegger's conception of dwelling *as a staying within the fourfold* can provide a realistic alternative to the nihilism of our age. By describing dwelling as staying within the fourfold, Heidegger attempts to re-appropriate the archaic view that what gives human building measure and ground is some more primordial building, the sacred cosmic order. Harries is concerned that this understanding of dwelling negates the liberating promise of technology and relies on too strong a sense of place. Harries thus warns against the desire to appropriate Heidegger's thought as the basis of a democratic architecture – it is too rooted in the archaic, and too opposed to technology, too attached to the allure of the local and of blood and soil.

conception of democratic architecture for post-apartheid South Africa.[45] It would be possible to explore these attempts to unpack further the possible meanings of the bridge metaphor in post-apartheid constitutionalism. However, perhaps an even better starting point for a Heideggerian discussion of the post-apartheid bridge metaphor is provided by Julian Young's recent attempt to translate Heidegger's architecture of ethical dwelling into the basic design philosophy of the movement towards 'local', 'regional' or 'ecological' architecture.[46] Young captures the ethical spirit of this new architecture in an explanation of the ways in which bridges and other buildings can give expression to the sky:

> A construction can be 'ready' for the climatic conditions inherent in its site either *brutally* – in virtue of the brute power of reinforced concrete – or else through the elegant use of minimal force. But minimal force technology is expressive. A bridge constructed as a thoughtful rather than a forceful response to the local weather *expresses* that weather. This, perhaps, is why suspension bridges are often so beautiful. They are, as it were, wind harps, instruments which allow the wind to sing its song.[47]

Young suggests that the suspension bridge should serve as the paradigm for an alternative understanding of space and architecture (opposing the paradigm of the highway bridge and abstract space).[48] A suspension bridge is able to give expression to the sky because its design is not absolutely dominated by a linear function or a static image. The same applies to other elements of the fourfold. A suspension bridge is able to give expression to the earth by intensifying one's awareness of the abyss that brought the bridge into being in the first place, thus intensifying one's awareness of the activity of bridging or being suspended in the in-between itself. In this way the suspension bridge produces a charged location with a strange intensity to which the hiker (the counterpart of Van der Walt's 'walker' and Kundera's 'ambler') constantly finds herself returning.

This allure of the suspension bridge is of course, precisely what André van der Walt claims should inform post-apartheid constitutionalism.[49] It is a call for constitutional law as an expressive and contextually rich 'minimal force technology'. From this perspective the function of the constitution and the essence of transformative constitutionalism

---

45 See for example Bert Olivier 'Heidegger and architecture: preliminary remarks' and 'The question of human dwelling: architecture between art and technology', both in Bert Olivier *Critique, architecture, culture, art* (1998) 23–46; 47–56; and Estelle Maré 'Democratic vs revolutionary architecture: General concept and guidelines for the future South Africa' in *The South African Association of Art Historians Ninth Conference July 1993 (Conference Proceedings)* 27–32. More generally, Johan van der Walt also relies on the idea of dwelling in the fourfold as an ethical mode of existence as the basis for a post-apartheid ethics of responsibility and reconciliation (see again his remarks in chapter one of this volume).

46 Julian Young *Heidegger's later philosophy* (2002) 91–121.

47 *Idem* 113.

48 *Idem* 108–109.

49 Van der Walt (n 5) 296: 'Here, the focus is not on the two spaces on either side of the abyss, but on the abyss itself – the bridge is functionally and essentially linked to and obtains its significance from the abyss beneath it, so that the bridge is not a temporary instrument for a single crossing, one way, but allows and invites multiple crossings, in both directions, since there is no inherent value attached to being on one side of the bridge rather than the other'. The value attaches in other words to being on the bridge itself, suspended in the in-between and the creative and imaginative energy which this experience releases. Bridging is Van der Walt's jurisgenerative alternative to the jurispathic effect which the erection of conceptual bridges has on law.

is to resist formalism and the brute force technology of rules; to ensure that the law remains in a state of suspension, that is, to keep the in-between status of the law open, to keep the 'not yet' alive, to ensure that even the most fundamental dualism of the legal order can be contested through dialogical politics.[50] The value of the constitution attaches not to the fixed doctrinal position or rule which it enshrines, but to the way in which it enables legal rules that were regarded as fixed, objective, true and necessary to become suspended. The value of the constitution thus attaches to the act of suspension or bridging itself. This act is valuable, according to Van der Walt, because it releases an 'energy'[51] that stimulates the jurisprudential imagination to produce more complex and imaginative responses than 'the two places between which we have [thus far] chosen to choose'.[52] This anti-foundational and imaginative openness, which is also the mark of the minimal force aesthetic of ecological architecture (of which the new Constitutional Court building is an excellent example, to jump ahead in my discussion) is the essence of transformative constitutionalism as Van der Walt understands it.

However, what is missing from Van der Walt's celebration of legal creativity and the power of the jurisprudential imagination, is any reference to the limits of this imaginative constitutionalism.[53] In this regard it is worth noting that the sight of a suspension bridge spanning a seemingly groundless abyss resonates closely with the examples that Immanuel Kant provides, not of beautiful scenes in nature, but of experiences of the sublime – the '*astonishment*, amounting almost to terror, the awe and thrill of devout feeling, that takes hold of one when gazing upon the prospects of mountains ascending to heaven, deep ravines and torrents raging there, deep-shadowed solitudes that invite to brooding melancholy, and the like'.[54] What is significant about these sights is that the

---

50 In chapter two of this volume Karin van Marle distinguishes between 'monumental' and 'memorial' approaches to constitutional norms and judgments. This distinction resonates closely with the distinction between brute force and minimal force technologies which I introduce here. In chapter five, Henk Botha develops a conception of complex equality in which the constitutional rights discourse approximates the 'memorial' or 'minimal force' architectural aesthetic which is invoked here.

51 Young (n 46) 304.

52 *Idem* 296. André van der Walt 'Closure and openness on difference and democracy: a response to Justice Johan Froneman' (2001) 12 *Stell LR* 28 at 39 argues that a decisive distinction in post-apartheid constitutionalism lies 'between the judges who take part in the transformative process, but who want to get the new order and its accompanying legal system established and developed as soon and as completely as possible and to confirm and entrench this new system as clearly and systematically as possible, so that everyone knows how things stand and how they work; and those who are willing to suffer the anxiety and the discomfort of continual change and openness'.

53 The same can be said about Henk Botha's equally powerful celebration of the centrality of the creative legal imagination in transformative constitutionalism. Botha 'Metaphoric reasoning'(n 5) simply assumes that the metaphoric nature of law by itself ensures that a ready source is available for the imagining of alternative worlds. The only requirement is that we move our focus from rules to metaphors and embrace the metaphoric structure of law and legal argumentation. All objectivity will then be exposed as simply a failure of imagination. The alternative would be twofold: to use existing metaphors more creatively and to imaginatively invent new ones. Given the plenitude of constitutional meaning(s), very few real crises or problems beset this imaginative constitutionalism.

54 Immanuel Kant *The critique of judgement* (1952) 120–121. Other examples include 'the broad ocean agitated by storms' (92), 'shapeless mountain masses towering one above the other in wild disorder' (104), 'bold, overhanging, and, as it were, threatening rocks', 'thunderclouds piled up the vault of heaven, borne along by flashes and peals', and 'the high waterfall of some mighty river' (110). These are all examples of the unimaginable might or magnitude of nature.

creative human imagination encounters its limits in them, precisely because it is unable to capture the magnitude or might of nature fully. Here there is no serene sense, comfort or closure of place involved. In these sights or events the unimaginable or unpresentable is encountered, resulting in both anxiety (the vastness or power of nature threatens to overwhelm the imagination) and exhilaration (the mind is not overwhelmed but fortified in its ability to think and form ideas, thus confirming the superiority of reason over sensibility). On this basis Kant presents the sublime as a negative presentation of the unpresentable (in his case the ideas of reason and thus the whole of morality).[55]

If Van der Walt's celebration of bridging is linked to the experience of the sublime, a slightly different understanding of transformative constitutionalism announces itself. Rights do not serve as the opportunity for the imaginative release of the normative essence of a richly depicted context. There is no closure, or normative comfort to be had in the context. Contextualisation makes the ability to exercise reflective judgement imaginatively possible and impossible at the same time. It is an aporetic undertaking. Constitutionalism must take this aporetic nature of a contextually rich constitutional politics of interpretation seriously. Constitutionalism must take the limitations (as opposed to the power) of the imagination as its starting point.

The outlines of such a constitutionalism can be derived from the reading of the Kantian sublime undertaken by Jean-François Lyotard. Lyotard defines the *postmodern* as a response to the Kantian sublime which is best illustrated as praxis by artistic and avant-garde modernism.[56] In modernist art, but also in law and politics, the postmodern is characterised by the paradoxical testimony through acts of presentation that the unimaginable or unpresentable exists. From this perspective the task of transformative constitutionalism would be the same as that ascribed by Lyotard to the artistic avant-garde: a constant 'scrutiny of the pictorial techniques used to instill a belief in [reality]' coupled with a constant exposure of 'the artifices of presentation that allow thought to be enslaved by the gaze and diverted from the unpresentable'.[57]

This starting point informs Lyotard's critique of both classical liberal legalism (formalism) and its republican alternatives (imaginative or deliberative constitutionalism). On the assumption that every poetics (discourse pragmatics) implies a politics, Lyotard introduces three contrasting approaches to constitutional politics.[58] In terms of premodern constitutionalism, the answer to the question of justice is provided by the politics of the model. Plato asserted that claims to justice (prescriptive statements) could be justified with reference to the truth (descriptive statements). Constitutional disputes are likewise

---

55 *Idem* (n 54) 127.

56 Jean-François Lyotard *The postmodern explained: Correspondence 1982–1985* (1992) 1–16.

57 *Idem* 12.

58 Jean-François Lyotard and Jean-Loup Thébaud *Just gaming* (1985) 19–43.

to be settled with reference to authoritative descriptions of legal concepts. In terms of modern constitutionalism, by contrast, the answer to the question of justice is provided by the politics of autonomy. Rousseau and Kant both asserted that a prescriptive statement is just, only if those subject to it could be regarded as its authors. In terms of discourse pragmatics, modern constitutionalism posits the democratic or republican subject as both the sender and the addressee of the same prescriptive statement. Justice is thus defined without recourse to discourses of truth but relates purely to discourses of freedom. The important point is that justice still forms part of a representational discourse, but that discourse is now understood as a discourse of self-representation.

The postmodern approach to constitutionalism claims that the answer to the question of justice is the politics of paganism. Paganism is simply the belief that there are gods. In paganism no maker of statements or teller of stories is therefore ever autonomous. Every speaker is first of all a listener. The impossibility of translating listening into speaking without remainder, and the slippages involved in the process, become the focus of politics. Justice is no longer defined as a form of representation, but in terms of the limits of presentation, the sublime and the unpresentable.[59] In terms of discourse pragmatics the postmodern is captured by the Jewish understanding of Yahwe's prescription to Abraham: because no image can or may be made of Yahwe, He (God) arrives only as a voice that addresses and thus radically positions Abraham as an addressed subject. The senders and the addressees of prescriptive statements are radically asymmetrical and cannot be interchanged (as in the Platonic pragmatics of scientific truth) nor dialogically made to overlap (as in the republican pragmatics of autonomy). Any attempt to this effect comes up against a *differend*.

In terms of discourse pragmatics the *differend* describes the structural (or post-structural) limit between two discourse positions or statements. For example, the *differend* marks the limit between the addressed 'you' and the addressing 'I' (or put differently, between prescriptive statements and descriptive statements). However, it is crucial to understand that the *differend* is not simply a difference between two positions or pragmatics. The *differend* does not exist in the abstract and cannot be conceptually unpacked in the form of a series of conceptual dualisms. The *differend* is only indicated by the feeling of the sublime, which is an experience of the limit which is encountered when an attempt is made to present one pragmatics in terms of another, for example when a sighted person tries to present through sounds to a blind person what a colour looks like. The same applies when an attempt is made (essential and necessary as it is) to present the pragmat-

59 On this ground Dwight Furrow (*Against theory: Continental and analytical challenges in moral philosophy* (1995) 136) sets Lyotard and Levinas apart from both traditional legalism and recent attempts to mediate law pragmatically (Rorty) or narratively (Nussbaum). Every attempt to ground justice in the (re)description of existing law and legal categories, no matter how imaginatively or narratively employed, fails to capture the paradoxical dynamic of justice, obligation and responsibility. It remains an attempt to derive justice from law. Both Lyotard and Derrida recognise the necessity to do so (justice which would not include a reference to democratically legitimate law would forsake the right to be called justice), but both seek to draw attention to the *differend* or *differance* at the heart of this derivation, that is the slippages and displacements which are involved. Rules do not convert to imaginative stories or dialogues but to aporias and *differends* (see below).

ics of ethics (being obliged) in terms of the pragmatics of law (justifying obligations). In all these cases an essential slippage occurs. In all these cases the *differend* arises as the limits of the presentable, and thus as a negative presentation of the unpresentable in the act of presentation itself.[60]

Johan van der Walt and Henk Botha have recently formulated an approach to constitutional interpretation which comes close to the postmodern constitutional *praxis* of negative representation suggested by Lyotard.[61] Their version of constitutionalism rests on the assumption that the counter-majoritarian difficulty is irresolvable.[62] The gap between constitutional adjudication and democracy arises, not because constitutional adjudication overshoots actually instituted democratic politics, the mandates of which should be narrowly constructed, but because constitutionalism can never sustain a fundamental precondition of the democratic political community, namely plurality.[63] Van der Walt and Botha suggest that the Constitution should paradoxically be read as the constitution of 'a community without community'.[64] On this basis they argue that the limitation of rights should be understood as the provision of *unjust* reasons for constitutional norms.[65]

With this version of post-apartheid constitutionalism we have, through our exploration of the bridge metaphor which was introduced into South African jurisprudence by the interim Constitution, arrived at essentially three different approaches to transformation and constitutionalism. In the first approach the rights entrenched in the constitution are *defined* in an abstract way as fixed boundaries. The idea is to exclude certain claims logically in advance and entrench the gains that have been made since the bridge which led into the new South Africa was crossed. The second approach to constitutionalism is derived from attempts to rehabilitate a more embodied movement

---

60 See the complex discussion of phrase regimes, presentation and the inevitability of the *differend* in Jean-François Lyotard *The differend: Phrases in dispute* (1988). The links which Lyotard establishes between the Jewish interdiction against presentation, the sublime and postmodern constitutionalism radicalise the critique of Cartesian visuality and abstract space which informs van der Walt's and van Marle's understanding of post-apartheid constitutionalism in chapter one and two of this collection respectively. This radical critique of the hegemony of vision in the Western political tradition is a defining characteristic of French thought after the failed student revolts of May 1968, or what has been described as the flight from Mao to Moses (see the extensive discussion of this body of thought in Martin Jay *Downcast eyes: The denigration of vision in twentieth-century French thought* (1994) 543–586).

61 Johan van der Walt and Henk Botha 'Democracy and rights in South Africa: Beyond a culture of justification' (2000) 7 *Constellations* 341. See also chapter one of this collection in which Johan van der Walt links the idea of negative representation with the politics of reconciliation.

62 *Idem* 350.

63 *Idem* 352. In other words, constitutionalism is beset by a *differend* because it must translate the ethical relationship between two individuals (radical asymmetry) into the legal relationships between three or more individuals (radical symmetry). In the words of Johan van der Walt (*Tangible mais intouchable, la loi du tact, la loi de la loi* (2002) 102), constitutionalism must translate the 'e-normous' responsibility to the Other into constitutionally justified norms to others.

64 Van der Walt and Botha (n 61) 351. On another occasion Johan van der Walt ('The quest for the impossible, the beginning of politics: a reply to Dennis Davis' (2001) 118 *SALJ* 463 at 466) explicitly aligns this understanding of constitutionalism with the avant-garde modernism which Lyotard celebrates as the paradigm of postmodern political, legal and moral discourse: 'The modernist desire for reality found expression in the constant destruction of available styles. This destruction held vacant the place of truth in art. The irreducible non-representability of the people is [similarly] the condition for politics'.

65 Van der Walt and Botha (n 61) 352.

through space and time. This approach resists the conceptual closure of constitutional discourse by reinterpreting transformative constitutionalism as an act of bridging, that is as a suspension of doctrinal certainties. The challenge posed by constitutionalism is to *delimit* an open spectrum of right claims imaginatively in a variety of concrete contexts.[66] But if the reinterpretation of the bridge metaphor opened new possibilities for dialogical and republican constitutionalism, it also opened the door for an exploration of the limits of republican constitutionalism by highlighting the feelings of the sublime sparked by suspension bridges. From this third perspective, constitutional review is an attempt to activate the *differends* besetting constitutional discourse. Constitutional norms, once understood as rules, have been reconceived, first as open-ended radial categories, and then as aporias (*differends*).

It might be claimed that this discussion of the bridge metaphor has lost most of its pertinence at the close of the first decade of democracy, as the bridge metaphor has dated and is no longer the central architectural reference point of post-apartheid constitutionalism. That honour has now been granted to the new Constitutional Court building, which has, much more powerfully than any constitutional text could ever metaphorically have done, literally introduced a new set of architectural designs and images into South African law. Besides the obvious point that such a claim would itself confirm the hegemonic position of the linear interpretation of the bridge metaphor in South African law, it greatly understates the extent to which the design of the new building is directly implicated in the critique of abstract Cartesian space and the spatial aesthetic of law introduced above. However, this claim does force the issue of the architectural framing of post-apartheid law into the foreground. How does the new Constitutional Court building, which is also said to capture the spirit of post-apartheid constitutionalism, resonate with the different bridges of post-apartheid constitutionalism? In particular: how does the design respond to the attempts to conceive of democratic politics and constitutionalism beyond the confines of Cartesian models of space, vision and subjectivity?

3.3 Clearings

The main approach to the entrance of the new Constitutional Court building leads from the north up the Great African Steps. These steps leading up Constitution Hill are symbolically flanked on the left by the glass wall of the Constitutional Court building and on the right by the stone wall of 'Number Four' prison (one of the preserved buildings of the original prison site on which the court building is situated).[67] This is

---

66 The distinction between the *definition* and *delimitation* of rights is that of Van der Walt and Botha; see (n 61) 355.

67 This juxtaposition is a key feature of the design of Constitution Hill. The history of 'Number Four' prison and its relationship to the rest of Constitution Hill is discussed in Lauren Segal (n 3). The bridge metaphor also informs other design elements of the new constitutional precinct. Consider, for example, the following symbolic re-appropriation of the ramparts around the old Fort: "No longer needed for surveillance, intimidation or incarceration, the ramparts now serve as a vantage point over Constitution Hill, the city of Johannesburg, and South Africa in the process of transition. They serve as a bridge between the difficulties of the past – as represented by the derelict prison buildings – and the possibilities of the future – as represented by the Constitutional Court" (18).

a dramatic architectural re-enactment of the divide between the past and the future, the old and the new, apartheid and democracy. As such, it resonates closely with the bridge metaphor that was originally introduced into post-apartheid constitutionalism through the interim Constitution of 1994. The only difference is that this time there is no mention or sight of any bridge. In fact, it would appear that the completion of the Constitutional Court building, which is situated on the democratic side of the divide, has rendered the continued existence of a bridge or talk of a bridge obsolete. Given the dominance of the linear conception of transformation in post-apartheid jurisprudence, this should have been expected. The new Constitutional Court building is a clear confirmation that the dividing boundary between the past and the future has been crossed and that the bridge that made that crossing possible has been demolished (as Van der Walt correctly predicted it would be).[68]

However, there are also features of the Great African Steps that suggest that the architecture of the new Constitutional Court building could be approached from a completely different angle. The steps do not follow a linear and directional path up the hill, but wind along the contours in a fashion deliberately intended to resonate with the cattle paths that lead up the many hills of rural South Africa. The steps are similarly sheltered from the sun by the indigenous thorn trees that can be found scattered across the South African veld. The enclosed space of the Great African Steps is therefore not merely a functional or instrumental means of approaching the court entrance, nor merely a symbolic expression of a conceptual dividing line cutting through abstract space; it is also, and primarily so, an attempt to create a more embodied sense of place centred around material references. In this way the winding footpath that is cut into the Great African Steps recalls the idea of constitutionalism as a long or slow walk, which was briefly introduced above.[69] It suggests a radically non-Cartesian approach to space even before the building is entered. It soon becomes clear, however, that the design of the building sets out to produce a material sense of lived space as the essence of what is regarded as legal or public space. What happens when this alternative spatial aesthetic is celebrated and brought to bear on the aesthetics of law? The different ways in which this question can be answered are explored in this second part of this discussion.

Nearly all commentators on the building have concentrated their attention on the alternative philosophy of space and building which informs the design. This philosophy stood out from the outset. Justice Albie Sachs, who was a member of the jury responsible for the selection of the final design, explains that the design won the international competition primarily because of the new approach to building and space which it expounded.[70] The confines of this chapter do not allow me to explore all the dimensions of this alternative understanding of space and architecture fully. The discussions of the building already undertaken in architectural circles will have to stand

---

68 Van der Walt (n 5) 260.

69 See the text corresponding to footnotes (n 20) to (n 25) above.

70 Albie Sachs 'Foreword', in Sabine Marschall and Brian Kearney *Opportunities for relevance: Architecture in the new South Africa* (2000) xi. See also the comments in Albie Sachs (n 4).

in for this purpose.[71] Suffice it to say that the design philosophy can be understood in Heideggerian terms as an example of 'performative architecture',[72] or as 'democratic architecture',[73] 'regional architecture',[74] 'ecological architecture',[75] or more generally as

71 Many of the distinctive design features are extensively discussed in Wessel le Roux 'From acropolis to metropolis: The Constitutional Court building and South African street democracy' (2001) 16 *SAPR/PL* 139. See also the special feature on Constitution Hill and the Constitutional Court in (2003) 8 *Urban Green File* 18–27 and the discussions by Marschall and Kearney (n 70) and Lipman (n 77) mentioned below.

72 At the end of the 1980s Bert Olivier (n 45) presented the idea of performative architecture as a possible basis of post-apartheid architecture. He derived this concept of architecture from Heidegger's critique of the Cartesian conception of extended space, as precluding human dwelling. Olivier insisted that human beings cannot live in the homogeneity of endless space. As living bodies we demand heterogeneity and boundaries, periods and regions. Olivier regarded apartheid South Africa as an extension of the technocratic age of endless space in which buildings are mass produced out of standardised materials and the city becomes reduced to a 'drab, architecturally largely uniform suburban zone' (48). This technocratic functionalism cannot serve human dwelling. Neither can its radical opposite, namely architecture producing striking images to be viewed from a distance, or aestheticism. Olivier suggested that architecture, traditionally regarded as neither pure technology nor pure art, is ideally situated to point post-apartheid South Africa beyond the impasse of modernity. Following Karsten Harries, he suggested that the key lay in a return to the ontological function of building. Building should be re-thought as a way of articulating our human mode of dwelling (being), our sense of place and thus our ethos. Buildings should not be viewed primarily as objects in abstract space, but as to be inhabited as lived spaces. At its most general level, only architecture which contained a performative element had any potential as a place of dwelling. Performative architecture opened itself as 'uncompleted architecture' to its inhabitants or users, much as a musical score opened itself as an essentially uncompleted product to its performers. Dwelling is per definition foreclosed by aesthetic or technocratic architecture (in which image and function, as opposed to human creativity and improvisation, dominate the design). A key element which contributes to the performative potential of a building is the use of natural light (29). Like Mugerauer (n 73) and Young (n 45), Olivier referred explicitly to the use made of natural light and skylights by architects like Alvar Alto and Louis Kahn (29). The use of natural light in the design of the Constitutional Court building can now be added to this list. The play of light reveals the infinite moods of architectural shapes and surfaces. It undermines any uniform conditioning of human responses to the utilitarian or aesthetic regimes of buildings. Instead it opens up an inexhaustible variety regarding the discovery of colour, light and warmth in brick, stone and wood (33). However, like Estelle Maré (n 73), Olivier never fully developed these ideas into a new conception of civic architecture for post-apartheid South Africa. He simply accepted that public architecture lent itself more readily to an aesthetic or monumental architecture of the image, and on that basis located performative architecture in houses and churches (53). The significance of the new Constitutional Court building lies precisely in the fact that the design team effectively conceived a new generation of public buildings as performative architecture.

73 At the beginning of the 1990s, on the eve of the transition to democracy, Estelle Maré (n 43) made a call for 'democratic architecture' in post-apartheid South Africa as opposed to the 'revolutionary architecture' which she feared would dominate post-apartheid culture. Maré described 'revolutionary' architecture as buildings and monuments commissioned to express the ideology of the new regime, at least during an initial stage of political image-building. In this case buildings are approached as free-standing and self-contained objects and striking edifices. 'Democratic architecture', by contrast, sought to facilitate dwelling in a meaningful human life-world. In this case buildings are approached as place-creating environments supporting the creativity of people. In short, Maré understood the democratisation of architecture as a shift from power-centred architecture to people-centred architecture. In spite of her general comments about a possible post-apartheid architecture derived from Heidegger's writing, Maré's only detailed study of dwelling in architecture remains restricted to temple architecture (Estelle Maré 'Myth and architecture: Heidegger's fourfold in Greek, Shinto and Christian architecture (1992) 24 *Acta Academica* 30). It is an open question whether she would regard the new Constitutional Court building as an example of democratic architecture as she originally conceived of it.

74 Robert Mugerauer, in 'Architecture as properly useful opening' in Arleen B. Dallerly and Charles E. Scott (eds) *Ethics and danger: Essays on Heidegger and continental thought* (1992) 215–226; and *Interpretations on behalf of place: Environmental displacements and alternative responses* (1994) 65–120, derives the idea of regional or local architecture from Heidegger. Mugerauer argues that an architecture of dwelling would be an architecture that begins by holding itself back, or keeping itself in reserve. In this architecture buildings would no longer function as expressions of an ego of

'relevant architecture',[76] or even as 'critical regionalism'.[77] In all cases there is agreement that the new paradigm conceives of space in embodied terms as a lived or practical, and therefore continuously shifting and changing, reality, and no longer as an abstract geometrical construction dominated by abstract images or functions.

It is significant that Albie Sachs, one of the leading justices on the bench of the Constitutional Court, understands this shift away from image and function in very non-Heideggerian terms as a rationalisation of culture and architecture. Sachs regards the design and architecture of the building as an example of 'critical modernism'.[78] According to him, the Constitutional Court building undertakes a restoration of the critical rationality of modernism against two of its later mutations: the crass commercialisation (or what he calls the 'clumsy arbitrariness') of postmodernism, on the one hand, and the aesthetic self-projection of functionalism and the international style, on

---

artistic subjectivity, nor as products for consumption or aesthetic experience (217). Buildings would be regionally sensitive responses to the ways in which other human beings have responded to the natural, human and sacred realms (218). As an example of such an architecture of self reserve, Mugerauer refers to the Kimbell Art Museum in Fort Worth by Louis Kahn. The building responds to its natural environment firstly through the use of light. By providing slits in the roof, the interior of the museum is not subjected to uniform light (as if it is merely an extension of abstract space) but to natural light in its daily and seasonal rhythms and variations. Secondly, the museum is not so much an object as the occurrence of a site where other events are allowed to occur. Here the building withdraws in order to provide an opening for other ontological events (i.e. dwelling) to occur. According to Mugerauer, this kind of architecture will be the result 'when, together, people take up their problems and ideals and talk with one another as may occur in community marketplaces, at the kitchen table, or with an interviewer who genuinely listens. Clearly, things are not seen globally in these cases, but in terms of specific places which we usually call 'locality' and 'region'. Thus, planning and building take place in the midst of what is local – within local traditions, materials, skills, needs, animal and plant life, climate, dress, customs, foods, dialects, and so on' (68-69). The Constitutional Court building embodies all the elements Mugerauer celebrates and could thus serve as an even better example of public architecture conceived of as regional architecture.

75 Young (n 46) enlists Heidegger in the name of ecological architecture. The way buildings make use of natural light (or in his terms 'gather the sky') is a key element of this type of architecture. The use of natural light is one of the most important design features of the Constitutional Court building and largely defines the nature of the spaces inside the building. By contrast, Young claims that the modernist shopping centre is such a depressing place because it blocks out the ever-changing natural light and replaces it with the monotonous and oppressive uniformity of fluorescent light. What he calls 'authentic builders' will refrain from isolating the building in this way from the natural rhythms of the sky. Young, like Mugerauer (n 74) and Olivier (n 45) refers in this regard specifically to the use of skylights by Alvar Aalto. According to Young, similar considerations apply to the blocking of the natural flow and shifting vibrations of natural air. Authentic builders will, wherever possible, abhor the uniformity of air-conditioning (112). Again, the Constitutional Court building could serve as an example, as it relies for a large parts on a passive (natural air-flow) conditioning system.

76 Marschall and Kearney (n 70) 134. Marschall and Kearney helpfully identify six defining principles of the new architecture, all of which can be traced in the architecture of the Constitutional Court building (as they themselves point out). These are: enhancing community participation; subjecting architectural image to local appropriateness; approaching architecture as process rather than product; approaching architecture as a combination of high and low technologies; ensuring architectural legibility; and ensuring environmental responsiveness.

77 Alan Lipman *Architecture on my mind: Critical readings in design* (2003) xvii. Lipman describes the Constitutional Court building as the 'promise of a fresh, confident South African architecture' (74). He hails this architecture as an alternative to the 'banality of contemporary South African architecture' (xi). By this he means the thrall of faked-up materials, the superficial borrowing from European styles (such as Tuscan), the use of quick-fix, unreliable and cheap building materials, the re-cycling of neo-classicisms and the yearning for imported status (all features of postmodernist consumerism and globalisation). By contrast, regional designers 'seek to interpret and give expressive form to local identities; to distinctly local ways of living, of constructing and of using buildings' (xvii). Critical regionalism is about the materiality of 'space, light and organisation, not style, charm or whimsy' (xiii).

78 Sachs (n 70) xii.

the other. The new architecture is explicitly presented by Sachs as an alternative to the technical mastery, domination and exploitation of the environment made possible by instrumental rationality and pitifully expressed in the urban environment inherited from apartheid. In contrast to this environment, Sachs regards the new building as the catalyst for a 'new rationality to emerge'.[79] As he sees it, the basis of this 'new rationality' is an inclusive human dialogue and interaction. The Constitutional Court building proves that architectural solutions to the challenges posed by the development and political reconstruction of post-apartheid South Africa will only emerge when 'a multiplicity of new imaginations are drawn into the dialogue'.[80] The Constitutional Court building therefore introduces an architecture that is characterised by its 'participatory processes', not its 'spatial forms', as Alan Lipman succinctly puts it.[81] From this perspective the new Constitutional Court building is the architectural equivalent or expression of the shift from instrumental to communicative rationality. It represents a new way of finding solutions to architectural design problems, not through the technical mastery and skill of the architect alone, but through processes of community participation and intersubjective deliberation.

None of the discussions of the building that have already been undertaken has included an attempt to relate the design philosophy of the Constitutional Court building, and the new sense of space which it enacts, directly to the aesthetics of constitutional law. The fact that the building is designed as, and around, a courtroom, has largely been lost from sight. However, the building with its architectural design not only affects the post-apartheid aesthetics of space, it also affects the aesthetics of post-apartheid law. It does so, implicitly, by rehabilitating a non-monumental sense of space and by celebrating the very materiality, performativity and complexity that André van der Walt and Van Marle wish to rehabilitate as the essence of constitutionalism.[82] The design also affects the aesthetics of post-apartheid law in a more explicit manner. It does so through the iconography of justice, which it self-consciously celebrates.

The iconography of justice implicit in the design has received equally little attention in the discussions of the building that have been undertaken thus far. This is not surprising as the iconography of justice has over the years received very little or no attention from South African legal scholars, mainly because legal formalism holds that law exists purely in the form of formally realisable written rules. However, legal semiotics suggests otherwise.[83] The written texts of law have a symbolic, rather than an immediately semantic or linguistic content. The written text is, in addition, only one

---

79 *Ibid.*

80 *Ibid.*

81 Lipman (n 77) xiii.

82 See again van Marle (n 22) and her discussion of the difference between monumental and memorial constitutionalism in chapter two of this collection. The attempt by Sachs (n 70) to interpret this new spatial aesthetics in terms of the Habermasian categories of critical theory (the shift from instrumental to communicative rationality) is only one way of understanding this complexity. However, it allows the building to be celebrated in jurisprudential terms as a sign of the shift from the conceptual logic of legal formalism to the deliberative dialogue of republican constitutionalism in post-apartheid South Africa, or from instrumental rationality to communicative rationality.

83 Goodrich (n 1) 209–259.

medium through which law is communicated. A rich collection of symbols, rituals, images and icons mark the appearance of law as legitimate (as opposed to merely de facto) power. Law is experienced as a system of images, not as a system of rules. It is a mythology that should be pursued through its emblems and images. An important task of courtroom architecture is to enhance and support this iconic order and thus to stage the appearance of the law.[84]

Given the connection between the iconography of the blindfolded Justitia and the cultural configuration of Western modernity (as it was set out by Martin Jay in the discussion above), it is significant that when the South African Constitutional Court was established in 1994, a deliberate decision was taken to distance the court from this long history.[85] South African artist Carolyn Parton was approached to design a logo for the court which could introduce a uniquely South African iconography of justice. As Justice Albie Sachs puts it, the intention was to 'move away from the tired old symbols of the scales of justice to an iconography rooted in Africa and recognisably our own'.[86] This iconography had to reflect three things: (1) that the court is a place of protection for all people, (2) that the court is of Africa and (3) that the court is rooted in history

Clashing icons. Barbed wire on top of the old prison wall, juxtaposed with a new logo on top of the Constitutional Court building.

---

84 *Idem* 222–224.

85 For a fuller discussion of this history see Denis E Curtis and Judith Resnik 'Images of justice' (1987) 96 *Yale LJ* 1727–1772.

86 Quoted by Leigh Darrol in 'Justice Albie Sachs – about the Constitutional Court' (2003) 8 *Urban Green File* 27.

and struggle.[87] The logo eventually produced by Parton depicts a group of people gathered under a tree. The constitution is, in other words, allegorically presented as a big tree, rooted in the African soil providing protection and shelter for everybody in the community.

The shift in the iconography of justice from the mechanical image of balancing scales to the organic image of an indigenous tree reinforces the shift from abstract space to lived space which informs the design of the building. The balancing scales, a highly sophisticated piece of technology and the symbol of technocratic rationality, is replaced as the ground of justice with people gathering to engage in deliberation, a symbol of communicative rationality. The new logo depicts law as an organic and dialogical process rather than as a set of pre-determined logical outcomes. The new logo expresses law in relational rather than in spatial terms.[88] The republican community under the tree is seemingly tied together only by shared practices of dialogue and reflective judgement. This image of justice suggests an approach to rights in which constitutional disputes are not settled by definitions, but by democratic contestation. Rights are like the tree depicted on the logo. They provide shaded clearings of public space in the otherwise harsh political landscape where dialogue and political contestation can occur. As Van der Walt states with reference to Jennifer Nedelsky: to lay claim to a right is only the beginning and not the end of public discussion; rights do not trump, they just provide openings or clearings for debate.[89] In the place of the abstracted male gaze of the blindfolded Justitia (Jay), what is encountered here are the situated and embodied plurality of perspectives that characterise the public sphere or clearings of flourishing political communities. The logo of the court institutes the question of plurality (the precondition of politics and justice) as the key question of constitutionalism.[90]

The justices of the Constitutional Court deliberately decided in 1994 to move away from the figure of Justitia and the abstract perspectivism it implied as the basis of their jurisprudence. When the design of a new Constitutional Court building became a reality in 1997 it gave them an opportunity to entrench this shift. The cover of the *Brief and conditions* of the competition for a design was adorned with the logo of the court and became a visible reference point for the entire project. The winning design more or less directly translated the logo and the idea of the court and rights as trees into the architectural design of the building itself. Justice Sachs explains that he was immediately attracted to the final design precisely because 'it had the friendly feel of Africa, a vivid intimation of justice in the open air and under a tree'.[91] A rich variety of architectural

87 Maurice 'Tributes to the Constitution: The art of the court' on *Constitutional Court of South Africa: Art collection* (CD-Rom: distributed at the opening of the Constitutional Court building, 21 March 2004).

88 Darrol (n 86) 27 quotes Justice Sachs as he explains that the allegorical depiction of the constitution and Constitutional Court as a big African tree 'speaks of openness and transparency, and of responsibilities – as the people protect the tree, so the tree protects the people, as the tree is nurtured and respected so it will grow'.

89 Van der Walt (n 5) 302. See also Jennifer Nedelsky 'Reconceiving rights as relationships' (1993) 1 *Review of Constitutional Studies* 1 at 16.

90 We have already seen above that modern (republican) and postmodern conceptions of constitutionalism divide precisely on the question of how the constituting plurality of our (the/a) political community is to be understood and protected.

91 Sachs (n 70) xi.

features work together to sustain this metaphoric depiction of the Constitution and the Constitutional Court.

Large steel replicas of the court's logo are prominently mounted either against, or on top of, the outside walls of the building. These metal trees are clearly visible both from inside and outside the building. Carolyn Parton's original logo appears as the only iconographic reference at the entrance to the court chamber (the *Brief and conditions* stated explicitly that 'ornate details and heavily imposed symbolism should be avoided').[92] The strategic placement of these logos serves to highlight and re-enforce the central metaphor around which the whole design is structured. The iconic tree of constitutionalism is further translated into a variety of physical features of the building. The main entrance to the building is provided through a series of very narrow and very tall engraved wooden doors which fold open to reveal the interior of the building. The vertical lines of these doors allude to the tall trunks of a cluster of big trees. The use of natural sunlight is a key element of the design in this regard.[93] The entrance foyer itself is filled with diffused sunlight from all sides, including the roof, from where narrow rectangular slits let in streaks of natural sunlight. The resulting effect is a moving pattern of alternately shaded and brightly lit patches, much like the soft light falling and moving through the leaves of a big tree. As the sun changes its position during the cycle of the day, the shapes and shades of the foyer are transformed as is the ground under a tree. If the slitted roof of the foyer forms the canopy of a cluster of trees, the trunks are provided by three sets of pillars, which are grouped together and slanted sideways (like trees in a forest). Each pillar is decorated with mosaic patterns in the hues of the forest: brown, green and blue. A number of leaf-patterned chandeliers are suspended between the pillars. These serve both to diffuse and to hide the artificial lights needed to supplement the streaks of natural sunlight filtering into the interior.

The court chamber is more evenly lit by artificial light, but the pattern on the carpet replicates the pattern of shade and light found on the ground under the foliage of a tree bathed in bright African sunlight. The openness and horizontality characterising the clearing under a tree are also replicated in the court chamber. The justices and the public are seated on the same level. The seats of the other officers of the court are lowered in such a way that any person who stands up to argue her case will be on the same eye level as the seated justices and public. As is the case under a tree in the open veld, there are no fixed structures to separate the various groups of people assembled in the court chamber. The public gallery gradually transforms into the desks and chairs of the officers of the court, which in turn flows into the bench of the judges themselves. The justices behind the bench are not backed up by any further architectural support. They are not the final word in a bureaucratic hierarchy. The landscape stretches out, as

92 *Brief and conditions of the competition for the new Constitutional Court building of South Africa* (1997) 19.

93 Recall the discussions of the use of natural light in buildings by Olivier (n 45), Mugerauer (n 74) and Young (n 46). It is not only the use of natural light that enhances the performative dimension of the architecture. The building relies for large parts on a passive cooling system, and the Exhibition Foyer ends in a completely open enclave where rain and wind and sun are allowed to enter the building (the enclave is now netted in order to keep birds from flying into the building). These are all key design elements which the new ecological architecture celebrated.

it were, into the empty and completely unstructured space behind their backs. They sit as if in the open veld, with literally no other support than the dialogical fellowship of the semi-circle which they constitute with the rest of the community who have gathered in the clearing.

The sense of openness characterising the gathering is strikingly reinforced by a narrow horizontal window that encircles the chamber and all its occupants at eye level. The window makes movement of people on the outside of the building constantly visible and establishes the greater horizon of this gathering in the general community. To rely, once again, on Justice Sachs's interpretation of the building, the ambience in the court chamber was deliberately created in order to symbolise the fact that law and justice 'arise from dialogue'.[94]

The logo and architecture of the Constitutional Court ground justice and law on the dialogical practices of the democratic community. It powerfully inscribes the clearing as the key architectural metaphor of post-apartheid constitutionalism (in the place of the older bridge metaphor). As such they underscore the shift from metaphors grounded in conceptions of abstract space to metaphors grounded in conceptions of dialogue (which Henk Botha identifies as a defining feature of post-apartheid constitutionalism), with all the implications that that shift entails for the aesthetics of post-apartheid law.[95]

A number of people have made use of the Constitution Hill project to present the Constitutional Court not only as one clearing or public space among many in the post-apartheid political landscape, but as the foremost example of such clearings or as the most important site of democratic politics in post-apartheid South Africa. The Constitutional Court building was from the very outset of the project billed as 'the first major public building of the new era of constitutionalism and democracy'.[96] The court building was soon assigned the task to 'physically dramatise the transformation of South Africa from a racist, authoritarian society to a constitutional democracy'.[97] Following these claims, it is understandable that the winning design boldly announced the building as 'a new symbol for a new democracy'.[98] The tone set by these early statements about the symbolic importance of the building has also found resonance in the way the building has been depicted in the popular press. 'The pinnacle of our democratic development',[99] 'democracy cemented in bricks and mortar',[100] 'the cornerstone of democracy',[101] and 'a national *lekgotla*'[102] are but some of the headlines and acclamations that have been used to describe the symbolic significance of the new building.

94 Sachs (n 4) 27.

95 Botha 'Metaphoric reasoning' part 2 (n 5) 20–36.These implications have already been addressed above in the discussion of imaginative constitutionalism. See also the discussion of the right to privacy below.

96 Remark by Jeff Radebe, Minister of Public Works in his Preface to *Brief and conditions* (n 92) 17.

97 Sachs (n 4) 29.

98 Andrew Makin *Design memorandum* (1987) cover page.

99 *This Day* (2004-03-22) 2.

100 *Northcliff Melville Times*, week ending (2003-09-19) 28.

101 'Souvenir Supplement: Constitution Hill' in *Sunday Times* (2004-03-21) 3.

102 *Idem*.

The foyer of the Constitutional Court building. The sun-streaked public place is a clearing between trees. The entrance to the Courtroom is on the left; an old stairwell of the former prison to the right.

The high stakes invested by post-apartheid South Africans in the symbolic capital of this court building stand in marked contrast to the processes of symbolic re-configuration which have recently played themselves out in other contexts of political transformation. Architecturally speaking, the need to 'dramatise transformation physically' has resulted in the design of highly symbolic new parliament buildings. Two spectacular examples of this process are provided by Enrique Marsalis's new Scottish parliament building in Edinburgh[103] and the Reichstag in Berlin, which was first wrapped by Christo and then visibly and dramatically redesigned by Norman Forster.[104] The fact that in post-apartheid South Africa the Constitutional Court building has been hailed as the most important symbol of democracy, at the expense of a new or altered parliament building, is therefore highly significant.

---

103 Deyan Sudjic and Helen Jones (eds) *Architecture and democracy* (2001).

104 Michael Wise *Capital dilemma: Germany's search for a new architecture of democracy* (1998); and Bernhard Schulz and Norman Foster *The Reichstag: Sir Norman Foster's parliament building* (2000).

Constitutional theory has been dominated over the past decades by attempts to delineate, restate, and dissolve what is commonly known as the counter-majoritarian difficulty. Given these debates, the architectural attempt not only to celebrate the Constitutional Court as a democratic institution, but to elevate it to the status of the paradigmatic institution of post-apartheid democracy, is highly problematic. In one of his early essays, Frank Michelman responded to the counter-majoritarian debate by locating the deliberative or discursive republican community in the American Supreme Court.[105] To date, this court-centred version of republicanism provides the best theoretical support for the claims made by the architectural project around the South African Constitutional Court.[106] According to Michelman, the authority of the Constitutional Court rests not on the past acts of the republican or constitutional community (as Bruce Ackerman had claimed earlier), but on the active self-government or practical reason of the justices of the court themselves. The Constitutional Court justices represent by their own self-government the community's missing self-government, by their practical reason the community's missing dialogical self-modification: '[T]he courts, and especially the Supreme Court, seem to take on as one of their ascribed functions the modelling of active self-government that citizens find practically beyond reach'.[107] However, this kind of judicial self-government is undermined by 'talismanic invocation of authority'.[108] According to Michelman, the self-government of the people through constitutional review is only possible if 'every norm, every time, requires explanation and justification in context'.[109] Judicial self-government therefore calls for practical reason which, in turn, involves an open and imaginative dialogue; a dialogue that Michelman understands as a self-modulating encounter with otherness.[110] From this perspective, rights are not abstract entitlements that can be conclusively defined, but rather the medium and the occasion for the dialogical self-government of the people.[111]

With this theory Michelman somewhat uncomfortably found himself in the company of Ronald Dworkin, who also claimed to have diffused the counter-majoritarian difficulty with his idea of a moral reading of the American Constitution.[112] These two defences of the power of constitutional review generated a series of critical responses during the 1990s, all of which have called for a more restrictive approach to the role and status of the Constitutional Court. These critiques range from Antonin Scalia's attempts to narrow the scope of judicial review by means of textualist constitutional interpre-

105 Frank Michelman 'Traces of self-government' (1986) 100 *Harvard LR* 5.

106 Michelman's work has been particularly influential in South Africa. See for example the recent collection of essays dedicated to his intellectual labours, Henk Botha, et al. (eds) *Rights and democracy in a transformative constitution* (2004).

107 Michelman (n 105) 74.

108 *Idem* 76.

109 *Ibid*.

110 Frank Michelman 'Law's republic' (1988) 97 *Yale LJ* 1496 at 1526–1527.

111 Frank Michelman 'Dilemmas of belonging: Moral truth, human rights, and why we might not want a representative judiciary' (2000) 47 *UCLA LR* 1221 at 1224. Michelman's self-governing political community falls somewhere between coercive communitarianism and liberal pluralism, unanimity and tolerance.

112 Ronald Dworkin *Freedom's law: The moral reading of the American Constitution* (1996) 1–38.

tation,[113] to Mark Tushnet's calls for a complete abolition of constitutional review.[114] Whether made in the name of a conservative or radical politics, these calls share the idea that popular participatory politics should be afforded a more decisive importance in constitutionalism (relative to the importance ascribed to the Constitutional Court and constitutional review). Against the background of this critique, the unbridled celebration of the Constitutional Court as the paradigmatic clearing or public space and thus the foremost symbol of democratic politics in South Africa assumes added significance. It implies the absence of other significant deliberative clearings in post-apartheid politics and thus turns the very possibility of the dialogical gathering of the constitutional community into a pressing constitutional issue.

Nevertheless, the design philosophy, iconography and jurisprudence informing the architecture of the Constitutional Court building work together to form a powerful aesthetic consolidation of the imaginative and dialogical constitutionalism as discussed in the context of the bridge metaphor. On the level of design, the building has been said to be an example of regional or community-based architecture vested in concrete deliberative processes rather than abstract images or functions. On the level of iconography, the building concretises the image of justice as the outcome of an inclusive and deliberative gathering of the community in a clearing under a tree. Finally, on the level of jurisprudence, the building has been hailed as the only remaining site of (virtual) dialogical self-government by the people. In all three cases, the dominant associations are those of inclusiveness, openness, accessibility, friendliness, sheltering, dialogue, respect, equality, plurality and mutual recognition. On the whole, the Constitutional Court building is a powerful statement against all forms of the culture of authority, and determinant closure of constitutional debate and politics.

A number of constitutional writers have suggested that the Constitutional Court's privacy jurisprudence presents the best example of constitutionalism when rights are metaphorically conceived of as trees or clearings for public deliberation. Jacques de Ville, one of the most ardent champions of a republican reading of the South African constitution, cites the privacy judgments in *Bernstein v Bester*[115] and *National Coalition of Gay and Lesbian Equality v Minister of Justice*[116] as two examples in which the Constitutional Court has explicitly adopted a republican approach to the interpretation of human rights.[117] In both these cases the court rejected a spatial approach to privacy in

113 Antonin Scalia *A matter of interpretation: Federal courts and the law* (1997) 3–47.

114 Mark Tushnet *Taking the Constitution away from the courts* (1999) 9–14; 57–65;154–176. Tushnet calls for a 'populist constitutionalism' in which the 'thin constitution' will be protected by popular legislative politics freed from the distorting influence of 'judicial overhang'. Other critiques include Cass Sunstein's calls for a minimalist approach to constitutional review: *One case at a time: Judicial minimalism on the Supreme Court* (2001) 24–45, about which see Iain Currie 'Judicious avoidance' (1999) 15 *SAJHR* 138. Chris Roederer 'Judicious engagement: theory, attitude and community' (1999) 15 *SAJHR* 486; and Albie Sachs 'Book reviews' (2001) 51 *Univ Toronto* LJ 87); and Emilios Christodoulidis' calls for reflexive politics as opposed to contained or constitutional politics 'Self-defeating civic republicanism' (1993) *Ratio Iuris* 64 and *Law and reflexive politics* (1998). The recent debates around a Bill of Rights for Britain have also tended to restate the virtues of participatory majoritarianism against the virtues of constitutional review (see for example Jeremy Waldron's critique of 'judicial aristocracy' in *Law and disagreement* (1999) 248).

115 *Bernstein v Bester* 1996 (4) BCLR 449 (CC) para 67.

116 *National Coalition of Gay and Lesbian Equality v Minister of Justice* 1998 (12) BCLR 1517 (CC).

117 De Ville (n 6).

The courtroom. The room is the architectural expression of the promise that justice will be dispensed at an open gathering under a tree.

favour of an associational approach. The associational approach understands the right to privacy as a radial (or graded) concept with both core and peripheral areas (rather than as a bounded category). The core is constituted by intimate associations and the periphery by a variety of more impersonal associations. The spatial approach, by contrast, understands privacy as the right to be left alone within clearly defined private places or behind definite boundaries.

The associational approach to privacy resonates closely with the architectural depiction of rights as clearings under trees. Henk Botha has recently celebrated the court's privacy jurisprudence precisely because of the greater possibilities it allows for the dialogical contestation of constitutional meaning and categorisation.[118] Where the right to privacy is still conceived in terms of rigid boundaries, both with reference to what it apparently describes in the 'real world' and the way it operates in legal argu-

118 Botha 'Metaphoric reasoning: part 2'(n 5) 32–33. Botha distinguishes between 'rigid categorisation' and 'relational categorisation'. He explains the difference between these two approaches as follows: 'a rigid categorisation approach assumes that law is neutral; that judges can avoid becoming embroiled in moral and political controversies; that justice is blind and legal meaning disembodied. Against this view, proponents of a relational, dialogic conception of rights recognise that there are different ways of looking at the world; that legal distinctions do not reflect pre-existing boundaries, but depend on the perspective of those making them'. This implies in turn that 'the content, reach and permissible limitations of rights are determined through an ongoing process of public dialogue. By conceiving rights as dialogue, we declare our readiness to listen to other viewpoints, to enter into discussions over our own beliefs, to open ourselves to the possibility of a dialogical modulation of deeply held convictions and prejudices' (24–25).

ment, it precludes the possibilities of transformative constitutionalism.[119] It literally and figuratively allows the bearer of the right to slam the door in the face of the republican community. "If I want to watch pornography or engage in gay sexual activity in the privacy of my home, that is of no legitimate concern to you." The spatial approach to privacy can therefore, at best, achieve a measure of tolerance between otherwise indifferent individuals.[120] On the basis of the associational right to privacy, by contrast, it is possible to vindicate publicly (as opposed to merely tolerate privately) the value of gay intimate relationships.[121] This is precisely what the Constitutional Court has done. If this act of public vindication is understood as an act of dialogical self-modulation, as Michelman suggests, then it reflects a measurable transformation of the political community. Hence the excitement shown by De Ville and Botha about the republican character and potential of the court's privacy jurisprudence.

However, the privacy jurisprudence that De Ville and Botha hailed as the touchstone of the very post-formalist republican jurisprudence supported by the architecture of the Constitutional Court building has subsequently spawned the judgments delivered in *S v Jordan*.[122] In this case the Constitutional Court used the same privacy jurisprudence to remove prostitutes unsympathetically from the celebrated open gathering of the constitutional community. In the process the court did not even manage to secure the threshold of a tolerant community grounded on a liberal conception of spatial privacy. The judgment completely belies the idea that the right to privacy serves metaphorically as a sheltered clearing under a tree and thus as an opening where a plurality of different voices can be heard. There is no indication in the judgment of any willingness to engage

---

119 The point is grasped even by Dworkin (n 112) 31, who points out that 'whether great constitutional issues provoke and guide public deliberation depends, among much else, on how these issues are conceived and addressed by lawyers and judges. There is little chance of a useful national debate over constitutional principle when constitutional decisions are considered technical exercises in an arcane and conceptual craft'.

120 Anthony Kronman 'Living in the law' (1987) 54 *Univ Chicago* LR 835 situates the democratic community somewhere between indifferent tolerance on the one hand (crude liberalism) and enforced unanimity on the other (crude communitarianism). The spatial approach to privacy is unable to move post-apartheid society beyond the threshold of crude liberalism. In all likelihood it still captures the dominant understanding of both privacy and rights in South Africa's mushrooming gated communities, walled-in golf estates and fenced-off suburbs. The very existence of the Constitutional Court in down-town Johannesburg represents a complete negation of this urban landscape and the ideal of the tolerant liberal community (if that) which it physically institutes. The location of the court was chosen precisely as a statement against the re-fortification, re-segregation, re-privatisation and re-militarisation of the post-apartheid city. Constitution Hill is conceived as a network of open streets and vibrant public spaces imbued with the virtues of inner-city street life: publicity, inclusive differentiation, variety and eroticism. The court, in turn, is metaphorically understood as a republican gathering place (not as a bridge guarding determinant legal boundaries), as I have been trying to explain above.

121 This was precisely the basis of the defence of the right to privacy which Michael Katz ('Close encounters of the third kind: privacy, equality and the expression of homosexual preference' (1996) 12 *SAJHR* 308 at 320) formulated earlier against the claims made by Edwin Cameron ('Sexual orientation and the Constitution' (1993) 110 *SALJ* 450) that the right to equality and non-discrimination formed the only basis upon which homosexual activity could be regulated in the post-apartheid era. According to Cameron, the right to privacy would not be sufficient to break the societal discrimination against gay people, firstly because it would only protect homosexual conduct in private places like the home, and secondly, because it would subtly reinforce the idea that homosexual intimacy is shameful and improper and best confined to the bedroom (464). Katz rejected this spatial conception of the right to privacy and suggested the very associational approach to privacy which was subsequently adopted by the Constitutional Court.

122 *S v Jordan* 2002 (6) SA 642 (CC).

openly with the sometimes disturbingly different stories about, and perspectives on, sex and womanhood which the prostitutes in question tried to introduce into the public constitutional conversation. The justices, on the contrary, preferred to decide the case on the basis of unexamined middle-class stereotypes and male fantasies about female sexuality.[123] A prostitute, it held, could receive no or only scant protection from the right to privacy because when she has sex she is not 'nurturing relationships or taking life-affirming decisions about birth, marriage or family; she is making money'.[124]

The contrast between the callous prostitute flaunting her sexuality to make money, and the devoted wife dedicating her sexuality to married life and procreation can hardly be drawn in a starker fashion. With this statement the court follows in the footsteps of its American counterpart in *Bowers v Hardwick* by confining the right to privacy to the good sex associated with the heterosexual family.[125] The middle-class family becomes the paradigm of the intimate associations that are protected at the core of the right to privacy. The image of the devoted wife, which has faithfully served to sustain this patriarchal institution at the heart of oppression in society, is once again enlisted by the court, this time to silence the dissenting voices of prostitutes (as it has been to co-opt and neutralise the potentially disruptive energy of gay and lesbian sexual desire).[126]

The exclusion of prostitutes from the clearing of the welcoming constitutional community follows closely in the footsteps of a number of other marginalised figures of South African society who have suffered the same fate.[127] The Constitutional Court's treatment of these figures has forced some constitutional writers to complain about the court's tendency to fall back onto 'reasoning based on stereotypes' at crucial moments during the adjudication of constitutional disputes.[128] This is an important point of internal critique. It implies that when it comes down to the hard work of constitutional interpretation, the court is not always as open and responsive to difference and otherness as the flowery republican rhetoric and imagery that have sprung up around the design of the new Constitutional Court building would have one believe. However, the judgments in *Jordan* cut much deeper and raise more fundamental questions about the quest to formulate a post-Cartesian conception of space and jurisprudence for post-apartheid South Africa.

3.4 Labyrinths

In theoretical reflections on the spatial configuration of modernity, the figure of the prostitute is frequently associated with an alternative and subversive sense of space. Jane

---

123 Wessel le Roux 'Sex work, the right to occupational freedom and the constitutional politics of recognition' (2003) 120 *SALJ* 452 at 462.

124 *S v Jordan* (n 122) para 83 (per O'Regan J and Sachs J).

125 Michael Engleman '*Bowers v Hardwick*: the right of privacy – only within the traditional family?' (1987—88) 26 *Journal of Family Law* 373.

126 Pierre de Vos 'Same-sex sexual desire and the re-imagination of the South African family' (2004) 20 *SAJHR* 179.

127 See for example the treatment of single fathers in *President of the Republic of South Africa v Hugo* 1997 (4) SA 1 (CC), and of mystic lawyers in *Prince v President, Cape Law Society* 2001 (2) SA 388 (CC).

128 Gretchen Carpenter ('Of prostitutes, pimps and patrons – some still more equal than others?' (2004) 19 *SAPR/PL* 231 at 248) criticises the hold on the legal imagination of stereotypes about sex and gender.

Rendell, for example, describes the figure of the prostitute as a subversion of patriarchal conceptions of space.[129] Patriarchy, she explains, establishes gendered identities by relating men and women differently to space. Men own women and space as commodities or private property. Women are owned as property and confined in space. Men move through abstract space as rights-bearing subjects. Women are moved through abstract patriarchal space as commodified objects. Given this patriarchal context, the figure of the cyprian or prostitute – the mobile female body resisting its containment in patriarchal space – presents an alternatively gendered representation of space. As a moving female body, the prostitute flouts the patriarchal rules for women's occupation of space. Her movement is transgressive and creates differently gendered or female spaces within the public domain of the city.

Scott Lash also positions the figure of the prostitute centrally in his critique of the abstract conceptions of space characterising modernity.[130] Lash grounds his call for 'another modernity' in the re-exploration of gothic and labyrinthian urban spaces within the confines of the grid-like baroque city. This alternative gothic city 'operates out of cellars, in the shadows of skyscrapers. It is a city and a space which signifies through the complexity of its towers, alleys and paths, through the gestures of its dark figures, lepers, prostitutes'.[131] Lash describes this labyrinthian city as a city of the real (as opposed to the symbolic). It is a city (*a polis*) that evades representation and unified images or embodiments of itself. This city only signifies as one moves through it and encounter and stage micro events with concrete objects and figures.

Rendell and Lash both enlist the disruptive spatial configurations associated with the figure of the prostitute (the radical materiality of feminine and gothic space) in their critique of abstract Cartesian space. However, the difference between the meaning that they attach to the figure of the prostitute and that presented by the court in *Jordan* highlights a difference in the way the complexity and materiality of post-Cartesian space are understood in each case. The judgment in *Jordan* is therefore not simply a failure to live up to the idea of rights as clearings (as the internal critique would imply) but is itself a precondition for the idea that the materiality of space is best understood as a clearing for political dialogue and representation. This judgment, more than any other, highlights the fact that the Constitutional Court continues to regard the South African political community as an abstracted unity, which can only be maintained as an imagined presence if the constant confrontation with the material and labyrinthian spaces of the real, marked by the body of the prostitute, is effectively avoided. After *Jordan* the post-apartheid constitutional community has become an empty abstraction which remains at heart captured by the visual culture of the baroque and the Christian

129 Jane Rendell 'Ramblers and Cyprians: Mobility, visuality and the gendering of architectural space', in Louise Durning and Richard Wrigley (eds) *Gender and architecture* (2000) 135–154. In this regard, Rendell relies heavily on the discussion of the patriarchal construction of space by Luce Irigaray *This sex which is not one* (1985) 170–191.

130 Lash (n 27).

131 *Idem* 85.

dream of an embodiment of God. South Africa's democracy will then not be a street democracy but will remain inscribed into the modern politics of presentation.

Transformative constitutionalism might require more than a new image or presentation of the democratic community as a dialogical community, coupled with the development of a relational conceptions of rights. Transformative constitutionalism might require precisely the confrontation with the materiality of the political community which the metaphor of rights as clearings seems to avoid. It might require no less than a critique of presentation. Van der Walt and Botha's celebration of a constitutionalism of negative presentation, which was briefly introduced above, moves in this direction. They claimed that the very plurality, which is a pre-condition for politics, is necessarily destroyed by politics. Constitutionalism can therefore not be grounded on any present understanding or presentation or imagination of the political community (whatever the content given to those understandings, presentations or images). Every attempt to constitute the community on the basis of a rights discourse can at best be regarded as a negative presentation of that community, that is, as a sign that the true plurality constituting the political community has yet again slipped away. In this postmodern understanding of constitutional review, the constitution has no ground or central clearing. Constitutionalism is beset by a *differend* between ethics and law, which continuously transposes justice into the not here, not this, not yet.

How can such a constitutionalism find architectural expression? I have already explored the possibilities that the metaphor of the suspension bridge offers in this regard. In order to conclude the discussion, I briefly introduce one proposal that has been put forward as the basis of the courtroom architecture of postmodern constitutionalism. This proposal can be derived from Jacques Derrida's reading of Franz Kafka's well-known fable *Before the law*.[132]

In this fable, a man from the country arrives at a building in the city where the court is located. It is a very special building, one apparently designed with openness and accessibility in mind because it contains a large number of gates. In fact, every visitor to the court has a special gate set aside and kept ready for his or her arrival. Having found his gate, the man from the country wants to enter the building. He asks the security guard on duty whether he can enter. The guard replies that it is possible to enter but not just yet. The man peers through the open gate to the inside and is told that he is merely at the outside gate of the building. The interior is made up of a labyrinthian network of further gates and hallways, each opening onto another and guarded by doorkeeper after doorkeeper, each more powerful than the other. The man waits his whole life for permission to enter the gate and thus the labyrinth of law, but is constantly told that he cannot be let in just yet. When his immanent death makes further use of the gate obsolete (it was meant for him alone) it is shut by the guard.

---

132 Jacques Derrida 'Before the law', in Derek Attridge (ed.) *Jacques Derrida: Acts of literature* (1992) 181–220. The essay has been seminal in the development of a gothic jurisprudence in recent critical theory. See Les Moran 'Law and the gothic imagination', in Fred Botting (ed.) *The Gothic* (2001) 87.

Derrida reads Kafka's fable as a commentary on the quasi-transcendental conditions of law (justice): the condition of the normative possibility of law is the impossibility of ever gaining final access to the norms of the law.[133] Respect for the law (according to Kant a sublime feeling) is only possible as long as law is not fully grasped or brought under total human control. Both the origin and place of law must thus be impossible to reach, for law to be possible. For law to be law, law must become fictional or mystical: '[Law] appears as something that does not appear as such in the course of history. As all events, it cannot be constituted by some history that might give rise to any story. If there were any history, it would be neither presentable nor relatable: the history of that which never took place'.[134] Law must essentially remain an empty or non-place, an atopology. To try to fill this emptiness is the sign of totalitarianism.[135] This does not mean that positive law is here contrasted with the disembodied void of deconstructive justice. A labyrinth is not a disembodied emptiness but a place of constant dislocation. Here we encounter another image of the path of the law and what it means to walk along that path. In Derrida's words the labyrinthian nature of the courthouse architecture in Kafka's fable becomes the 'map of this forbidden path, no itinerary, no method no path to accede to the law'.[136] The guard has his back turned to the law in order to prohibit all presentations or embodiments of the law. The man from the country who faces the law sees no more than the guard or doorkeeper. The doorkeeper cannot see the law (he cannot even bear the sight of the other doorkeepers after him) and neither can the man from the country. Both see only other doors and other doorkeepers in an endless labyrinth. However, the prohibition from entering the place or clearing of the law is not an imperative constraint, but is what Derrida calls a *différance*.[137] It is an interruption and deferment of passage – the door is open – not a fixed or solid boundary around either a gathered community or an empty space. The discourse of the law therefore does not say 'no', but says indefinitely 'not yet'.

Derrida's reading of Kafka's fable and his depiction of the boundary of the law as a *différance* resonates closely with Lyotard's critique of the conceptual boundaries of law as *differends*. Both these descriptions amount to radical critiques of the humanist

133 This deconstructive paradox is further explored in Jacques Derrida 'Force of law: The "mystical foundation of authority"' in Cornell, et al. (eds) *Deconstruction and the possibility of justice* (1992) 5–60. Like Lyotard (n 60), Derrida argues that this paradox precludes the republican grounding of politics. See Jacques Derrida 'Declarations of independence' (1986) 15 *New Political Science* 7–15.

134 Derrida (n 132) 194.

135 See Jean-François Lyotard 'The survivor' in *Toward the post-modern* (1995) 144. This view of totalitarianism can only arise if the constitutional state, politics and law are approached as a limit to the infinite responsibility to the Other, or in Emmanuel Levinas' words, if the visual presentation or *image* (portrait) of the other is unsettled by the *Face* (a calling out to me) of the Other, if the Christian body of god is interrupted by the Jewish voice of god. See Emmanuel Levinas 'Philosophy, justice and love' in *Entre Nous: On thinking-of-the-Other* (1998) 103 at 105: 'It is in terms of the relation to the Face or of me before the other that we can speak of the legitimacy or illegitimacy of the state. A state in which the interpersonal relationship is impossible, in which it is directed in advance by the determinism proper to the state, is a totalitarian state. So there is a limit to the state. Whereas, in Hobbes's vision – in which the state emerges not from the limitation of charity, but from the limitation of violence – one cannot set a limit on the state'.

136 Derrida (n 132) 196.

137 *Idem* 203.

culture of vision and abstract conception of space which I introduced at the start of the discussion. Both move in the same direction as the design of the Constitutional Court building. However, the building still seeks to ground constitutional adjudication unproblematically in the dialogical gathering or presence of the community, an attempt for which the tree as metaphor provides the proper place. Derrida and Lyotard suggest that the appearance before the law as the freedom or rational will of the gathered community is a more complex and paradoxical event. The embodiment of the law has to be understood as a sublime event which can only be presented in a negative manner.

Staircases leading into and out of the old prison stairwell in the foyer.

Is it possible to find traces of this negative presentation of law and the constitutional community in the architecture of the new Constitutional Court building? One might also rephrase the question to ask whether the design bears any marks of the labyrinthian displacement of republican self-presentation.[138] The building is certainly designed as a gathering place and as a clearing, not as a place of dispersal and dislocation. It is an aesthetics of place that informs the design. Any suggestion to the contrary would do unjustifiable violence to what is attractive in the design in the first place. However, the foyer of the building is not simply a clearing in a forest prepared for the gathering of the post-apartheid community. It is also a rehabilitated prison site that still self-consciously bears the marks of trauma and exclusion. Inside the foyer, between the trees as it were, like the last remaining part of a gothic ruin, stands the original staircase of the demolished awaiting-trial prison where many political opponents of the apartheid regime were incarcerated, complete with barbed wire, prison bars and graffiti on its walls. The staircase at first sight appears successfully to contain the violence and the exclusion which were characteristic of the apartheid political order in space and time. Its presence in the new building seems to serve as a reminder that the old, abandoned position should never again be adopted. The past and the future are again neatly separated into an opposing dualism. When one begins to take a closer look at the staircase, however, one word in particular among the graffiti carved into the plaster at the bottom of the stairs captures attention: *welkom*. The inscription is in Afrikaans and means welcome. Having just arrived at the clearing in the foyer, one reads and acknowledges the greeting. Then one is suddenly beset with doubt. Was the inscription addressed to you? It is after all an inscription that once greeted those who were about to be cast into isolation, exclusion and silence. How can it without remainder also be directed at those who now arrive at this place on the basis of an altogether different invitation to participate in public debate?

The ambivalent manner in which the word *welkom* cuts across boundaries of time and place suddenly imbues the whole foyer with a sense of ambivalence. The labyrinth of language has collapsed the clear divide between the past and the present (and with it the structural centrality of the metaphors of bridges in the design). One simple word contains the markings of two different paths: the first leading up into the prison staircase and the second down into the Constitutional Court Chamber. As this single word splits into a double, the whole interior space of the Constitutional Court building suddenly assumes the disorientating and heterotopian character of the labyrinthian staircases depicted in Escher's *Relativity*[139] or even Giambattisa Piranesi's Carceri.[140] The deliberate lack of any hierarchy which can serve to organise the interior spaces that opens onto or out of the foyer, allows various stairs and passages to lead away without clear direction or destination (and with that collapses the structural centrality of the metaphors of clearing and gathering in the design). It is no longer apparent which of the many

138 The labyrinthian groundlessness of law need not be restricted to the republicanism of the civil law tradition. The same imagery can also effectively be employed to capture the mystical foundation of the law in time immemorial in the common law tradition. See in this regard David Evans's reading of Kafka's fable in 'Theatre of deferral: The image of the law and the architecture of the Inns of Court' (1999) 10 *Law and Critique* 1–25.

139 M.C. Escher *The graphic work* (1990) 67.

140 Andrew Robinson *Piranesi: Early architectural fantasies* (1986) 138–179.

'Welcome at B-Shift.' Detail from the graffiti on the wall of the old prison stairwell in the Foyer. Who is the host and who the hostage?

staircases, doors and floor levels will lead one to the clearing at the centre of the building. The downward slope of the exhibition foyer, for example, seems to lead deeper into the building, but when followed, in fact leads outwards and ends unexpectedly in an open courtyard on the inside of the building. The fixed boundaries between past and future, inside and outside, up and down, forward and backward, margin and centre, inclusion and exclusion, law and power have become displaced. What at first appeared to be a clearing and a fixed destination, has turned into a network of further paths along which those approaching the gathering of the constitutional community will again and again be dispersed. The constitution and the precinct of the Constitutional Court has become a labyrinth without centre.

If one were now once again to find one's way to the door of the court chamber, it would, on entering, no longer be possible to find the democratic community constituted there, or to see the justices as the personifications or embodiments of the self-governing republican community, as Michelman would have it. The robed justices can now be seen for what they are: not the embodiment of the law, but merely guardians marking further turns in the greater constitutional labyrinth. We have it on Kafka's good authority that we should be wary of the gatekeepers of the law.

BIBLIOGRAPHY: CHAPTER THREE

Books and articles

Benjamin, W. *The Arcades Project*. London: Harvard University Press, 2002.

Botha, H. and A. van der Walt, eds. *Rights and Democracy in a Transformative Constitution*. Stellenbosch: Sun Press, 2004.

Botha, H. 'Civic Republicanism and Legal Education'. *Codicillus* 41 (2000):23.

___. 'Freedom and Constraint in Constitutional Interpretation'. *SAJHR* 20 (2004):249.

___. 'Metaphoric Reasoning and Transformative Constitutionalism: Part 1'. *TSAR* (2002):612.

___. 'Metaphoric Reasoning and Transformative Constitutionalism: Part 2'. *TSAR* (2003):20.

Cameron, E. 'Sexual Orientation and the Constitution'. *SALJ* 110 (1993):450.

Carpenter, G. 'Of Prostitutes, Pimps and Patrons: Some Still More Equal than Others?'. *SAPR/PL* 19 (2004):231.

Casey, E. *Getting Back into Place: Toward a Renewed Understanding of the Place-World*. Bloomington: Indiana University Press, 1993.

Casey, E. *The Fate of Place: A Philosophical History*. Berkeley: University of California Press, 1997.

Christodoulidis, E. 'Self-Defeating Civic Republicanism'. *Ratio Iuris* (1993):64.

Cohen, F. 'Field Theory and Judicial Logic'. *Yale LJ* 59 (1950):238.

Currie, I. 'Judicious Avoidance'. *SAJHR* 15 (1999):138.

Curtis and Resnik. 'Images of Justice'. *Yale LJ* 96 (1987):1727.

Darrol, L. 'Justice Albie Sachs – About the Constitutional Court'. *Urban Green File* 8 (2003):27.

De Ville, J. *Constitutional and Statutory Interpretation*. Goodwood: Interdoc Consultants, 2000.

De Vos, P. ' Same-Sex Sexual Desire and the Re-imagination of the South African Family'. *SAJHR* 20 (2004):179.

___. 'A Bridge too Far? History as Context in the Interpretation of the South African Constitution'. *SAJHR* 17 (2001):1.

Derrida, J. 'Before the Law', in *Jacques Derrida: Acts of Literature*, edited by Attridge, D. New York: Routledge, 1992.

___. 'Declarations of Independence' *New Political Science* 15, 1986:7.

___. 'Force of Law: The "Mystical Foundation of Authority"'. In *Deconstruction and the Possibility of Justice*, edited by D. Cornell, D. Rosenfeld and M. Carlson. New York: Routledge, 1992.

Dworkin, R. *Freedom's Law: The Moral Reading of the American Constitution*. Cambridge: Harvard University Press, 1996.

Engleman, J.M. '*Bowers v Hardwick*: The Right of Privacy: Only within the Traditional Family?' *Journal of Family Law* 26 (1987–1988):373.

Escher, M. C. *MC Escher: The Graphic Work*. Berlin: Taschen, 1990.

Evans, D. 'Theatre of Deferral: The Image of the Law and the Architecture of the Inns of Court' *Law and Critique* 19 (1999):1.

Furrow, D. *Against Theory: Continental and Analytical Challenges in Moral Philosophy*. New York: Routledge, 1995.

Goodrich, P. *Languages of Law: From Logics of Memory to Nomadic Masks*. London: Weidenfield and Nicholson, 1989.

Hall, M. 'Earth and Stone; Archeology as Memory'. In *Negotiating the Past: The Making of Memory in South Africa*, edited by S. Nuttall and C. Coetzee, C. Cape Town: Oxford University Press, 1998.

Harries, K. *The Ethical Function of Architecture*. Massachussetts: MIT Press, 1998.

Harvey, D. *The Condition of Postmodernity: An Enquiry into the Origins of Cultural Change*. Cambridge: Blackwell, 1989.

Heidegger, M. *Basic Writings*. New York: Harper and Row, 1977.

Jay, M. 'Must Justice Be Blind? The Challenge of Images to the Law'. In *Law and the Image: The Authority of Art and the Aesthetics of Law*, edited by C. Douzinas and L. Nead. Chicago: University of Chicago Press, 1999.

Jay, M. *Downcast Eyes: The Denigration of Vision in Twentieth-century French Thought*. Berkeley: University of California Press, 1994.

Kant, I. *The Critique of Judgement*. Oxford: Clarendon Press, 1952.

Katz, M. 'Close Encounters of the Third Kind: Privacy, Equality and the Expression of Homosexual Preference'. *SAJHR* 12 (1996):308.

Kronman, A. 'Living in the Law' *University Chicago LR* 54 (1987):835.

Lash, S. *Another Modernity, a Different Rationality*. Oxford: Blackwell, 1999.

Le Roux, W. 'From Acropolis to Metropolis: The Constitutional Court Building and South African Street Democracy'. *SAPR/PL* 16 (2001):139.

___. 'Sex Work, the Right to Occupational Freedom and the Constitutional Politics of Recognition'. *SALJ* 120 (2003):452.

Levinas, E. *Entre Nous: On Thinking-of-the-Other*. London: Athlone, 1998.

Lipman, A. *Architecture on my Mind: Critical Readings in Design*. Pretoria: Unisa Press, 2003.

Lyotard, J. F. *The Differend: Phrases in Dispute*. Minneapolis, University of Minnesota Press, 1988.

___. *The Postmodern Explained: Correspondence 1982–1985*. Minneapolis, University of Minnesota Press, 1992.

___. *Toward the Post-modern*. Dublin: Humanities Press, 1995.

Lyotard, J. F. and J. L. Théboud. *Just Gaming*. Minneapolis: University of Minnesota Press, 1985.

Maré, E. 'Democratic vs Revolutionary Architecture: General Concept and Guidelines for the Future South Africa'. In *The South African Association of Art Historians: Ninth Conference July 1993 (Conference Proceedings)* 1993:27.

___. 'Myth and Architecture: Heidegger's Fourfold in Greek, Shinto and Christian Architecture'. *Acta Academica* 24 (1992):30.

Marschall, S and Kearney, B. *Opportunities for Relevance: Architecture in the New South Africa*. Pretoria: Unisa Press, 2000.

Michelman, F. 'Dilemmas of Belonging: Moral Truth, Human Rights, and Why we Might not want a Representative Judiciary' *UCLA LR* 47 (2000):1221.

___. 'Law's Republic'. *Yale LJ* 97 (1988): 1496.

___. 'Traces of Self-government'. *Harvard LR* 100 (1986):5.

Moran, L. 'Law and the Gothic Imagination'. In *Essays and Studies on the Gothic*, edited by F. Botting. London: Boydell and Brewer, 2001.

Mugerauer, R. 'Architecture as Properly Useful Opening'. In *Ethics and Danger: Essays on Heidegger and Continental Thought*, edited by A. Dallerly and C. Scott. Albany: State University of New York Press, 1992.

Mugerauer, R. *Interpretations on Behalf of Place: Environmental Displacements and Alternative Responses*. Albany: State University of New York Press, 1994.

Mureinik, E. 'A Bridge to Where? Introducing the Interim Bill of Rights' *SAJHR* 10 (1994):31.

Nedelsky, J. 'Reconceiving Rights as Relationships' *Review of Constitutional Studies* 1 (1993):1.

Olivier, B. *Critique, Architecture, Culture, Art*. Port Elizabeth: University of Port Elizabeth Publications Committee, 1998.

Rendell, J. 'Ramblers and Cyprians: Mobility, Visuality and the Gendering of Architectural Space'. In *Gender and Architecture*, edited by Durning, L and Wrigley, R. New York: Wiley, 2000.

Robinson, A. *Piranesi: Early Architectural Fantasies*. Chicago: University of Chicago Press, 1986.

Roederer, C. 'Judicious Engagement: Theory, Attitude and Community' *SAJHR* 15 (1999):486.

Sachs, A. 'Book Reviews' *University Toronto LJ* 51 (2001):87.

___. 'Judge and Jury' *South African Architect* 1 (1998):27.

Scalia, A. *A Matter of Interpretation: Federal Courts and the Law*. Princeton: Princeton University Press, 1997.

Schlag, P. 'The Aesthetics of American law' *Harvard LR* 115 (2002):1049.

Schulz, B. and Foster, N. *The Reichstag: Sir Norman Foster's Parliament Building*. London: Prestel, 2000.

Segal, L., ed. *Number Four: The Making of Constitution Hill*. Johannesburg: Penguin, 2006.

Sudjic, D. and H. Jones, eds. *Architecture and Democracy*. London: Laurence King, 2001.

Sunstein, C. *One Case at a Time: Judicial Minimalism on the Supreme Court*. Cambridge: Harvard University Press, 2001.

Tribe, L. 'The Curvature of Constitutional Space: What Lawyers Can Learn from Modern Physics'. *Harvard LR* 103 (1989):1.

Tushnet, M. *Taking the Constitution Away from the Courts*. Princeton, Princeton Universityersity Press, 1999.

Van der Walt, A. 'Closure and Openness on Difference and Democracy: A Response to Justice Johan Froneman'. *Stell LR* 12 (2001):28.

___. 'Dancing with Codes: Protecting, Developing and Deconstructing Property Rights in a Constitutional State'. *SALJ* 118 (2001):258.

___. 'The Quest for the Impossible, the Beginning of Politics: A reply to Dennis Davis' *SALJ* 118 (2001):463.

Van der Walt, J and Botha, H 'Democracy and Rights in South Africa: Beyond a Culture of Justification'. *Constellations* 7 (2000):341.

Van Marle, K. 'In Support of a Revival of Utopian Thinking, the Imaginary Domain and Ethical Interpretation' *TSAR* (2002):501.

___. 'Law's Time, Particularity and Slowness' *SAJHR* 19 (2003):239.

Waldron, J. *Law and Disagreement*. Oxford: Oxford University Press, 1999.

Wise, M. *Capital Dilemma: Germany's Search for a New Architecture of Democracy*. Princeton: Princeton Architectural Press, 1998.

Young, J. *Heidegger's later Philosophy*. Cambridge: Cambridge University Press, 2002.

Case law

Azapo v The President of the Republic of South Africa 1996 (4) SA 671 (CC).

Bernstein v Bester 1996 (4) BCLR 449 (CC).

National Coalition of Gay and Lesbian Equality v Minister of Justice 1998 (12) BCLR 1517 (CC).

President of the Republic of South Africa v Hugo 1997 (4) SA 1 (CC).

Prince v President, Cape Law Society 2001 (2) SA 388 (CC).

S v Jordan 2002 (6) SA 642 (CC).

FOUR

The Public Aspect of Private Property

André van der Walt

> But whereas inside the church certain pews
> were reserved for certain families,
> from generation to generation, regardless of merit,
> outside, considerations of civic worth applied.
> — Julian Barnes[1]

4.1 The Franciscan water

The fountain in the centre of Great Court, Trinity College, Cambridge, whose 'splash at midnight has been grateful to the ears of so many generations of dwellers in the Great Court',[2] was built in 1601–1602[3] when Thomas Nevile was constructing the court in its current form.[4] In his history of the college, Trevelyan noted that (when he wrote)[5] the water in the fountain was 'still the Franciscan water' emanating from an underground aqueduct installed by the Grey friars in 1325 to bring fresh water to their convent in the centre of Cambridge.[6] This may sound like just another quaint historical footnote from one of the guides to the Cambridge colleges, but the phrase 'still the Franciscan water' and the historical context to which it refers is enough to make a property lawyer sit up and pay attention.

---

1 The story of Mats Israelson' in *The lemon table* (2004) 23 at 25.

2 George Macaulay Trevelyan *Trinity College. An historical sketch* (2001) 22. The book was first published in 1943, with several enlarged and reset editions until the most recent edition of 2001 that I refer to.

3 Nevile was Master of the College 1593–1615. Trevelyan (n 2) 28–38. The Fountain was rebuilt on the original design, with some alterations, in 1715–1716. *Idem* 33; Nikolaus Pevsner *The buildings of England: Cambridgeshire* (1954) 171; Royal Commission on Historical Monuments: England *Inventory of the historical monuments in the city of Cambridge* Part II (1959) 213. Charles Benstead *Portrait of Cambridge* (1968) 149 mentions that it is a mystery who designed the Fountain, although it could have been Ralph Symons, who also built the Hall around 1605. For descriptions and photographs of the Fountain see Pevsner 171; Royal Commission on Historical Monuments: England (1959) 232-233; Benstead (1968) 149, 160 and the Trinity College webpage http://www.trin.cam. ac.uk/index.php?pageid=44&stop=4.

4 Trevelyan (n 2) 31. See further Benstead (n 3) 45, 147.

5 At the time of writing this chapter, the College website (n 3) mentioned that the Franciscan water was used for the Fountain 'until recently', because the Franciscan water is not used for the Fountain at the moment. According to Mr Paul Simm, the Junior Bursar, the discontinuation is a temporary measure necessitated by leaks in the pipe that have to be repaired. The original (probably stone) aqueduct has since 1325 been replaced by a thick lead pipe encased in oak, and this pipe has been damaged by building activity.

6 The convent stood on the site where Sidney Sussex College is now situated in Sidney Street. The College map shows that Trinity College still occupies land in a straight line from the Great Gate, across Trinity Street into Blue Boar Court, the Wolfson Building and Whewell's Court on Sidney Street, just across from Sidney Sussex College.

To get the water from the source to the convent the Franciscans had run an aqueduct from the Conduit Head spring some two kilometres to the west of the city, underneath the river and through what would later become the Trinity College Great Court. Trevelyan notes that the Warden and scholars of King's Hall, a predecessor of Trinity College situated in what is now the north-east corner of Great Court,[7] 'had had disputes with the friary, and had claimed to tap the water on its way through their grounds'.[8] When the friars built their aqueduct in 1325 it apparently ran along what used to be Childers Lane, a public lane that connected High Street (now Trinity Street) with the river,[9] so the water dispute probably emerged after 1433, and was in all likelihood precipitated by the 'privatisation' that took place when King's Hall obtained leave to close the eastern part of Childers Lane and to build a new row of King's Hall chambers on its south side, so that the Hall straddled what used to be a public lane[10] and changed it into a private pathway.

The water dispute was settled decisively when the aqueduct, together with the Franciscan land served by it, 'passed into the hands of Trinity' when Henry VIII founded the college in 1546. Trevelyan's laconic phrase refers to the fact that the Franciscan land in the centre of Cambridge – and the water transported there by the aqueduct – was dispossessed by Henry VIII during the campaign (1535–1539) when he dissolved all monasteries in England and Wales,[11] and it was subsequently given to Trinity as part

---

7 King's Hall was founded in 1317 by Edward II, incorporated by Edward III in 1337, and located in a private house first rented and then bought from Robert de Croyland, situated north of Childers Lane in what is now the north-east corner of the Great Court between the Great Gate, the Chapel and the Sundial. See Trevelyan (n 2) 11–12. The other predecessor of Trinity was Michaelhouse, founded by Hervey de Stanton in 1324 and situated in what is now the south-west corner of the Great Court. Trevelyan (n 2) 11–20 refers to King's Hall and Michaelhouse as 'proto-Trinity'.

8 Trevelyan (n 2) 22.

9 Royal Commission on Historical Monuments: England (n 3) 232–233.

10 What is now the Clock Tower (the Edward III Gate) used to be located further south, being the entrance from Childers Lane to the enlarged King's Hall after new buildings were erected to the north and west of the original de Croyland house during the fifteenth century. The present Great Gate was erected in 1490 to form the new entrance to the Hall once new buildings had been erected on the opposite side of Childers Lane. See Trevelyan (n 2) 15–16; Benstead (n 3) 45. Of course, the members of King's Hall could have laid claim to the water before Childers Lane was closed, when the aqueduct was still running along a public lane, but in that case they would have argued that the aqueduct and the water were public and not private, which would have changed the arguments on both sides.

11 Henry VIII was instrumental in the process of religious reform in England and Wales during the 1530s, partly because of the Reformation that was then taking place elsewhere in Europe and partly because of his private battle with the Church, originating when Pope Clement VII refused to annul Henry's marriage to Catharine of Aragon. Once he had installed himself as head of the English Church in the 1530s, Henry set about dissolving the monasteries and appropriating their property. This process, overseen by Thomas Cromwell from 1535 to 1537, not only entrenched Henry's victory in his religious battle with Rome, but also filled his empty coffers and allowed him to redistribute wealth in favour of the landed gentry. By 1539, seven years before Trinity was founded, 560 monastic institutions had been dissolved and their property appropriated and redistributed. The rich Dominican and Carmelite institutions would probably have been the main target rather than the poor Franciscan ones, but of course even the Franciscan monasteries owned valuable land, and they were dispossessed with the rest. Before Trinity was founded there was a threat that the colleges would also be dissolved and their property appropriated in terms of an Act of Parliament passed in 1544 that empowered the King to 'dissolve any chantry, college, hospital, etc, and appropriate its possessions'. See Trevelyan (n 2) 17. However, a commission appointed in 1546 reported in favour of the colleges, and Henry decided not to dissolve the colleges but rather to use monastic wealth to found a bigger and richer college than any other in existence at the time – Trinity.

of its founding endowments.[12] The solution of the water dispute was therefore brought about quite incidentally through a sovereign act of dispossession and redistribution of private property. What looked like a vaguely interesting bit of college lore about an ancient water dispute now appears to hide from view a complex mixture of political, social, religious and legal conflicts.

Disputes about water are notoriously difficult because of its great social and economic importance.[13] They are also theoretically interesting because of conceptual difficulties regarding the use, possession and ownership of water. Because of its limited availability and vital importance in sustaining human life, water inevitably invites speculation and dispute about competing rights, and the history of the Franciscan water prompts one to reconsider the validity and force of different views of property rights, particularly with regard to water but also in general. In fact, the very nature of water renders debates about property rights problematical. One only has to reflect for a moment on the notion that the water in the Trinity College Fountain was (at any given moment during the last five centuries) still 'the Franciscan water' – even when the water was, in fact, still brought from the source to the fountain via the Franciscan aqueduct,[14] this is clearly a troublesome phrase, as flowing water can only be controlled as property if it is contained in stable, identifiable units. For purposes of access to fresh water, this is obviously not a feasible way to acquire water rights and, as a rule, water disputes involve access to, and the use of, flowing water.

In the dispute about the Franciscan water, the friars would probably have considered it relevant that use of water from the Conduit Head source was possible only because they installed the aqueduct to get the water from the source to their convent, and they would have founded their claims to exclusive use of the water on their attempt at occupying or 'privatising' the water through the building of their aqueduct. On the other side, the Warden and fellows of King's Hall would probably have focused their claims to use the water on the fact that the aqueduct ran through their land, against which the Franciscans might have countered that the aqueduct was originally built along a public lane before it was closed and included in King's Hall property, and that they should not lose their established rights simply because King's Hall benefited from privatisation of a public lane.

To modern legal minds, each of these arguments carries some weight and it is quite difficult to decide which one is stronger – authority from various jurisdictions supports each of these conflicting arguments. So, how strong was the Franciscans' right to the water and did King's Hall have a legitimate claim to tap into it? How relevant are con-

---

12 Trevelyan (n 2) 21–22; Benstead (n 3) 147. Having used the stones of the former Franciscan monastery in the gradual construction of the new buildings (probably especially the Chapel) of Trinity, the College sold the land to Sidney Sussex in 1596, but retained the water. Benstead (n 3) mentions at 146 that the University, having used the Franciscan Friary for its commencement ceremonies, wanted the property when the Friary was dissolved by Henry VIII; the town wanted it as a hospital for the indigent poor; 'but Trinity had it'.

13 Trevelyan (n 2) 22 confirms that fresh water was rare and valuable in Cambridge before water was brought into the city by Hobson's Conduit, and therefore the Franciscan water was valuable at the time they built their aqueduct in 1325.

14 Trevelyan (n 2).

siderations of public access, individual effort, or ownership of land in property disputes about a scarce resource such as water? How relevant are the historical circumstances within which different rights and conflicts emerged? How should one explain Henry VIII's dispossession and redistribution of the convent property? In the next section, I argue that the answers to these questions depend on unacknowledged, often unconscious and contested assumptions and notions of what is individual and what common, what is private and what public. In addition, I argue that arguments about property disputes are undermined by an impoverished notion of the public.

In the next section, I illustrate my argument about the impoverished or thin notion of the public with reference to examples from case law relating to water disputes in a variety of jurisdictions. In the analysis of the case law I also attempt to conceptualise the ways in which current perception's of the public are defective and the impact this has on adjudication. In the section after that I explore one set of historical arguments about the origin of this shortcoming, and I point out its impact on the development of the conceptual and rhetorical strategies that are used when property disputes are discussed. In the concluding section I refer to contemporary views about the importance of changing perceptions of the public, and I discuss various proposals for ways in which such a transformation could be initiated or promoted.

4.2 Water disputes

Water disputes assume different forms in different contexts, and water issues are complex for historical and for contextual reasons. To name an example: in the Dutch provinces of the Netherlands, where South African Roman-Dutch common law originated,[15] the problem has always been to get rid of excess water, but South Africa is an arid country where access to limited water is the main source of disputes, and therefore Roman-Dutch water law has little meaning in contemporary South African law. Water disputes have also become more complex recently as a result of water's increasing role in transnational environmental issues, land use regulation, international law and globalisation.

I do not intend to enter into any of these aspects of water law, nor do I want to describe or analyse water law in any specific jurisdiction. Rather, I will refer to three examples of water-related case law from different jurisdictions to illustrate the central line of my argument in this chapter, namely that property rights issues cannot be regarded as straightforward private entitlement problems; that they are always hopelessly intertwined with, and complicated by their historical, social and political context; and that they are inevi-

15 I use the term to refer to the largely uncodified system of rules received from Roman-Dutch civil law as it was received in Holland during the sixteenth and seventeenth centuries, together with case law in which those rules have been explained, analysed and developed. In the process of development, elements of English law were imported, resulting in a mixed system that should be distinguished from English common law and from European civil law. For an introduction and references to further literature see Reinhard Zimmermann and Daniel Visser 'Introduction: South African law as a mixed legal system' in Reinhard Zimmermann and Daniel Visser (eds) *Southern cross: Civil law and common law in South Africa* (1996) 1–30.

tably thought about and discussed against a background of largely unacknowledged but strongly contested notions of private and public. Each of these examples also illustrates the fact that perceptions of the public aspect of property are thin or shallow, impoverished by the overwhelming importance of private interests in property thinking.

The first example comes from American constitutional property law and concerns access to bodies of public water for purposes of transport. In *Kaiser Aetna v United States*[16] the United States Supreme Court had to decide whether a private marina that had been opened up to the Pacific Ocean through private enterprise was navigable water of the United States and, if it was, whether the government had authority to grant public access to the marina by way of the federal navigational servitude, without having to pay compensation. The majority of the court decided that 'the imposition of the navigational servitude in this context will result in an actual physical invasion of the privately owned marina' and that the government would therefore have to pay compensation if it wanted to impose public access upon what was formerly exclusive private property.[17] In coming to this conclusion, the majority relied on a number of findings and assumptions.

First, it was held that the pond that was opened up to create the marina has always been considered to be private property according to Hawaiian state law,[18] and it was assumed that this finding must have a significant bearing on the outcome, in that the opening up of the marina to public access would establish an easing up in private property.[19] In other words, having decided that the marina was private property, the majority assumed that the owner of the marina was automatically entitled to unrestricted and exclusive ownership rights, including the right to develop the marina within the limits of state regulation and the right to exclude others from the marina. Moreover, since the marina was opened up to the Pacific through the private effort of the owner, the majority assumed that the public should not be entitled to the fruits of this private enterprise without compensation.[20]

The majority further assumed that, although the marina was subject to federal regulation under the Commerce Clause,[21] creating a right of public access to the marina

---

16 *Kaiser Aetna v United States* 444 US 164 (1979).

17 *Kaiser Aetna supra* (n 16) at 180 per Rehnquist J for the Court.

18 *Idem* 166, 179.

19 *Idem* 172.

20 In the Trinity College Fountain dispute, the Franciscans might have found the argument of the *Kaiser Aetna* majority sympathetic to their cause.

21 *Kaiser Aetna* (n 16) at 172–174. The majority never questioned the federal government's power to regulate navigable waters, nor the fact that the private marina was navigable and therefore subject to regulation, but it restricted the regulatory power of the government to the making and enforcement of navigation and safety rules within the marina (172, 174). Interestingly, the regulatory powers of the federal government with regard to navigable waters that could really cause harm without attracting compensation – such as the power to cut off riparian owners' existing access to navigable water through works necessitated by the public interest in free navigation – were practically defined out of the current case, which was declared to be closer to cases dealing with regulation of dry land than to cases dealing with 'real' navigable waters (176). In Swiss constitutional law it was recently decided that regulatory action that cut off existing access to public roads and waterways does not necessarily attract compensation, although the backdoor was left open for a compensation award in suitable cases: BGE 126 I 213. The Swiss constitution explicitly provides for compensation for unfairly harsh regulatory action. See further (n 38) below.

would – although legitimate – go further than mere regulation and establish a taking of property that requires compensation in line with the *Mahon* principle.[22] The majority supported this finding with reference to the main tests for compensable takings: public access would establish an actual (and permanent) physical invasion of private property;[23] would interfere with significant, reasonable investment-backed expectations with regard to the property;[24] and would deprive the landowner of 'one of the most essential sticks in the bundle of rights that are commonly characterised as property – the right to exclude others'.[25]

The navigational servitude and federal powers to enforce it are based on the Commerce Clause in the United States Constitution, and therefore it is inevitable that there would be a connection in this case between the interests of free commerce and the public interest in navigable waters, but even then the force with which the majority emphasised the Commerce Clause logic of promoting free interstate trade through free access to navigable waters by way of the navigational servitude, is striking.[26] In a sense, the majority opinion reduces the public interest in water to the upholding of free interstate commerce, which could, from a certain perspective, be seen as a private rather than a public interest because

22 *Kaiser Aetna* (n 16) at 178. In *Pennsylvania Coal Co v Mahon* 260 US 393 (1922), Holmes J first established the principle that the state cannot compensate for loss caused by every regulation, but that a regulation that goes too far will be treated as a taking and has to be compensated (as what would later be known as a regulatory taking). In *Penn Central Transportation Co v New York City* 438 US 104 (1978) 124 the court added that it would answer the taking question 'by engaging in essentially ad hoc, factual inquiries' with reference to certain factors, such as the economic impact of the regulation, the extent to which the regulation interfered with reasonable investment-backed expectations, and the character of the government action. See *Kaiser Aetna* (n 16) at 174–175 for a summary. In *Lucas v South Carolina Coastal Council* 505 US 1003 (1992) 1015–1020, Scalia J summarised the logic of cases where 'categorical treatment' of regulatory takings was justified and where the usual ad hoc, factual inquiries would therefore be unnecessary.

23 *Kaiser Aetna* (n 16) at 180. According to *Andrus v Allard* 444 US 51 (1979), such a physical invasion is a redline indication that a regulatory taking has taken place. Compare the subsequent decision in *Loretto v Teleprompter Manhattan CATV Corp* 458 US 419 1982.

24 *Kaiser Aetna* (n 16) at 180. See footnote 22 above.

25 *Idem* 176. This would indicate that the impact of the regulation was unacceptably harsh – see further (n 21) above.

26 See generally *Kaiser Aetna* (n 16) at 168–170. This emphasis on free navigation for the sake of interstate commerce is even more striking in view of the fantastical notion – apparently taken for granted but never discussed – that the importance of water for free interstate commerce could be anywhere near as significant today as it would have been a century or so ago, which underlines the unhistorical and context-free nature of the majority's approach to property.

27 The attitude I am referring to was characterised by the statement, with reference to *Berman v Parker* 348 US 26 (1954), that the US Supreme Court lacks 'any coherent and broadly accepted theory of the public good as more than an aggregate of private needs and wants', Laurence Tribe *American constitutional law* vol I (2000) 837. I discuss the notion of 'really public' aspects of property in a later section of the chapter below, but suffice for the moment to say that I understand the notion in the same sense as Kevin Gray and Susan Francis Gray 'Private property and public property' in Janet McLean (ed.) *Property and the constitution* (1999) 11–39 at 39, where they refer to 'those intangible and fragile values which alone assure freedom from widespread exploitation, exclusion and social alienation'; and Greg Alexander *Commodity and propriety: Competing visions of property in American legal thought* 1776–1970 (1997) 1–2, where he explains the assumption that humans are inherently social beings who depend on others to survive and to thrive, and who consequently owe each other obligations 'as an inherent incident of the human condition'. In this paradigm, property serves not only personal individual purposes but also the social purpose of facilitating the proper social order. What the proper social order is may be controversial and contested, but property cannot be understood without giving account of its relation to the common good in some way. I owe a great deal of my understanding of and concern about the public aspect of property and the concomitant problems with the relationship between private and public in property law to Greg Alexander.

it promotes common or shared private economic interests, rather than public concerns that transcend the private in the sense of economic interests.[27]

The minority in *Kaiser Aetna*[28] adopted a different attitude towards property and the navigational servitude. Their main concern was that the majority decision would have the Lockean result that private landowners could deprive the public of access to navigable waters simply by enhancing or improving the access to it.[29] Apart from this general concern, the minority used a different navigability test[30] and concluded that the marina (like the pond before being opened up) was always navigable water. The minority also insisted that the federal navigational servitude extends to all navigable water without exception or qualification,[31] because what is at issue in the navigational servitude is power, not property – the servitude safeguards the federal government's paramount control over water used in interstate commerce by limiting the states' powers to create conflicting interests based on local law.[32] As such, federal control does not depend on the nature of the water body, but purely on navigability and the 'corresponding commercial significance the waterway attains'.[33] Once again, the emphasis is placed on the interests of interstate commerce, but adding federal power and the relationship between the federal government and the states to the discussion moves it into another realm, where property issues are judged against the larger backdrop of the public sphere that transcends individual interests and commercial freedom (which is a collective form of individual interests).[34] By adding this consideration to the points for discussion, the minority changed the context within which the case was considered and the grammar of their opinion fundamentally.

The dissent further insisted that the navigational servitude extends to privately created or enhanced water, in other words also to navigable water that only became accessible to the public because of the improvements made by private landowners. The government's interest in imposing the servitude is that of maintaining the free common highways, which is an overriding interest, and therefore the majority was wrong to allow private developers, who are seeking their own benefit, to appropriate navigable waters to the detriment of the public interest in the name of freedom of commerce.[35] Extension of the servitude to privately created or improved water does not dispose of the compensation question, though – the compensation issue requires additional balancing of private and public interests.[36] However, according to the minority, earlier case law established that non compensable loss resulting from the imposition of the servitude relates directly or indirectly to riparian owners' access to, and use of, navigable waters.[37] In other words,

28 Blackmun J, with whom Brennan and Marshall JJ joined in dissent. See at 180–181 ff.

29 *Kaiser Aetna* (n 16) at 181.

30 *Idem* 181–184.

31 *Idem* 184–187.

32 *Idem* 187.

33 *Ibid.*

34 At least in the sense that it involves the functioning of the federal system and hence of democracy, and not just the interests of commerce. See (n 27) above.

35 *Kaiser Aetna* (n 16) at 191.

36 *Idem* 187.

37 *Idem* 189.

expenditure and investment purely aimed at securing or enhancing the landowner's enjoyment of or benefit derived from access to navigable waters cannot be recovered by way of compensation if that access should be lost or the value of the investment affected by the navigational servitude.[38] In drawing this difficult but real distinction between the public interest in free interstate commerce and purely private economic interests, the minority illuminated a very strong argument in favour of treating the public interest in the federal navigational servitude as something more than a purely economic interest; something that could have real civic or democratic significance.

The minority, finally, dissented on the authority of state private law in deciding this case. The majority assumed that the land (including the pond) was private property under state law, but in the minority view 'local law concerns rights of title and use between citizen and citizen, or between citizen and state, but does not affect the scope or effect of the federal navigational servitude',[39] and therefore the minority did not want the matter to be disposed of by principles of private law. Private law protects narrow private interests that are subservient to the overriding public interest in promoting and securing free interstate commerce and subject to the power of the federal government to promote that public interest. Even in balancing those private interests against the public interest it appeared that loss resulting from the imposition of the navigational servitude did not require compensation, since the loss was, in fact, caused by individual risk taking in promoting narrow private interests not protected by the compensation guarantee. This is directly in conflict with the majority view, which assumed the presence of private property rights and thereafter simply checked whether the regulatory action went too far, in which case loss caused by it automatically had to be compensated. In the minority opinion there is, in other words, a definite if vague and imprecise element that supports the idea that certain public interests, such as the federal navigational servitude, embody a facet of public-ness that transcends private interests.

Two aspects of the differences between the minority and majority opinions are significant for my purposes. First, the minority opinion does not reduce the public interest in public waters to freedom of interstate commerce; although it also emphasises free commerce as the basis of the servitude and the federal government's powers with respect to it, the minority's reference to federal power vis-à-vis the states and its contextual analysis of the circumstances under which compensation had been awarded in earlier loss of access cases hint at a greater awareness of the public interest in a deeper or richer sense, a public-ness that is important enough to transcend individual interests

---

38 This attitude roughly reflects the current state of German constitutional law, where it is also accepted that incidental benefits derived from the characteristics of land, such as direct access to public roads and waterways, do not form part of the property and cannot necessarily be regarded as rights that have to be upheld indefinitely; see André van der Walt *Constitutional property clauses: A comparative analysis* (1999) 154–155; *BVerwGE* 38, 209 at 219 (1971) (establishing that beneficial characteristics of land such as access to public roads and water do not belong to the property unless the owner reasonably relied on their continued existence when first using it). In Swiss law it was always accepted that loss of beneficial characteristics of land such as public access do not establish a ground for a compensation claim. But the recent decision in BGE 126 I 213 might have changed that; compare (n 21) above.

39 *Kaiser Aetna* (n 16) at 191, citing *Lewis Blue Point Oyster Co v Briggs* 229 US 82 (1913). This part of the minority opinion comes the closest to considering what I refer to as 'real public' aspects of property; see footnote (n 27) above.

as well as the collective individual interest represented by free commerce. Second, the minority's refusal to privilege state private law in determining the rights baseline from which the case was to be decided, and its balancing of public and private interests in access to navigable water, indicate a more nuanced approach to the complexities of the public-private relationship than is the case with the majority. In short, the minority opinion suggests that it is sometimes necessary to decide property issues with reference to values or considerations that transcend both private individual rights and the public interest in the narrow sense of common or shared economic or commercial interests.

The second example, the *Naßauskiesung* case[40] of 1981, is the most famous case on property rights in the German basic law. The case involves a constitutional property conflict between an individual holder of property and a federal law of 1976[41] that subjected all uses of groundwater to exhaustive administrative regulation and specified that landownership did not entitle the owner to use water in any way that normally required a permit. The plaintiff mined gravel on his land and had started to extract it from below the groundwater level. His application for a permit to continue mining was denied, as was his claim for compensation.[42] The question was whether the water law was constitutional in depriving him of the right to carry on with underwater excavation.

The central finding of the Federal Constitutional Court was that a person who felt disadvantaged by a statutory measure that affected his or her property could only claim compensation if there was a statutory basis for such a claim – if not, the correct remedy was to approach the administrative courts to have the infringement invalidated for not complying with constitutional requirements.[43] The *Groundwater* decision implies that it is impossible to claim compensation for regulatory takings in German law; when regulatory measures which normally do not provide for compensation have a disproportional impact on property rights, they may be invalidated for being in conflict with the constitutional requirements,[44] but they cannot be transformed into expropriations

40 *BVerfGE* 58, 300. For a further discussion of this case see Greg Alexander 'Property as a fundamental constitutional right? The German example' (2003) 88 *Cornell LR* 733–778 at 755–765. Donald Kommers *The constitutional jurisprudence of the Federal Republic of Germany* (1997) 257–261 refers to it as the *Groundwater case*.

41 *Gesetz zur Ordnung des Wasserhaushalts [Wasserhaushaltsgesetz B WHG] 16/10/1976 BGBl I p 3017.*

42 Existing rights were provided for by way of continuation of existing permits, issuing of new permits, or compensation for the loss of existing permits. The applicant did not have an existing permit because his operation had not involved water before the excavation reached the underground water level. The right that he lost because of regulation was therefore the right to keep on excavating underwater without a permit. Since he had no existing permit, he did not lose a permit and could not claim compensation.

43 See *BVerfGE* 58, 300 at 319–320. The property clause in Article 14 of the German Basic Law requires that expropriating laws specify the nature and extent of compensation. In terms of the decision an expropriation in terms of a law that does not specify the nature and extent of compensation is in conflict with the legality requirements and invalid. The power to test for constitutionality vests in the constitutional courts and the power to decide on legality in the administrative courts. The civil courts haves jurisdiction in matters concerning the payment of compensation.

44 Either because it is an expropriation that does not provide for compensation, or because it is a regulatory measure that goes too far and has disproportionate results. Since the *Naßauskiesung* decision, the German courts (especially the administrative courts) have developed a complementary doctrine in terms of which it is sometimes possible, if the authorising laws permit, that non-expropriating equalisation compensation (*Ausgleich*) could be paid by the regulating authority to prevent the impact of regulatory action from being so harsh that it is disproportionate and therefore invalid. This is not regarded as compensation for expropriation and does not change the nature of the infringement. The latest position, including the impossibility of claiming compensation for a regulatory taking and the possibility of receiving equalisation payments for certain regulatory infringements, was confirmed and set out authoritatively and clearly in *BVerfGE* 100, 226 (1999).

by the courts simply because of the extent of their impact and payment of compensation cannot be claimed or awarded for them.

The disputed water law removed groundwater from the sphere of private property rights altogether and subjected it to public regulation, without providing for compensation,[45] and it was therefore an out-and-out regulatory law that raised the question whether the negative impact it had on existing property rights could be justified. If it could not be justified, the law could be declared unconstitutional and invalid, but if it could, the landowner would have to bear the burden without compensation.

In discussing this question, the court first confirmed that, because of the social and public importance of establishing and securing a system of public water controls, it was justifiable for the water law to separate entitlements to use groundwater from private ownership of land, and to subject them to exhaustive public law regulation.[46] It was constitutionally justifiable to separate groundwater from landownership because there are strong reasons why water use should be regulated centrally and no reason why groundwater should belong to the landowner – all property does not necessarily have to be available for private individual ownership. Furthermore, although private rights may be affected when certain goods or categories of property (e.g. water, minerals or sensitive lands) are removed from the domain of private rights and subjected to exhaustive public regulation for the sake of protecting the public interest, doing so does not necessarily endanger ownership as an institution.[47]

In the case *a quo*, the Federal Court of Justice in Civil Matters argued that groundwater formed part of the land and therefore belonged to the landowner in terms of paragraph 905 of the Civil Code, but the Federal Constitutional Court disagreed and decided that

---

45 Except for instances where existing permits were lost, which was not in issue here because the applicant did not have a permit – he lost the right to excavate without a permit, and no provision was made to compensate that loss. See footnote 42 above.

46 See *BVerfGE* 58, 300 at 327–338.

47 *Idem* 339–340. In making this decision the court was confirming other similar decisions, where other categories of property were removed from the sphere of private rights for the sake of protecting the public interest. Examples are *BVerfGE* 24, 367 (removal of dyke property from private ownership to facilitate regulation that prevents flooding); *BVerfGE* 42, 263 (a private compensation fund established to compensate victims of the Thalidomide tragedy transformed into a public fund to facilitate public control). The removal of certain categories of things from the sphere of private ownership is not regarded as a form of nationalisation; art 15 of the German Basic Law allows for nationalisation in certain circumstances, but has never been used.

48 *Idem* 332–334. The position in South African law is now comparable to the German position. Since 1998 all water in South Africa has been removed from private ownership and subjected to public regulation: National Water Act 36 of 1998. Before that, private rights could exist with regard to water that occurred naturally on one piece of land. The preamble to the 1998 Act explicitly recognises the scarcity and uneven distribution of water, the history of discriminatory laws and practices that prevented equal access to it, and the government's responsibility in ensuring equitable allocation of water and water resource management that would ensure sustainability. In 2002 a similar law removed minerals and petroleum products from private ownership and replaced private rights with a permit system under regulatory control: Mineral and Petroleum Resources Development Act 28 of 2002. On the reform function and constitutional validity of these acts see André van der Walt 'An overview of developments in constitutional property law since the introduction of the property clause in 1993' (2004) 19 *SAPR/PL* 102–149 at 144–146. The English courts followed a different approach in the nineteenth century, declaring that use rights in underground percolating water were absolute. Accordingly, the House of Lords refused in *The Mayor, Aldermen and Burgesses of the Borough of Bradford v Pickles* [1895] AC 587 to even qualify that absoluteness with regard to malicious exercise of water rights: Michael Taggart *Private property and abuse of rights in Victorian England: The story of Edward Pickles and the Bradford water supply* (2002) 3.

the nature of flowing water did not fit in with the definition of land in the Civil Code and that the use of groundwater had always been regulated outside of private law.[48] The Constitutional Court also rejected the civil court's view that landownership included the right to exploit every conceivable and economically beneficial use of the property, and stated categorically that a conception of property that would privilege private law tradition over public law in determining the content of property in the constitutional context was not in accordance with the Constitution – the constitutional concept of ownership and the extent of constitutional protection of property cannot be derived purely from normal law, which is subject to the Constitution, but must be developed from the Constitution itself, read together with private and public law.[49] The Constitution obliges the legislature to establish a property order that recognises both the individual interests of owners and the public interest, which means that the legislature must establish suitable private law laws to regulate the relations between private persons, with due recognition of the public interest. Although private law and private interests have to be taken into account in determining the constitutional nature of ownership, the private law tradition (with its conceptual framework and underlying assumptions about the primacy of private individual rights) is not privileged in deciding the scope of the constitutional property clause.[50]

Based on this analysis, the court concluded that the water law did not deprive the applicant of established rights, but regulated the relationship between landownership and the right to use groundwater and, in doing so, established and outlined the position of individual landowners with regard to the use of groundwater. As far as new rights are concerned, the restrictive effect of this law does not create any problems, as the law simply determines what the nature and extent of new rights are. With regard to existing rights, the question is whether the law makes adequate provision for the regulation of existing rights, taking into account that it does not make provision for compensation for loss of non-permitted existing uses.[51] In this regard, the court referred to the fundamental importance of water: it has long been recognised in German constitutional law that the importance of water and the increasing complexity of conflicting claims on its use made regulation essential.[52] Moreover, since water flows and is not restricted to any single parcel of land, it is natural and increasingly necessary to subject it to encompassing public regulation. The nature and social significance of water therefore justify its regulation through a law such as the water law.[53]

The court further held that the separation of groundwater from landownership and the concomitant regulatory removal of water from the private property sphere are

49 *BVerfGE* 58, 300 at 335.

50 Note the similarity between this statement and the minority opinion on the authority of state law regarding private rights in *Kaiser Aetna* (n 16). See further on German law Theodor Maunz and Günther Dürig (eds) *Grundgesetz Kommentar* (2003) Vol II (Art 12–20) at pp 40–45 nr 35–42; compare on this aspect of the Groundwater case Alexander (n 40) 739. Regarding the debate on the private law baseline, see footnotes 155 and 156 below.

51 *BVerfGE* 58, 300 at 336, 337–338.

52 *Idem* 341, with reference to *BVerfGE* 10, 89.

53 *Idem* 343.

constitutionally unobjectionable as far as the property guarantee is concerned, because these steps do not make it impossible to use land economically. It is possible that some landowners may lose certain potentially profitable uses through the regulation, but Article 14 of the basic law does not guarantee every single profitable and valuable use of property, and in this particular case the negative effect of the law on landownership was not disproportionate.[54] In coming to this conclusion, the court formulated what has since become one of the central principles of constitutional property law in German law: when regulating the use of property the legislature is not restricted to a choice between leaving existing and exercised rights unaffected or else expropriating them against compensation. When the public interest requires it, the legislature can reform or amend individual positions, without compensation, even when such amendment causes individual loss, provided the specific measure is proportionate.[55]

It has become trite that environmentally sensitive and scarce resources such as water can be regulated by the state, even to the detriment of individual landowners, and this kind of statement would perhaps hardly raise a frown outside of strict libertarian circles today. In that respect the groundwater case is not unusual at all. However, it is remarkable for two findings that the court made in arriving at its conclusion: (1) that private law does not enjoy a privileged status when determining the nature and content of constitutional property rights and, (2) that not all property necessarily needs to be available for private rights, so that certain categories of property can justifiably be removed from the sphere of private rights if the public interest should require that.[56] Both these findings emphasise an aspect of property law that transcends the purely private or economic individual interest, and in doing so they bear a closer similarity to the minority opinion in *Kaiser Aetna* than to the majority.[57]

The third example resembles the Franciscan water dispute in that it also involved access to water from someone else's pipeline. It derives from South African private law,

---

54 *Idem* 346.

55 *Idem* 351. Although nothing of this nature is said in the *Groundwater* decision, and it would take this chapter too far off track to investigate the matter here because relevant cases were decided on non-property issues, the general social value system based on human dignity and social responsibility that was developed in the jurisprudence of the German Federal Constitutional Court could support the argument I am developing in this chapter. (Some of the key decisions in this regard are about housing and the landlord-tenant relationship, which may be a starting point for analysis.) Notions of human dignity, social responsibility and other fluid and ephemeral civic values concerned with living together in society would then enter into a constitutional property dispute to enrich the technical arguments based on private rights and public powers. See in general Maunz and Dürig (n 50) 186–191 on the 'social bond' or responsibilities of property ownership. See further in this regard the very illuminating discussion by Alexander (n 40) 745–753.

56 Margaret Jane Radin made a similar point about market-inalienability and commodification: see Margaret Jane Radin 'Market-inalienability' (1987) 100 *Harvard LR* 1849; *Contested commodities: The trouble with trade in sex, children, body parts, and other things* (1996). The point is also made by Alexander (n 27).

57 In the same spirit, one senses that the German court, and perhaps the minority in *Kaiser Aetna* (n 16), might have refused to decide the dispute about the Franciscan water purely with reference to either the occupation rights exercised by the Franciscans in building the aqueduct or the ownership rights of King's Hall deriving from its status as landowner – either bench might perhaps have insisted on looking beyond the established and acquired rights and asked questions about public interest (was this the only water available in town?), social and historical context (what was the effect of the closing of Childers Lane?) and, perhaps, civic worth and obligations.

58 *Zulu v Minister of Works, KwaZulu* 1992 (1) SA 181 (D&C).

in a case that was not supposed to be decided with reference to rights at all. In *Zulu v Minister of Works, KwaZulu*[58] the applicant, the senior prince and a former Prince Regent in the Zulu royal family,[59] applied for a court order to restore the piped water supply to his home. During his service as Prince Regent the applicant had a house built with private funds, some 800 metres from the royal residence, at the same time that the government developed a spring and installed a pump and a pipeline to bring water from the spring to the king's palace.[60] When the pipeline was installed, the applicant connected it to his own house, at his own cost but with the approval of the KwaZulu authorities. This situation continued until 1990, when the third respondent (the Department of Works), without prior notice, suddenly interrupted the supply to the applicant's house. Initially the third respondent merely closed a stopcock, but when the applicant had the stopcock reopened the third respondent severed the pipeline with a hacksaw.

The respondents' view was that the applicant had never had any right to be supplied with water free of charge by the KwaZulu government: he was allowed to use surplus water while it was available, but the demand for water in the royal complex had risen and no surplus water was available, and hence the respondents could terminate the supply of water from their pipes. The court seemed to agree with this view, deciding that the government had had no authority to provide free water in the first place and that it had exceeded its authority in doing so.[61] The applicant initially argued that he was entitled to water because his house formed part of the royal complex, but the court dismissed that argument,[62] and since he acknowledged that he had no contract with the government,[63] he resorted to a different strategy, claiming a spoliation order to force the respondents to restore the water to his house before argument on the merits could be heard.

The *mandament van spolie* is a unique possessory remedy, derived from Roman-Dutch law but amended and developed in South African law and now used to restore possession that was lost as a result of unlawful, extra-legal self-help. In the South African *locus classicus* the Appellate Division of the Supreme Court described the remedy as follows:[64] nobody can be allowed to take the law into his or her own hands, and if it should appear that anybody was dispossessed of property through unlawful self-help, the original possession has to be restored *ante omnia*, before the courts would hear argument about the parties' respective rights to possession. If the despoiler should succeed in a subsequent action on the merits, the previous possession would of course have been restored only temporarily, but it nevertheless had to be restored before argument

59 The applicant was the brother of the late Zulu King Cyprian Zulu, and when the king died in 1968 he was proclaimed Prince Regent until the successor, Prince Zwelithini, reached the age of majority in 1970. Once Prince Zwelithini was elevated to king, the applicant was removed from the office of Prince Regent, but he remained the senior prince.

60 At a later stage, the pipeline was improved and extended by the new KwaZulu government to bring purified water to nearby schools and the rest of the royal complex, which includes the residences of ministers and senior officials.

61 *Zulu* (n 58) at 185E.

62 *Idem* 184D–185E.

63 *Idem* 184D.

64 *Yeko v Qana* 1973 (4) SA 735 (A) at 739; see further *Nino Bonino v De Lange* 1906 TS 120 at 122.

on the merits could be heard, so as to discourage self-help and preserve law and order. This principle has been confirmed and applied in numerous decisions over the years, and it is now trite law that the applicant need not prove a property title or right, nor will the court consider such proof in cases of this nature: all that is required is proof of undisturbed prior possession by the applicant and unlawful dispossession by the respondent. The applicant's strategy in using the remedy was therefore to get the water supply, which had been dispossessed through self-help, restored before a case on the merits could be considered.[65]

However, the applicability of the spoliation remedy in cases concerning the intermittent use of immovable property or the services associated with it[66] has long been controversial. In *Bon Quelle (Edms) Bpk v Munisipaliteit van Otavi*[67] the Appellate Division of the Supreme Court decided that the spoliation remedy was appropriate for cases where use of water was terminated by unlawful self-help, provided the applicant could prove that she had previously enjoyed actual and undisturbed use of the water, since it was not possible in a technical sense to possess the flowing stream of water itself. It was also decided that, although the intermittent use of property or the use of water and similar services in cases such as this is often based on servitude, the applicant does not have to prove the existence of a servitude, since that would be contrary to the nature of the remedy. In *Zulu*, the Durban and Coast Local Division of the Supreme Court considered the fact that the applicant had applied for *ante omnia* restoration of the water supply and not for restoration of the damaged to the pipes installed by the applicant, enough to distinguish the case from the earlier water and electricity cases and to refuse the application.[68] The assumption clearly was that, although the applicant

---

65 Had the remedy been available the Franciscans would no doubt have been able to use the same argument to restore the *status quo ante*, without regard to the merits, should the fellows of King's Hall have acted on their threats and tapped into the water supply unilaterally and unlawfully.

66 Some early cases relate to self-help termination of servitude-like use of roads over land and the like, and hence the issue has become known as the 'servitude cases'; compare for example *Nienaber v Stuckey* 1946 AD 1049; *Shoprite Checkers v Pangbourne Properties* 1994 (1) SA 616 (W). A second group of cases relate to self-help termination of water and electricity services associated with occupation of the land; compare for example *Naidoo v Moodley* 1982 (4) SA 82 (T); *Froman v Herbmore Timber and Hardware* 1984 (3) SA 609 (W); *Bon Quelle (Edms) Bpk v Munisipaliteit van Otavi* 1989 (1) SA 508 (A). A third and most recent group deal with self-help termination of telephone or electronic connections to premises; compare *Tigon Ltd v Bestyet Investments (Pty) Ltd* 2001 (4) SA 634 (N); *Telkom SA Ltd v Xsinet (Pty) Ltd* 2003 (5) SA 309 (SCA). The *Naidoo v Moodley* and *Froman v Herbmore* decisions sparked academic debate about the applicability of the *mandament van spolie* in these cases; see for example André van der Walt 'Three cases on the mandament van spolie' (1983) 100 *SALJ* 689–699; André van der Walt '*Naidoo v Moodley* 1982 (4) SA 82 (T)' (1983) 46 *THRHR* 237-240; Marius De Waal '*Naidoo v Moodley* 1982 (4) SA 82 (T)' (1984) 47 *THRHR* 115–118; André van der Walt 'Nog eens *Naidoo v Moodley* – 'n repliek' (1984) 47 *THRHR* 429–439; Jean Sonnekus 'Mandament van spolie – kragtige remedie by kragonderbreking?' (1985) *TSAR* 331–338; Duard Kleyn 'Die mandament van spolie as besitsremedie' (1986) 19 *De Jure* 1–16; Jean Sonnekus 'Besit van serwituutbevoegdhede, mandament van spolie en logika' (1989) *TSAR* 429–442; André van der Walt 'Die mandament van spolie en quasi-besit' (1989) 52 *THRHR* 444–453; 'Toepassing van die mandament van spolie op onroerende sake' (1986) 49 *THRHR* 223–232; '*Bon Quelle v Munisipaliteit van Otavi* 1989 1 SA 508 (A)' (1989) 31 *Codicillus* 65–66. See more recently André van der Walt and Phillip Sutherland 'Dispossession of incorporeals or rights – Is the *Mandament van Spolie* the appropriate remedy?' (2003) 15 *SA Merc LJ* 95–108.

67 *Bon Quelle v Munisipaliteit van Otavi* 1989 (1) SA 508 (A).

68 *Zulu* (n 58) at 186F–H.

could perhaps prove possession and spoliation with regard to the pipes, he could not do so with regard to the water.

The court in *Zulu* recognised that this remedy does not depend on (or even allow consideration of) proof of rights,[69] but nevertheless found it impossible to acknowledge that the applicant had possession of the water, for purposes of the *mandament van spolie*,[70] when it would clearly not have been lawful to restore the water supply to him.[71] However, the court succumbed to logical error here – although unlawfulness of the government's action in providing the water free of charge could indeed be relevant to the availability of the remedy, its potential relevance relates to the unlawfulness of the dispossession,[72] not the factual question whether the applicant indeed used the water or not.[73]

The court's logical error could be blamed on doctrinal sloppiness, but the unwillingness to grant the spoliation order also indicates an almost intuitive feeling that certain instances of unlawful dispossession cannot be dealt with in terms of the *mandament van spolie* because of contextual factors that resist its application. The servitude applications of the *mandament van spolie* are never simple and when they involve discontinuation of public services such as water or electricity the issues become even more complex. The remedy serves public policy purposes in discouraging unlawful self-help,[74] and hence one could argue that the same or other public policy purposes could weigh against its application in certain cases. I do not want to suggest that the *mandament van spolie* should not apply in cases where the state provides and then discontinues services, because the remedy does apply against the state[75] – my point is rather that the

69 *Idem* 187G–H.

70 In a long section ending at 190F–H, the court concluded that 'the applicant's use of water did not constitute the use of a servitutal right' and that 'any right which the applicant might have had to have water supplied to him did not constitute an incident of his possession or control of a corporeal thing (ie his dwelling house)'. Both conclusions are open to disagreement on the facts, and the logic employed to reach them could have resulted in a different decision in *Bon Quelle* if applied there. See further 187F–G: 'The applicant never had possession of the water'.

71 At several points the court remarked on the fact that the government did not have the power to supply water to Zulu free of charge, which could be an (irrelevant) indication that the applicant could never have acquired a right to receive water: see for example 185C, 186D, 190I. The court's attitude is supported by concern, also expressed by authors such as Kleyn and Sonnekus (n 66), that unrestricted expansion of the remedy to instances of so-called quasi-possession could result in the remedy being abused to effect restoration of contractual claims (in the guise of incorporeal things). Recent case law illustrates the fact that those concerns were not entirely misplaced and suggests that it is indeed possible to expand the restorative function of the remedy to instances that would be better served by contractual and delictual remedies. See *Tigon Ltd v Bestyet Investments (Pty) Ltd* 2001 (4) SA 634 (N); *Telkom SA Ltd v Xsinet* (Pty) Ltd 2003 (5) SA 309 (SCA); compare Van der Walt and Sutherland (n 66) 95–108.

72 If the supply of water were unlawful it would not be unlawful to terminate it.

73 Considering the lawfulness of providing the water to him in this regard amounts to asking about the lawfulness of the use or the existence of a right, which is impermissible.

74 This proposition has met with some resistance based on the fact that the *mandament van spolie* is a possessory remedy, but that does not mean that it serves proprietary rather than public policy purposes, and in fact the sources are quite clear about the purpose of the remedy. See in general André van der Walt 'Die mandament' (n 66); 'Toepassing' (n 66); 'Die funksies en omskrywing van besit' (1988) 51 *THRHR* 276–296, 508–514.

75 The most obvious instances of application of this remedy against the state are the so-called squatter cases during the apartheid era, when some courts attempted to resist or at least limit the government's implementation of large-scale evictions and forced removals in the process of establishing separate race group areas. The first and most famous of these decisions is still *Fredericks v Stellenbosch Divisional Council* 1977 (3) SA 113 (C).

kind of public service provided, its social importance and the specific circumstances under which it was supplied and terminated, could combine to indicate that unlawful termination of certain services for certain reasons might be better controlled through other regulatory remedies[76] and not through the *mandament van spolie*. The unease with which the servitude and services applications of the *mandament van spolie* left some courts and commentators prompted the conceptual argument that the remedy was inapplicable because the applicant did not have possession, but perhaps the matter should be considered from another, contextual, vantage point, focusing on policy reasons why other control mechanisms are sometimes better suited to prevent or remedy unlawful termination of certain services. Policy analysis of this kind should, in fact, extend to the separate question whether unilateral termination of services, without formal legal process but in accordance with either a contract or a set of regulations, could be unlawful in some instances and lawful in others, depending on the nature of the services, the personal circumstances of the recipient, and other contextual factors.

The suggestion that the applicability of the *mandament van spolie* in termination of services cases could depend on contextual considerations needs more careful analysis and substantiation than is possible here, and I leave it for another occasion, except for the following general remarks. Based on existing case law, it seems clear that dispossession of houses (eviction) without legal process is socially and legally more problematic than unilateral power cuts for non-payment; and that unilateral termination of services for non-payment is more problematic when it concerns fresh water supply for residential purposes than when it concerns telephone or other electronic services. In the same spirit, it should be possible to argue further that some unilateral dispossessions of services are not necessarily unlawful in the absence of legal process, and that they may be better controlled by other means than the *mandament van spolie*.[77] The point is that the availability of a specific remedy in each of these cases is very much a policy call and not a technical argument that could be solved by mechanical deduction, which supports the central argument in this chapter, namely that disputes about water use rights can often not be solved through mechanical or deductive reasoning about individual rights and entitlements because those disputes often require consideration of open, contextual and contingent policy issues.

From this point of view, the *Zulu* decision is unsatisfactory in several respects, even if one ignores the conceptual muddles referred to earlier. One point of criticism is that unilateral discontinuation of water sources previously supplied by the government or its agents – lawfully or not – is more problematic than when other services such as electric-

---

76 Contractual, administrative, or constitutional remedies, to name a few examples.

77 Questions that remain are, for instance, whether the same exclusion should apply to private providers of the relevant public services; and which factors should be taken into account when deciding which kinds of services should be excluded in this way. A first preliminary thought is that some guidance could be gleaned from the constitution and the various social and economic reform laws, many of which emphasise special compassion when dealing with weak and marginalised groups such as children, the elderly, and households headed by women or children. A second idea is that special areas of care could be identified by concentrating on what are regarded as basic and fundamental services in the constitution and in various reform laws; such as housing and provision of clean water for domestic consumption.

ity or telephone lines are concerned and stricter control over such cuts seems desirable. A second point is that discontinuations of water supplies are as easily remedied as they are committed if the court should grant a (temporary) spoliation order, and just as easily repeated if the supplier should win a subsequent case on the merits. A third point is that temporary restoration of water supply (while proceeding with a case on the merits) is unlikely to cause much loss for the supplier, whereas discontinuation of water supply could have disastrous results for those who depend on it for daily sustenance. All these considerations weigh in favour of being lenient towards restoration, and therefore the *mandament van spolie* seems like a useful and suitable remedy for cases where *ante omnia* restoration of specifically domestic water supply is applied for, following an alleged unlawful self-help dispossession of previously actually enjoyed use of water from that supply. However, these are all more or less technical points that should occur to any court considering a spoliation application.

A more difficult question is whether the courts, in applying such a policy-dominated remedy, should not be more aware of wider policy-relevant contextual matters. In the *Zulu* case, for instance, one is left with the feeling that the court concluded too easily that the KwaZulu government had no duty or power to supply services free of charge 'to all and sundry',[78] and (although it was strictly irrelevant in this case) that the applicant had no right to claim continued supply of water. This conclusion seems unsupported by the circumstances surrounding the applicant's initial acquisition of the water: though living in his own private house he was Prince Regent when he was allowed to tap into the royal water supply and after the young prince became King, the applicant remained in his position as senior prince (and therefore state official). Even in the absence of a dispute about property rights, these circumstances could arguably entitle the applicant to more concern about the abrupt termination of the water supply he had enjoyed for more than twenty years, not to mention general humanitarian concern about his access to suitable water after the water supply had been cut off. However, apparently the court did not consider these aspects important and they played no role in the decision.

The problem with the decision is that it is formulated strictly in terms of the acquisition of private rights and the lawfulness of state action that creates rights, while the facts of the case hint at contextual circumstances and civic processes that were taking place outside the narrow realm of private rights and the public power to grant them. Given the fact that the remedy is a policy instrument that could at most have temporary effects, one cannot but conclude that the decision was impoverished by its private rights orientation and its lack of awareness of, and sensitivity towards, public and civic concerns that go beyond private rights and even beyond the extent of formal public law powers. In this respect the South African *Zulu* case demonstrates the poverty of

78 The court's phrase. See *Zulu* (n 58) at 185D–E.

79 One question not raised is whether the political-historical context played any role in the events that led up to the case. KwaZulu became a self-ruling 'independent' homeland under the apartheid government on 1 February 1977 in terms of Proc R11 of 1977, issued in terms of the Self-Governing Territories Act 21 of 1971; the homeland system was terminated and the former homelands abolished by the new government on 27 April 1994: s 1(1) of the 1993 interim Constitution

traditional private property orientated rights talk and the importance of wider, historical, social, political[79] or civic contexts in deciding property disputes.

From one perspective, none of the three cases discussed above is remarkable. Any number of cases from these jurisdictions or from many other countries around the world could be cited to make the point that water disputes involve both private and public interests, or that water is too scarce and important to decide disputes about it simply on the basis of individual rights.[80] However, these cases are more interesting than that. Four preliminary observations are in order at this stage.

First, it is significant that there was an attempt in all three cases to have the dispute solved within the framework of private law, with varying degrees of success. In *Kaiser Aetna*, the Supreme Court majority decided the matter on the basis of its assumption that the marina was private property in terms of state law and the minority dissented, arguing that state private law should not dispose of the matter so easily. In the groundwater case, the civil court *a quo* decided the matter on the basis that the applicant's rights to groundwater had to be evaluated in terms of his ownership of the land, of which the water was said to form part, but the Federal Constitutional Court rejected this argument explicitly and held that a constitutional concept of property had to be developed with due recognition, but not on the exclusive authority of private law. In *Zulu*, the applicant conceded that he could not claim a private law right to the water but nevertheless attempted to have his water supply restored temporarily by way of a unique private law remedy, and the court decided the matter with reference to the question whether the state had the power to grant the right claimed by the applicant.

The second point follows from the first: deciding the matter in terms of private law means that private property rights feature centrally and the dissenting voices that refused to decide water disputes on this narrow basis stand out. The majority opinion in *Kaiser Aetna* took the private law landownership of the marina as its point of departure, while the minority took the opposite view and regarded the public interest in free inter-

---

declared that the Republic of South Africa would be one sovereign state, and s 1(2) declared its territory to be as set out in Sch 1, where the nine new provinces are described (see also s 124(1)). KwaZulu (the homeland before 1994) and KwaZulu-Natal (the province since 1994) was plagued by political strife and unrest, and deep political divisions continually resulted in violent struggles between and within families, communities and localities. Mutual recriminations and disagreements about participation in the apartheid-dominated homeland government system during the apartheid years resulted in acrimonious disputes, even and perhaps especially in the ranks of tribal leadership and those surrounding the Royal House. Whether such a social or political struggle perhaps inspired or exacerbated the events that led to the case is unclear, but the court did not even consider the possibility.

80 There are no South African constitutional cases on water regulation yet, but there are many other water and scarce resource cases that could have been referred to. For German law, the dyke regulation case mentioned in footnote 47 would have served the same purpose. For US law, *Lucas v South Carolina Coastal Council* 505 US 1003 (1992) and the recent *Tahoe-Sierra Preservation Council, Inc v Tahoe Regional Planning Agency* 535 US 302 (2002) would have been just as useful. Another interesting case to discuss here would have been *The Mayor, Aldermen and Burgesses of the Borough of Bradford v Pickles* [1895] AC 587; for an exhaustive analysis of the case see Michael Taggart *Private property and abuse of rights in Victorian England: The story of Edward Pickles and the Bradford water supply* (2002). The case bears interesting resemblances to the Franciscan water dispute discussed in the introductory section of the chapter: by threatening to use his land in a way that would shut down the water supply that supplied the town's water, Pickles apparently tried to force the Corporation of Bradford to pay him for the water that originated under his land and that the Corporation sourced from the spring on adjacent land to supply water to the city of Bradford. The House of Lords held that it was not unlawful for a landowner to use his property to the detriment of others or the public interest, even if such use was malicious.

state commerce as an overriding right that should only be balanced against the private interest to determine whether compensation was due, not to decide whether the servitude applied. In this regard, the minority's analysis of the private riparian landowner's status as a participator in using public navigable waters is particularly interesting. The applicant in *Groundwater* relied very strongly on his ownership of the land on which the water occurred, and the civil court was satisfied that landownership disposed of the matter. However, the Federal Constitutional Court refused to privilege private law and the rights created by it in considering the nature and scope of constitutional rights and therefore placed less emphasis on the private right, preferring to focus on constitutional justification for the separation of landownership and water rights envisaged by the water law. The *Zulu* case is particularly interesting, because the nature of the unique private law remedy the applicant relied on prescribed that rights should not be considered at all, but the refusal of the application leaves a sense of the court having been very aware of the fact that the applicant did not and could not, in its view, have a right to the water. Since the unique character of the remedy derives from its policy-orientated focus on discouraging public violence and self-help, the decision is unsatisfactory both because of the court's unwarranted focus on the absence of rights and for its failure to focus on real public policy concerns.

The third aspect of interest is the role and status of the public interest in deciding these cases. In *Kaiser Aetna*, the majority and the minority differed on the status and weight of the public interest in this case, although both associated the public interest (understandably in the context of the case) with free interstate commerce and the Federal Government's powers under the Commerce Clause. The majority employed a conceptual approach, first classifying the marina as private property according to state law and then reducing the public interest issue to deciding whether a particular regulatory act would constitute a compensable taking under the rule in *Pennsylvania Coal v Mahon*. Accordingly, the public interest was reduced to the state's police power in regulating the use of private property and the limits of such regulation, before it 'goes too far' and becomes a regulatory taking. The minority regarded the public interest in free commerce as an overriding interest that transcended private economic interests, and wanted to balance private and public interests to see whether private landowners should receive compensation for improvements made to enhance their access to navigable waters. In *Groundwater*, the constitutional nature of the case and the public interest bound up with it was kept in the foreground by the Constitutional Court, particularly in its refusal to privilege private law principles and private rights in determining the legitimacy of a regulatory law intended to promote the public interest in water resource management. The court's explanation of the legitimacy of excluding certain categories of property from the sphere of private rights is particularly enlightening. The public interest was identified with effective and sustainable but proportionate and reasonable public management of water as a scarce resource. In *Zulu*, the remedy applied for is private but has a strong 'public' or policy focus, and the irony is that the applicant probably lost because the court focused too strongly on private rights and not enough on the civic or public context within which the case emerged. In so far as the public interest played a role it was reduced to the government's powers to grant services free of charge, while the public or civic aspect of the applicant's position as Prince Regent and the interest in preserving public peace against self-help were underplayed.

A final observation that emerges from these cases is that water disputes are not only difficult and complex because of the interaction of private and public law, and the tension between private rights and the public interest, they are also difficult because these conflicts and tensions can never be decided by way of reliance upon more or less mechanical deduction from rules and rights, whether private or public. They always involve policy decisions that reflect deeply contested visions of what is private and what is public in the first place, and therefore the problem I am discussing here is more than finding the right balance between individual and collective[81] (or private and public) interests. My point is that the very distinction between private and public is unstable and contested because the orthodox definition of *property* itself is unstable and contested, and that historical developments have left an impoverished and eroded concept that reduces the public to public control and harmonisation of private individual economic interests. Of course, the notions of public and of private are just as unstable and contested as the distinction between them, and hence it is possible to identify examples of *public law* that, in fact, protect private interests and of *private law* rules that are, in fact, infused with public consciousness. However, despite these pockets of visible or obvious mutual cohesion and infusion, we tend to work within an impoverished analytical framework that is inclined to privilege the private and reduce the public to a secondary, subservient function. In the next section I argue that the Franciscans and their unique attitude towards property played an important role in this development, and so I return to the Franciscan water dispute by way of an historical detour.

4.3 Franciscan property disputes

At roughly the same time that the Franciscans were installing their aqueduct in Cambridge, the Franciscan Order itself was involved in internal dogmatic disputes about property: disputes that would influence the future development of legal and philosophical thinking about private rights – and especially private property rights – fundamentally. Stated very simply, much of the current difficulty in giving proper

81 This is the reason why I am not even mentioning debates about communitarianism; I am not trying to get a better or different balance between individual and collective, but arguing that the terms in which we discuss the current balance are impoverished because we are not taking into account an aspect that could or should change the whole debate in some fundamental way. What that aspect is and how I see it is discussed in the last section of the chapter below, and see (n 27) above; see further (n 152) below. A useful perspective on the poverty of both traditional communitarian and libertarian views of the public-private problematic in property is given by Hanoch Dagan and Michael A. Heller 'The liberal commons' (2001) 110 *Yale LJ* 549–623, especially at 554: relying on the private/public distinction as a sharp dichotomy, theorists from these theoretical backgrounds have traditionally chosen between liberal and communitarian solutions to the tragedy of the commons problem, overlooking the possibility of a synthesis that could mediate liberty and cooperation. Dagan and Heller propose a model of the 'liberal commons' that could effect such a mediation (see at 553). See in the same vein Hanoch Dagan 'The craft of property' (2003) 91 *Cal LR* 1517–1571. I am indebted to Greg Alexander and Hanoch Dagan for some of the insights and refinements of my argument in this footnote and in the accompanying paragraph.

82 Of course the Franciscans' claim that they did not own any property complicates even further evaluation of King's Hall's threat to tap into the Franciscan water and Henry VIII's subsequent dispossession of the convent's land and aqueduct.

account of the public interest in property disputes can be traced back to the fact that the Franciscan friars denied that they had any property rights at all.[82]

In living up to the testament of their founder, the Franciscan Order[83] attempted from the second half of the thirteenth century onwards[84] to develop a coherent doctrine of apostolic poverty, which would allow them to maintain that they did not have property rights[85] in anything,[86] while still being able to use the things required for daily life in the monasteries. The early Franciscan position was set out in the bull *Exiit* issued by Pope Nicholas III in 1279: simple use (*usus facti*) of things is distinguished from ownership (*dominium*)[87] in that simple use does not establish ownership in things because it does not involve free disposal through gift or trade. By placing the emphasis on disposal through alienation or exchange as the essential characteristic of ownership, the Franciscans could deny that they ever acquired property and so they could adhere to their rule of poverty while still being able to use the necessities of everyday life. In effecting this slight but significant shift of emphasis towards alienation and disposal in the definition of ownership, the Franciscans aligned themselves with the pre-Accursian

---

83 Often known by the initials OFM, standing for Ordo Fratrum Minorum or Friars Minor, to reflect their stance of living in apostolic poverty according to the legacy of their founder, St Francis. The Franciscans arrived in the UK around 1220.

84 Roughly from around 70 years before the Franciscan water pipe was installed and King's Hall was founded on the present site of Trinity College. The initial Franciscan position was settled by 1279, ie 50 years before the aqueduct was installed, see below.

85 The Franciscan poverty debate included discussion of concepts such as *dominium* and *ius*, and therefore concerns ownership in the narrower sense and property rights in the wider sense.

86 For this section I have made extensive use of Richard Tuck *Natural rights theories: Their origin and development* (1979). The Franciscan story features at 20–31. I focus on Tuck's book not only because it is a brief and useful overview of the relevant history, but also because it was the first source for discussion when Johan van der Walt and I started the weekly discussions (in 1993) that developed into the regular meetings of the Pretoria discussion group. Costas Douzinas in *The end of human rights: Critical legal thought at the turn of the century* (2000) ch 2–5 adopts a slightly different approach toward this history, arguing that the classical Greek and Roman notion of a natural right was a 'methodological principle' with a corrective or critical edge that undermined established, sedimented societies, looking for the just answer in each individual case. See at 68. The religious naturalism that developed from Thomas Aquinas onward undermined the critical potential of this classical view of natural law and justice (60). From the late Scholastics on, it also moved away from the search for justice in each individual case and became associated with a power that every person has, thereby establishing the modern notion of natural human rights as powers belonging to individuals (61). The main difference between Douzinas' and Tuck's view of the history is that Douzinas blames the extreme individualism of Renaissance rights theories on the nominalism of the Franciscans, such as Scotus and Ockham (61–62) However, it is equally possible to argue that the individualism of the late medieval and early modern theories of rights was a result of the Thomists and late Scholastics locating the foundation of rights in human nature, which inevitably results in extreme individualism. See footnote and surrounding text. At the same time, the nominalism of the Franciscans and their focus on civil laws as social artifacts would have pushed them towards a stronger emphasis (at least as far as rights and property are concerned) on society as the source and context of rights, whereas the religious naturalist arguments of the late Scholastics would have resulted in extreme individualism, in which property (and other natural rights) are seen as pre-societal individual powers derived from the divine nature of man. I am quite attracted to Douzinas' view of classical natural rights' critical potential in undermining sedimented social institutions and traditions, and I take note of his explanation of how this critical edge was blunted by the religious naturalism of the Thomists, but for purposes of this chapter I adopt the view that it was this same religious naturalism rather than the Franciscans' nominalism that supported the emergence of early modern individualist and subjectivist theories of rights, property and the state. See further Maximiliane Kriechbaum *Actio, ius und dominium in den Rechtslehren des 13. und 14. Jahrhunderts* (1996).

87 Including *proprietas, possessio, ususfructus* and *ius utendi*.

88 Tuck (n 86) 21.

Romanist tradition in terms of which ownership was associated with a social or civil community rather than with a pre-societal natural state.[88] In modern terminology, they saw property as a conventional rather than natural institution, and associated it with the social arrangements that allow an individual to alienate property within a social and economic system that accommodates trade and exchange.

During the late thirteenth and early fourteenth century, the Franciscans' practice of living in apostolic poverty caused intense controversy between them and their rivals, the Dominicans.[89] Franciscans such as Duns Scotus[90] defended the poverty thesis set out in the bull *Exiit*, but the Dominicans resisted the ideal of apostolic poverty – and the papacy had to retreat from its original support for it – because it had radical critical implications: if some people in the Church could live this simple life without property, others could do so as well, which would raise questions about the sometimes opulent lifestyle within the Church.[91] The Dominican attack against the Franciscans assumed the form of an argument that individual ownership existed in the state of nature. Thomas Aquinas argued, for instance, that *dominium* was a pre-societal, natural human faculty and not merely a social convention. In 1329 Pope John XXII issued the bull *Quia vir reprobus* in support of this position, declaring that man's ownership of his possessions in the state of innocence was similar to God's dominium over the earth as creation – the notion of ownership as something pre-societal and natural to man was thus founded on divine law. William Ockham countered this change of direction within the papacy by again tying the existence and value of ownership to human or social institutions, defining *ownership* in terms of the possibility of enforcing the right through litigation.[92] The right to use things in the natural state could be called a *right*, he conceded, but that right cannot be enforced in a court as *dominium* can, and thus *dominium* is a social and conventional right and not a natural right. This allowed the Franciscans to follow their rule of poverty without directly coming into conflict with the new papal orthodoxy.

The difference between the Franciscans and the Dominicans was therefore that the former described ownership as a social or conventional right created for, and upheld by, social institutions, whereas the latter developed a natural law theory that described ownership as natural and essential to human beings, prior to, and independent of, social institutions. The Franciscan approach was based on and therefore orientated towards,

---

89 *Idem* 20–31. Tuck's thesis is that this controversy was the source of late medieval natural rights theories and a main issue for the discussion from which later natural rights theories developed.

90 Scotus *Quaestiones in Librum sentatarium* 15.2 in *Opera omnia* XVIII (1637; Tuck refers to ed. Paris 1894); Tuck (n 86) 21. Duns Scotus argued that natural law was in fact against individual ownership, because common use was the best possible arrangement for the pre-societal state of innocence. As a fundamentally civic right, *dominium* was necessarily a private right including the entitlement to exchange and defend one's property against interference, even against those in need. Since the Franciscans were supposed to live the simple life of innocence, this kind of *dominium* was not available to them, but since it was not the kind of use they made of things necessary for their existence in their everyday lives in the monastery, this was no great deprivation for them.

91 Tuck (n 86) 22.

92 William Ockham 'Opus nonaginta dierum', in Ralph Bennett and Hilary Offler (eds) *Opera politica* II (1974) 287–368; Tuck (n 86) 22–23 refers to ed. Manchester 1963.

the social origins and character of property, which means that property arrangements were conventional, limited by, and further amenable to, changes in their social context. In the Dominican theory, ownership was not the creation of social intercourse or civil law, but rather a basic fact on which social and political relationships had to be posited[93] – an approach that has obvious conservative and individualist implications for property and for political theory. Property rights were pre-societal, pre-conventional and pre-legal institutions of nature, and hence the establishment and development of society, convention and law had to start out from, and be limited by, recognition of these pre-existing rights.[94] The poverty debate died out in the fourteenth century with Ockham and during the fifteenth century there is little evidence of serious opposition to the Dominican natural rights theory. The most significant development was initiated by Jean Gerson, who described ownership as a natural human faculty or power,[95] which forged the vitally important link between property, human will and power. As Tuck indicates,[96] this enabled Gerson to assimilate ownership with liberty, establishing a significant link between ownership and sovereignty.[97] The Gersonian version of natural rights theory reigned supreme by the second decade of the sixteenth century and was developed further into the classic natural rights theories of the seventeenth century.

The Renaissance brought new perspectives and challenged the Gersonian natural rights theory. Humanist lawyers found it impossible to talk about natural rights,

---

93 Tuck (n 86) 24.

94 *Idem* 29. In language that the majority of the US Supreme Court in *Kaiser Aetna* (n 15) would have appreciated but the German Federal Constitutional Court would have rejected, the Dominicans argued that property rights were not created by the law of society, but by the law of nature, and therefore private property rights enjoyed a privileged status in social or constitutional (conventional) debate. The history of the Franciscan poverty debate explains the development of modern natural rights theory that probably influenced the US court in their decision, just as it influences all contemporary human rights and private law thinking. A possible explanation for the German court's different attitude is provided by Ruti Teitel *Transitional justice* (2000) at 16–18: comparative analysis of judicial attitudes towards transformation and the rule of law in post-World War II Germany and post-1989 Hungary reveals that the former rejected prior law on moral grounds, sacrificing security and continuity for the sake of equal enforcement in criminal prosecutions and searching for what was morally right as the controlling rule of law value; while the latter tended to opt for security of pre-existing rights and criminal forbearance. Contextual analysis shows that these different attitudes can be explained by the relative backgrounds: Hungary after totalitarianism was looking for bright line positive security after the demise of state power, while Germany operated within the security of relatively untainted pre-existing case law and in reaction against Fascism. In Germany, natural law was associated with the jurisprudence of the Third Reich courts and rejected, and the straightforward search for what was morally right in the new constitutional order came easily; in Hungary the need for security of pre-existing rights was more pressing and the new constitutional order had to be subjected to it. In other words the Germans opted for a 'Franciscan', conventional approach and the Hungarians for a 'Dominican', natural rights approach. In Teitel's view, neither a natural rights nor a positivist approach is essential for transitional justice, as the social construction of the rule of law mediates its transitional function (19-20). It should be noted that Teitel refers to the Hart-Fuller debate and that the conventional approach does not translate into positivism directly; the history of positivism includes further development that cannot be investigated here.

95 Jean Gerson *Oevres complétes* III ed Glorieux (1962); Tuck (n 86) 25–26.

96 Tuck (n 86) 26–27.

97 In chapter one of this collection Johan van der Walt critically discusses the hold which this and other expressions of sovereignty have over the South African political and constitutional imagination.

98 Tuck (n 86) 33.

and preferred to concentrate on 'humanly constructed law' and civil remedies rather than on natural law.[98] Natural life was associated with brutish, animal-like behaviour, while social or civil life was associated with reason and eloquence.[99] Human societies progressed from the brutish state of nature through the adoption of civil law; the *ius gentium or ius civile* is a product of civilisation.[100] As Tuck notes, '[m]any texts in the Digest supported the view that most phenomena of the moral world were post-natural', and the Humanists simply accepted the classical view that real moral relationships were the product of civilisation.[101] Moral relationships only became possible on the basis of social compacts, which are necessary for the survival of society, and all rights are therefore civil rights that guarantee civil remedies.[102] In principle, Humanism should have supported the Franciscans against Thomist orthodoxy, but the Humanist revival of conventionalism was short-lived because of the work of late Thomists such as Molina and De Soto and their Calvinist follower, Hugo Grotius.

Like the Humanists, the Spanish Dominicans Francisco de Vitoria and Domingo de Soto defined *ius* objectively as what is allowed under law and associated rights with remedies,[103] but they attempted to reconcile this with Thomist notions of natural property rights[104] through greater concern for the welfare of men and the limitations of what men were free to do with their property, rather than the emphasis on liberty that was typical of the earlier Gersonian natural rights theories.[105] They therefore placed more emphasis on distributive justice and on the claims of the needy against the wealthy, in keeping with their Thomist roots.[106] By the 1520s the subjective Gersonian natural rights

---

99 On this point humanist lawyers referred back to Cicero *De inventione* 1.2 (Loeb ed. p 4–6). See Tuck (n 86) 33. They also relied on Roman law, which was concerned with civil remedies rather than with natural or human rights. See Max Kaser *Das römische Privatrecht* 1er Abschnitt: *Das altrömische, das vorklassisiche und klassische Recht* (1971) at 225 '... bleibt jedoch zu beherzigen, daß den Klassikern, die weder eine Theorie des subjektiven Rechts noch einen durchgebildeten Anspruchsbegriff besitzen, solche Fragestellungen noch nicht zugänglich waren.' See further also Philip Thomas *Textbook of Roman law* (1976) 4–5. The exact dating of the notion of subjective rights is a controversial issue but not necessary to discuss here.

100 Tuck (n 86) 34.

101 *Idem* 34. Andreas Alciatus thus saw the task of the law as preservation of the civilised and sociable life. See Tuck (n 85) 36 with reference to Alciatus *Omnia opera* II (Basle 1546). Alciatus distinguished between *ius gentium* and *ius civile* on the basis that the former referred to the unpredictable and arbitrary rule of primitive kings, whereas the latter consisted of settled law that controlled everything, including the magistrates. However, both were human and therefore civilised or social law, as opposed to natural law. See Tuck (n 86) 37.

102 *Idem* 40.

103 *Idem* 48–49.

104 Referring back to medieval notions of *dominium utile*, which was associated with classical Roman usufruct but regarded as a form of *dominium* according to feudal law. See Tuck (n 86) 48. The poverty debate developed parallel to and intertwined with a debate about feudal property, which ended in the latter being abolished. See Kriechbaum (n 86).

105 Tuck (n 86) 49. This also refers back to the medieval definition of ownership by Bartolus de Saxoferrato ad D 41.2.17.1 (n 4): 'Dominium est ius de re corporali perfecte disponendi nisi lege prohibeatur'. For comments on this definition and its influence see André van der Walt 'Bartolus se omskrywing van dominium en die interpretasies daarvan sedert die vyftiende eeu' (1986) 49 *THRHR* 305–321; 'Der Eigentumsbegriff', in Robert Feenstra and Reinhard Zimmermann (eds) *Das römisch-holländische Recht: Fortschritte des Zivilrechts im 17. Jahrhundert* (1992) 491–526.

106 Tuck (n 86) 50.

107 That is, this was the status by the time that Henry VIII dissolved the monasteries (1535–1539) and established Trinity College (1546). See Tuck (n 86) 29; 50. Given his struggle with Rome and his association with Reformation ideals, Henry VIII and his associates would have been influenced by the Humanist rather than the Thomist movement towards objectivism.

theory had started making room for a Humanist and Thomist form of objectivism with its focus on man-made, social or civil laws.[107] However, by the 1580s a new generation of late Scholastic theorists started moving back towards the notion of natural rights, at least partly under the influence of theoretical debates about slavery. The impetus for this new movement came mainly from Portugal and the Netherlands, the main figures being Luis de Molina (a Jesuit) and Hugo Grotius (a Calvinist). Molina forged a new connection between *ius* as a human faculty and the faculties of free will and disposition, thereby reverting to the Gersonian position where rights were intensely individual and subjective and much more closely connected with liberty than with welfare.[108] He completely ignored the recent legacy of Humanism, and his theory looks like 'an ideology of mercantile capitalism',[109] which is understandable considering the importance of trade (and especially the slave trade) for Portugal at the time. With Molina, late Scholastic rights theory therefore reverted to Gersonian notions of property as a natural human faculty closely associated with the exercise of free will and disposition.

The early Calvinists were Humanists, and although they combined their Humanism with a strong sense of the omnipotence of God and his part in human affairs,[110] they nevertheless focused on social rather than natural man as the bearer of rights,[111] being concerned with human law designed by society for social utility (either under man's own initiative or under the command of God), and not with natural law.[112] Hugo Grotius grew up in this Humanist and Calvinist tradition, but like Molina he evidenced close ties to mercantile interests, especially in his first work, *De iure praedae*.[113] Grotius linked the Scholastic and Humanist theories of rights by denying the existence of private ownership in the state of nature, but simultaneously developed the notion of human sovereignty and the natural right of acquisition of property through first occupation, thereby cleverly combining his Humanist respect for Roman law (which recognised occupation as an original form of acquisition), and his interest in Scholastic notions of the human will and ownership as a human faculty. The inherent human right to use the material world naturally develops into the civil institutions of private property, through the process of physical occupation and man's exertion of labour on or alteration of natural objects.[114] Grotius subscribed to the atomistic theory of the state and of property that naturally follows from the natural rights theory, and this atomistic perspective has significant implications for later perceptions of private and public, as is explained by Tuck:

---

108 Tuck (n 86) 53; Luis de Molina *De iustitia et iure* I (1614).

109 *Idem* 54.

110 So that political life was the direct creation of God after the Flood, and not the creation of fallen man, which could have moved them in the direction of the Dominican theory of natural rights.

111 Tuck (n 86) 43.

112 *Idem* 44.

113 De *iure praedae* was written in 1607, but only one chapter was published as *Mare liberum* in 1609. The whole book was only published in 1868 in the ed. of Hamaker. See Tuck (n 86) 59.

114 Tuck (n 86) 61; Hugo Grotius *De iure raedae* ed. Hamaker (n 113) 216–217. The seas, for example, were not naturally private property, but man was able and had a natural right to occupy and so establish private property over them. See Van der Walt (n 105) 488.

> This was true also of his theory of property: private individuals and states were interchangeable with respect to property, and a state's boundaries were the same kind of thing as the boundaries of a private estate. In some ways, such an assimilation of the private and public realms was characteristic of all rights theorists from Gerson onwards; for by attributing rights of *dominium* or a kind of sovereignty to individuals in a state of nature, they immediately made the distinction between the two realms fluid and in effect purely a question of numbers.[115]

Tuck's explanation underlines the effect that atomism has on the distinction between private and public, particularly in a conceptual paradigm where human natural faculties play such an important role: the public realm (including the state) is reduced to a larger collection of the smaller unit, the human individual. This perspective has inevitably impoverished perceptions of the public, which is eventually associated only with the security of the boundaries between individual interests.

Grotius' *Inleidinge,*[116] the first natural-rights based 'reconstruction of a legal system in terms of rights rather than laws',[117] explains that the natural human faculty of contracting – like the property about which men contract – predated civil law, and that the civil law only stepped in as a corrective to preclude certain bad bargains.[118] Primacy is moved away from the civil laws to the natural faculties and the individual will, in line with Molina.[119] In *De iure belli ac pacis*, Grotius moved away from the conception of law as the observation of justice to law as the injunction to respect other people's rights – the law of nature was to preserve peace, which is only possible if people respect each other's rights.[120] In this construction, Grotius again cleverly combined his Humanist respect for the Roman maxim *sic utere ut alienam non laedas* and his Scholastic atomist view that society consists of individuals whose rights would conflict if the boundaries between them were not respected and properly regulated.

Tuck fails to mention another innovation of Grotius in the *Inleidinge*, which is the final destruction of the feudal category of *dominium utile* and the construction of the modern distinction between ownership and limited real rights. In a short passage,[121] Grotius explains the distinction between *dominium directum and dominium utile* as two distinct forms of ownership, but with reference to the classic distinction between *dominium plenum and dominium minus plenum* he proceeds to dismantle it: both are forms of incomplete ownership, but for the sake of clarity we agree to call the one with the greater value ownership and the other one 'rights'. This reveals Grotius' Humanist roots, but also his inclination towards natural rights – the right to acquire property pre-

---

115 Tuck (n 86) 63.

116 *Idem* 66; Folke Dovring, et al. (eds) *Inleidinge tot de Hollandsche rechts-geleertheid* (1619–1621) (1952).

117 See Tuck (n 86) 67. On the other hand, Grotius also moved away from distributive justice and would completely abandon it in *De iure belli ac pacis*, which shows his closer proximity to Lessius and De Molina than to the earlier Dominicans. See Tuck (n 86) 67. *De iure belli ac pacis* was completed in 1625, a good edition is De Kanter-van Hettinga-Tromp (ed.) (1939).

118 Tuck (n 86) 69.

119 *Idem* 70.

120 *Idem* 72–73; refer to Prolegomena 8–10, 18.

121 Dovring, et al. (n 116) 151. See further André van der Walt 'Der Eigentumsbegriff' (n 105) 492–493.

dates civil law, but convention and civil law can refine the categories in which property rights are discussed. In making this distinction Grotius laid the foundation for the basic distinction upon which property law in all modern, Roman-law-based civil codes and systems of private law still relies, namely between ownership and limited real rights. From now on, individual private ownership would be associated with individual will, sovereignty and autonomy, while all other rights in property would be downgraded to derived rights, created by and subject to the will of the owner.

The Franciscan ideal of apostolic poverty sparked the religious dispute between the Franciscans and the Dominicans, and eventually resulted in the development of the still dominant theory of property as a pre-societal, natural right. Ultimately, this dispute about power in the Church is the source of the idea, previously encountered in my discussion of the majority opinion in *Kaiser Aetna*, the civil court *a quo*'s decision in *Groundwater* and the background assumptions of the court in *Zulu*, that the existence of private property rights is a baseline consideration that, once proven, asserts a fundamental right that predates and therefore trumps public interests in the absence of overriding public interest. In view of this approach, the function of the state and the role of the public interest in property disputes are also reduced. First, the state has a duty and correlative power, transferred to it by the collective of individuals, to solve private property disputes by making laws to protect and ensure mutual respect for individual property rights – the public interest in law is reduced to the duty to uphold society through enforcing the private law maxim *sic utere ut alienum non laedas*. Second, the state has a limited capacity to restrict individual property rights in exceptional cases (as *ultima ratio*) for the sake of the public interest, provided a convincing case is made for departing from the normally inviolate status of private rights. The natural privilege of private property and the reduced status of the public interest still constitute the grammar of property disputes today.

This approach is obviously in conflict with the idea that property rights are social or civil artefacts, and thus subject to further social, political and policy redefinition and amendment, espoused by the Franciscans for their own religious reasons and encountered in the minority opinion in *Kaiser Aetna* and in the Federal Constitutional Court decision in *Groundwater*. The differences between the two approaches and the radical implications of privileging one of them emphasise the contested status of private property rights and their fraught relationship with state power and the public interest. However, they also illustrate the main point in this chapter, which is expanded on in the next section: discussions on property utilise an eroded and impoverished notion of the public. One can almost say that the public is completely absent from property discourse, because the social and analytical skills that are needed for a proper consideration of the public or civic aspect of property have been lost. In what follows I describe this absence as the result of being bombarded with too much private property or, to adapt a phrase from Jonathan Franzen: being constantly confronted by 'the Imperial Fountain'.

4.4 The imperial fountain

The media now routinely saturate public life with the minutiae of insignificant private lives. On television and in the popular press one is invited into the homes and lives of 'celebrities', and when public figures object to the constant invasion of their privacy, the apparently insatiable public appetite for vicarious living is satisfied by focusing on instant pseudo-celebrities; unknown private individuals who publicly exhibit their intimate physical and emotional trials and tribulations for the opportunity of playing a lead role in the cage[122] of 'talk shows' and 'reality shows'. Martin Amis[123] referred to this phenomenon as 'karaoke fame', an astute phrase that captures the element of public posturing that attracts unwilling attention to supposedly unique or outrageous aspects of otherwise insignificant private lives to alleviate the burden of an unconnected, purely private existence.[124]

Jonathan Franzen has argued that not private but public life is under threat, that it is being colonised and overwhelmed by the private.[125] In his view, privacy, 'the new American obsession', is far from being threatened – instead, privacy is valued more and protected better than ever before, and, in fact, it is the public sphere that is threatened.[126] Our sense of privacy functions, so Franzen argues, to keep the public out of the private *and* to keep the private out of the public, and while 'we're flat-out *drowning* in privacy', private life is 'brutally invading the most public of public spaces': 'Privacy is protected as both commodity and right; public forums are protected as neither. Like old-growth forests, they're few and irreplaceable and should be held in trust by everyone. The work of maintaining them gets only harder as the private sector grows ever more demanding, distracting, and disheartening.'[127]

---

122 With apologies to Pink Floyd 'Wish you were here' on *Wish you were here* (1975) 8 Sony Music Entertainment Inc 1975.

123 Martin Amis *Experience* (2000) 6 n H.

124 In Hannah Arendt's view, both the total absence of a private space to which one can retreat for intimate business and the total lack of real public appearance beyond the daily cares of intimate, private life signify an inhuman existence. See Hannah Arendt *The human condition* (1958) 64. Arendt's thinking about politics and public space is also discussed in chapter one of this collection by Johan van der Walt and chapter two by Karin van Marle.

125 Jonathan Franzen 'Imperial bedroom' in *How to be alone: Essays* (2002) 39 at 52.

126 *Idem* 39–54. When I refer to 'our' thin perception of the public and the need that 'we' should feel for a thicker version, I am of course not saying that every author is affected – or affected equally – by the malaise described by Franzen. The analysis below demonstrates that there are property theorists who are more successful than others in imagining and verbalising a thicker perception of the public aspect of property, just as there are others who are less successful in this regard.

127 Franzen (n 125) 53. Quotations in the preceding paragraph are from 48, 51. Franzen is echoing Hannah Arendt here. See Arendt (n 124) 59: 'The reason for this extremity [the mass phenomenon of loneliness] is that mass society not only destroys the public realm but the private as well, deprives men not only of their place in the world but of their private home, where they felt sheltered against the world and where, at any rate, even those excluded from the world could find a substitute in the warmth of the hearth and the limited reality of family life'. Compare at 60–61: 'It seems to be in the nature of the relationship between the public and private realms that the final stage of the disappearance of the public realm should be accompanied by the threatened liquidation of the private realm as well. Nor is it an accident that the whole discussion has eventually turned into an argument about the desirability or undesirability of privately owned property … [because] property apparently possesses certain qualifications which, though lying in the private realm, were always thought to be of utmost importance to the political body.'

I refer to the privacy debate because I think that Franzen's inversion of the commonsense, orthodox hierarchy of private and public also applies to the public–private dynamic in the property sphere; that (with apologies to Franzen) despite claims to the contrary, 'we are flat-out drowning in private property', that 'private property is brutally invading the most public of public spaces'. My point is that thinking about property is so overwhelmed by the omnipresence and the inviolability of private property that one is no longer able to conceptualise or even imagine the public aspect of property in a deep sense, or even to see how private law is (justifiably) infused with a consciousness of, and commitment to, deeper and larger public interests that transcend the individual and the economic. In human consciousness and language the public has been reduced to the place where private property is upheld, protected and only in exceptional cases ceremonially sacrificed for the public good, with much fanfare and suitable compensation.

In property theory, the counterpart of anxiety about the erosion of privacy is the popular notion that private property is under threat from increasingly aggressive and invasive government interference and regulation, particularly in the areas of land use planning and environmental conservation. In reform-orientated jurisdictions, fears about the erosion of private property intensify in view of reformist legislation and government programmes that support or promote land reform. Generally speaking, the impression created in the popular press is often that developments since the World Wars have tended to erode, undermine, hollow out and generally threaten private property by subjecting it to increasing state regulation and interference, insufficiently justified by reasons of public interest or benefit. In fact, however, the case studies in the previous section of the chapter (and many others like them) indicate that property is indeed protected very strongly today, particularly because of the tendency to constitutionalise the protection of property. The case studies illustrate the fact that thinking about property is dominated and shaped by a private property paradigm, and that it takes a real effort of will and imagination to ensure that the public interest in property features at all in property disputes. When one does think of the public in the sphere of property, one tends to see it as a threat to private interests and nothing more. Private property rights talk therefore tends to centre on discussions of how to keep the public out of the private, while ignoring or resisting the public-minded notion of keeping the private out of the public or – what amounts to the same thing – recognising and appreciating the public aspect of private property.

Many property lawyers would claim that account is taken of the public when property is discussed. The majority in *Kaiser Aetna* considered the public interest in the protection of free interstate commerce through the imposition of the navigational servitude; it also decided that the private marina was subject to federal regulation. However, upon reflection the public aspect of property in that case was reduced to the question whether upholding of the federal navigational servitude would affect private ownership of the marina so deeply as to establish a regulatory taking that required compensation – private rights remained firmly centre stage. Similar attitudes appeared from the decision of the civil court *a quo* in *Groundwater* and from the *Zulu* case. This is an extremely thin version of the public interest in property, and one typical of liberal thinking: what poses as the public amounts to little more than the commonality or the harmonisation of private interests. In this kind of thinking, private property interests come first; they mutually define and bind each other, and when one of them is subjected to disproportionate loss for the sake of the other, compensation is paid to spread the burden equally. What is presented as the public is no more than private individual interests standing together for mutual benefit and protection.[128]

Perception of the public interest in property has been impoverished to the extent that it is unthinkingly associated with the economic, albeit in a large-scale sense that includes the economic interests of all or a large number of people considered together. Like Grotius and the late Scholastics, the difference between the private and the public is seen as a matter of scale, nothing more. The modern, liberal conception of rights has so impoverished the understanding of the public realm that it is hard to imagine that the public could be substantively different from the private; that it could have something to do with transcending, non-economic interests that do not also, on a smaller scale, feature in the private sphere. Similarly, it is hard to see how and why private law is (and should be) infused with public and civic consciousness. According to popular belief, private property is under threat from unwarranted public interference, but in my view property is valued higher and protected more strongly than ever before, and it is the public aspect of property that enjoys insufficient recognition, respect and protection. Current concern about the threat against private property is inspired by what C.B. Macpherson described as 'possessive individualism',[129] a view of rights and of property that is characterised and dominated by individualism to such an extent that critics portray all rights as alienating and destructive of community.[130] As Sarat and Kearns describe it, 'rights-based individualism' is 'suspicious of the political realm' and

---

128 One could perhaps describe this as a purely economic (as opposed to a constitutional or, in Gregory Alexander's terminology, a proprietarian) view of the public, which would make the point clearer. Johan van der Walt 'The critique of subjectivism and its implications for property law: Towards a deconstructive republican theory of property', in Gerrit van Maanen and André van der Walt (eds) *Property law on the threshold of the 21st century* (1996) 115–159 at 115–119, distinguishes between a strictly economic and a constitutional understanding of property in pre-nineteenth century Western Europe; according to the civil-law economic understanding, property was a private right in which economic liberty and political liberty were separated from one another, while according to the common-law constitutional understanding, it was a constitutional right in a system that still unified economic and political liberty. During the nineteenth century these two understandings merged and property became understood as economic liberty throughout. See further Alexander (n 276).

129 C.B. Macpherson *The political theory of possessive individualism: Hobbes to Locke* (1985). James Penner *The idea of property in law* (1997) provides an example of a related property theory that combines and justifies elements of the 'possessive individualist' view of property. First, exclusivity is described as the central characteristic of property: the inherent interest in property law is the interest in exclusively determining the use of things (39, 48–49). On this basis, the whole of property law can be explained with reference to use and exclusion, our interest in the use of things justifying exclusion as the formal essence of the right (71). Secondly, distributive concerns are excluded from the sphere of property: once we understand the true scope of property we realise that distributive practices do not form part of the law of property (37). Finally, the description of property is based on the inherent features of 'the material itself'. The conclusion that distributive concerns fall outside the sphere of property is based on Joseph Raz's principle of individuation, according to which the organisation of law is an inherent feature of the legal material, because the categories of law 'reflect the individuation of act-situations according to the fundamental human interests that are at stake' and that are recognised by law as important enough to generate laws in the legal system. Since exclusive determination of use is the central characteristic of property, distributive concerns are not included in the organisation of the law of property.

130 Austin Sarat and Thomas Kearns 'The unsettled status of human rights', in Sarat and Kearns (eds) *Human rights: Concepts, contests, contingencies* (2002) 1 at 5.

therefore conceives rights as something prior to, or outside of it, in the sense that the very language of human rights demands grounding for rights in something timeless and universal.[131] It is not surprising that any context-driven social or economic policy that fails to bow to this rights-based individualism and elects to impose social or public limitations upon property is seen as a threat that deserves rejection, avoidance or at the very least restriction to the unavoidable minimum.

What is clearly needed is a broader more layered understanding of the public than that of 'rights-based individualism' if we are to consider property disputes more profitably and responsibly.[132] A broader notion of the public has to be free of the 'suspicion of the political' and has to be substantively different from the private instead of just as a matter of scale. What I have in mind when I refer to the public aspect of property is this: in the *Zulu* case discussed earlier I am left with a haunting and elusive sense of something that is missing from the decision, something that was not included in, or disposed of, by the talk about private rights and public powers.[133] In that case, I think this something relates to the complex social and political context that surrounds the institution of royalty, the complex relations of care that exist within traditional family and social structures, and the civic functions fulfilled by the Prince Regent, the royal house and those serving it with everyday necessities such as fresh water. I cannot shake off the sense that the court's talk of private rights and public powers in the *Zulu* decision fails to comprehend and account for the social and political nuances in full, and therefore I am uncomfortable with the result of the decision and the reasoning. What bothers me about this decision is that the deeper social or political or civic aspects of the property relationships within which the dispute arose have not been explained or

131 *Idem* 9.

132 At the same time, we need a thicker view of the private, including a better perspective of the way in which the private (and private law) inevitably is (and should be) infused with public consciousness. There are many examples of how private property law is (or used to be) infused with this kind of public spirit. I am indebted to Greg Alexander for reminding me of this point and of one example. Joseph Singer *Entitlement: The paradoxes of property* (2000) 87–91 explains how nuisance law (as opposed to trespass law) is private law imbedded in public consciousness. A second example is offered by Dagan (n 81) 1517–1571 and Dagan and Heller (n 81) 549–623, who discuss examples from the spheres of family property and condominium property to much the same effect.

133 As was already clear from my 'Un-doing things with words: The colonisation of the public sphere by private-property discourse' (1998) *Acta Juridica* 235–281, I owe a heavy debt to Hannah Arendt (n 124) and our discussions of this book in the Pretoria discussion group for my view of the public. See Arendt (n 124) 58: 'To live an entirely private life means above all to be deprived of things essential to a truly human life: to be deprived of the reality that comes from being seen and heard by others, to be deprived of an "objective" relationship with them that comes from being related to and separated from them through the intermediary of a common world of things, to be deprived of the possibility of achieving something more permanent than life itself.' In Arendt's analysis, it is the exterior appearance of property that is important for the public realm – the interior aspect of property relates to the household and has no public significance because it remains hidden. The exterior appearance of property 'as it appears in the realm of the city through the boundaries between one household and another', that was previously an actual space and that used to be associated with the law itself, is a boundary line, a 'kind of no man's land' between the private and the public, sheltering them from each other (63) (but also binding them to each other?).

taken account of at all, and in that sense the public aspect is absent from the decision. The decision and the law, in the sense of the doing of justice, are impoverished by this absence.[134] The German Federal Constitutional Court in *Groundwater* and the minority opinion in *Kaiser Aetna* hinted at something similar when they referred to the public interest in connection with democratic government that transcends the harmonisation of individual interests.

My point is really quite simple, perhaps even trite: although the public interest is often mentioned in discussions on property disputes, it is done in terms of a severely impoverished and truncated notion of what 'the public' involves, and more often than not what is called the public interest is nothing more than the commonality of individual economic interests. The question is: is it possible in law to take deeper social, political or civic contextual factors into account, or do they fall outside the scope of what property law can and ought to do?[135] Should the Nominalist[136] or atomist conclusion that there is no such thing as public or civic interest be accepted; that all one has is the individual interest and, in some instances, a commonality of individual interests? Is it true that the public interest is exhausted by consideration of the common individual interests of all individuals together or, if they cannot agree on their common interests, by the majority interest? What would such a conclusion imply for the *Groundwater* decision, where the court seems to have accepted that there is something beyond the individual and the collection of individuals; or for the South African *Zulu* decision, where the court seems to have ignored what might have been seen as transcending civic or public contextual factors?

Law in the Roman-Germanic tradition is heavily influenced by a conceptual and analytical paradigm according to which private law protects the private against private threats, while public law protects it against state intrusions – neither protects the public interest in the richer or deeper sense referred to above. In this sense, private property rights are characteristically defensive and private ownership of land provides the quintessential

---

134 As my rhetoric in this paragraph perhaps indicates, there are deconstructionist aspects to the notion of the absence of the public that I am not addressing in this chapter. Johan van der Walt (n 128) 115–159 offers an elegant if still exploratory argument in favour of a deconstructive republican perspective that would disclose the contingent, the irreconcilable, the displacement in the encounter between the private and the public around property (157). He has expanded on this topic elsewhere, including in chapter one of this collection. See also 'The future and futurity of the public-private distinction in view of the horizontal application of fundamental rights' in Johan van der Walt *Tangible mais intouchable, la loi du tact, la loi de la loi* (2002) 101ff; Johan van der Walt 'Progressive indirect horizontal application: Towards a co-operative relationship between common law and constitutional law jurisprudence' (2001) 17 *SAJHR* 341–363; 'Piracy, property and plurality: Re-reading the foundations of modern law' (2001) *TSAR* 524–547; 'Blixen's difference: Horizontal application of fundamental rights and the resistance to neo-colonialism' (2003) *TSAR* 311–331.

135 Taggart (n 48) points out that the court in *The Mayor, Aldermen and Burgesses of the Borough of Bradford v Pickles* [1895] AC 587 ignored the fact that the local municipality was not a commercial corporation but a creature of statute and a guardian of the welfare of the inhabitants of Bradford, and thereby ignored the public aspect of the dispute completely, treating it as a business transaction between private parties, which resulted in the vested landownership interest trumping the interests of the water users. See further, with regard to the history of water law in England, Joshua Getzler *A history of water rights at common law* (2004).

136 I am aware of the potential contradiction in my own view of the Franciscan position on law as a social construct, and here it may seem as if I agree with Douzinas that this view inevitably results in atomism. However, in (n 86) above I set out a different interpretation that, to my mind, opens up a more nuanced reading.

metaphor, not only for all property rights, but for all private rights, which are portrayed as fences or barriers much in the way that private land is physically fenced in against unwanted intrusion and external threat.[137] A large section of this chapter is dedicated to examples that illustrate the fact that there is more to property, even private property, than purely private interests and collective interests of an economic or utilitarian nature. The examples I have chosen demonstrate that the 'more than', the superfluous elements I have referred to as 'the public aspects of property' are concerned with overarching or transcendent common interests; interests that constitute, nourish or advance democracy, morality, humanity and civility. In one sense, my central argument in this chapter is that one tends to forget these aspects of property because (and when) one forgets the social origin, the civil nature, of property as a social construct and instead portray it as a natural, pre-societal characteristic or power of the human individual.

To a very large extent, this false picture of property as a pre-societal human characteristic and individual power has become embedded and entrenched in the traditional dichotomy of private law and public law that is still so strong in civil law jurisdictions. However, not everybody accepts the view of property advocated by 'rights-based individualism', despite its popularity. Contemporary critics of the classic liberal view of rights reject the impoverished view of the public.[138] Some of these critics deny that human rights 'define a unitary, universal condition' and emphasise the contextual and contingent aspects of rights,[139] while others argue more specifically that property theory is too focused on individual autonomy and exclusivity, and that more attention is required for what can only be described as the public or civic or political aspects of property.[140] However, taking into account the social or economic – and even political – context within which property functions is not enough for the development of a more layered notion of the public, because even contextually, socially and politically sensitive legal analysis can result in a property theory that is utterly devoid of any sense of the public in the deep sense mentioned earlier. In a sense, contextual and truly socially aware legal theory was perhaps indirectly responsible for some of the thinnest and bleakest versions of possessive individualism on record.

In the most authoritative and exhaustive analysis of this problem in recent literature, Gregory Alexander[141] describes the development of legal scholarship in the United States during the last decades of the twentieth century as the 'gradual decline of legal analysis based on the premise that law is an autonomous discipline and the concomitant rise of policy-focused writing',[142] with the result that increasing attention is paid to political,

---

137 This metaphor is brilliantly explained and exploited by Carol Rose *Property and persuasion: Essays on the history, theory, and rhetoric of property* (1994).

138 An animating feature which informs this and the other chapters in this collection is the attempt to rethink a richer view of the public and its implications for post-apartheid politics and constitutionalism.

139 Sarat and Kearns (n 130) 11.

140 It is impossible to survey all the relevant sources here. Significant examples not discussed in this chapter are Joseph Singer and Jack Beerman 'The social origins of property' (1993) 6 *Canadian Journal of Law and Jurisprudence* 217–248; Hanoch Dagan *Unjust enrichment: A study of private law and public values* (1997); Singer (n 132); Laura Underkuffler *The idea of property: Its meaning and power* (2003); Dagan (n 81) 1517–1571.

141 Alexander (n 27).

142 *Idem* 305.

social and economic context, and the effect of policy and politics on law. Increasingly, law is regarded as an instrument of social control. In addition, Alexander sees the major characteristic of the last decades of the twentieth century as a steady growth of the commodificationist idea 'that the basic, if not the sole, purpose of property is the satisfaction of individual preferences through market transactions',[143] combined with what he describes as an extraordinary rise in the influence of economic analysis in legal thought. The result is that the rhetoric of property has shifted towards almost exclusive talk of property in terms of entitlements in goods, signifying a substantive shift of interest towards property's potential to create wealth, that is, property purely seen as market commodities. In this context, property has only one kind of value, and that is exchange value in the market.[144] In this view, the public is reduced to the interests of the market, and the market is nothing more than the place where individuals gather to trade in property.

Alexander describes this view, which corresponds with what has been described as the liberal or the 'possessive individualist' view above, as the 'commodificationist' or commodity view of property, contrasting it with what he calls the 'propriety' or political view,[145] and one main theme in his book is that the history of legal thought about property reveals a dialectic between the two.[146] In his view, the recent dominance of the commodity view does not imply that the dialectic is over and that commodification rules – he predicts that 'a more civically orientated consciousness' will again manifest itself, judging from tendencies already visible in the late 1990s when he wrote.[147] Alexander uses the term 'propriety' in following Carol Rose,[148] who used it to describe property as 'the material

---

143 *Idem* 380.

144 *Idem* 381–382 explains that two factors contributed to the shift towards the commodificationist view of property: the Realists' destroying the Blackstonian concept of property as absolute dominion over a thing, replacing it with the disaggregated, more explicitly social bundles-of-rights notion that was much more amenable to the exchange-value entitlement view of economic analysis; and 'the growing acceptance within American legal thought of the view that substantive values, moral, political, and legal, are inherently subjective and nonrational', and that they should therefore be kept separate from scientific legal analysis.

145 Alexander (n 27) describes the 'propriety' view of property as the 'civic conception of property' (associated with Thomas Jefferson) according to which property rights are social rather than natural creations. On the basis of this premise, the civic republican approach attempts to describe the proper relationship between society and property: because society creates property rights it also continually controls them. In Alexander's words (27), 'such a [usufructuary] notion of ownership presupposes an integration of individual and society, private and public', and property is seen as an end to republican self-government rather than an end in itself. In American republican thought of the eighteenth century, individual interests were subordinate to the common welfare of the polity. In American republican thought protection against the government was not a major function of property, since there was no categorical opposition between individual and polity; republicans rather saw property as a necessary resource to facilitate an active public life for each citizen. John Greville Heard Pocock 'The mobility of property and the rise of eighteenth-century sociology' in *Virtue, commerce, and history* (1985) 103 explains that citizens possessed property to be autonomous, as autonomy was necessary to develop virtue as an active participant in political, social life. During the period described by Alexander, this view of property within the republican tradition shifted and developed, but it always maintained an element of integrating political ideals of democracy with the purely economic ideals of wealth-creation, looking for 'a mode of private ownership of property that instantiates a civic vision' (385).

146 In chapter five of this collection Henk Botha draws an analogous distinction between a privatised (or dignity based) conception of equality and a political (or complex) conception of equality.

147 Alexander (n 27) 384.

148 Rose (n 137).

foundation for creating and maintaining the proper social order, the private basis for the public good.' In this view, the human being is an inherently social being who depends on others to survive and to thrive, and interdependency means that humans owe one another obligations 'as an inherent incident of the human condition'. What the proper social order is may be controversial and contested, but in the civic view property always functions within a certain perspective of it and cannot be understood without taking it into account in some way. In other words, property has a public, civic or 'propriety' aspect to it that transcends individual economic interests, and that involves interdependency and the common obligations that result from it. In a propriety or civic conception of property consideration and account of those aspects must be given.[149]

Kevin Gray and Susan Francis Gray[150] provide a practical example of the way in which the civic view of property that Alexander refers to could develop. In exploring the suggestion[151] that the distinction or relationship between public and private in property should not be seen as a direct conflict or a strict dichotomy but rather as two extremes on a continuum, they investigated three spheres of so-called quasi-public property,[152] and

149 This would form part of the post-apartheid responsibility which Johan van der Walt describes in chapter one of this collection.

150 Gray and Gray (n 27) 1–39. See further Kevin Gray 'Property in thin air' (1991) 50 *Cambridge LJ* 252–307.

151 Made by Stanley Benn and Gerald Gaus 'The public and the private: Concepts and action' in Stanley Benn and Gerald Gaus (eds) *Public and private in social life* (1983) 25.

152 Gray and Gray (n 27) 20–38: shopping malls and civic commercial centres (20), enclosed or gated residential communities (31), privatised public service utilities (36). I am deliberately not discussing the issues surrounding gated residential communities or common interest communities in this chapter, because they involve conceptual and analytical dilemmas that would take the discussion too far off the track I have decided to follow (but see André van der Walt 'Enclosed property and public streets' (2006) 21 *SAPR/PL* 3). For the time being, the following brief and rather summary observations will have to do in lieu of a proper discussion. First, there are substantial differences of opinion about the potential of common interest communities for realising ideals relating to the public or communal life; compare Paula A. Franzese 'Does it take a village? Privatisation, patterns of restrictiveness and the demise of community' (2002) 47 *Villanova LR* 553–593 with Dagan and Heller (n 80) 549–623. Although Franzese describes homeowners' associations as 'private governments', 'de facto state actors' who should be required to satisfy due process, equal protection and first amendment guarantees (582), she approaches the matter from what I have here described as the impoverished private-law paradigm, insisting that the building or fostering of community through (for example) common interest communities is 'best left to informal networks and social capital' and that it should not be the work of formal structures such as legislators and courts (589). Accordingly, her discussion of community in terms of 'social capital' (567–569) and 'systems of reciprocity' (569–571) is inherently coloured by the private-interest economic language of efficiency, wealth maximisation and individual utility. Community is nothing more than a more efficient, larger group of individuals with similar or harmonious interests. Notions of 'connection and civility' (558) denote nothing more than individual interests functioning efficiently and optimally, with minimum conflict, in a communal setup. By contrast, Dagan and Heller approach the common interest community from their perspective of the 'liberal commons', which is strongly informed and shaped by deep-level, inherent public notions of democracy and public-ness that transcend (but are harmonised with) individual autonomy and private interests as well as communal economic interests in efficiency and wealth maximisation (590–594, 582–586). Dagan and Heller also refer to the notion of 'social capital' and their analysis is strongly influenced by a critical take on economic analysis; but even though they describe the function of the law as a 'background role', a 'safety net' that reinforces and guides human and social behaviour (554, 577), there is nothing of Franzese's strong privatism that would restrict the function of the law to the minimum; indeed, they regard the guiding role of the law in facilitating the creation of 'liberal commons' property as crucial (see e.g. 609–620). See further in a similar vein Dagan (n 81) 1517–1571. My reluctance to discuss the common interest community as an example is caused by the fact that I am uncomfortable with the assumption that what I have described as a thicker notion of the public can or should be collapsed into Dagan's (admittedly thick and public-, even civic-minded) notion of the 'liberal commons'. Obviously the two concepts have a lot in common, and the model proposed by Dagan and Heller certainly leaves room for instances of a 'liberal commons' that are much more private (marriage) and others that are much more public (ratepayers' associations?) in nature, with space for variation in between. My concern is

argued that these forms of property are located much further towards the public end of the spectrum than orthodoxy would have one believe was possible. They note that it is particularly private lawyers who tend to think that private and public property are separated by a deep chasm with enormous political significance, while, in fact, it has become increasingly difficult or impossible to uphold the distinction with clarity and consistency.[153] This is particularly so since the orthodox private perspective is already undermined by the deep subtext of 'propriety' that has always pervaded the social and legal definition of property in the sense that the 'allocation of differing quantums of property' to various holders is based on 'collective perceptions of the social permissibility or public merit attributable' to various kinds of competing uses of resources.[154] However, they accept that a private-right-biased perception of property as an absolute and exclusive right is deeply embedded in private law orthodoxy, and they set about dismantling it, emphasising the importance of underlining the public nature of property:

> At stake are rival perceptions of the political good. … [In striking the right balance between competing individual and collective goals, between private and public interests, we choose between] the self-regarding entrenchment of individual advantage and the promotion of rather different life patterns of 'connectedness' which consciously strive for the maintenance of some degree of social cohesion and mutual regard.[155]

In view of their analysis of the three spheres of 'quasi-public property', Gray and Gray conclude that increased vigilance in preserving the public interest – in this case through the 'infiltration within traditionally private law domains of something akin to public law controls' – may 'provide a key to the preservation of those intangible and fragile values which alone assure freedom from widespread exploitation, exclusion and social alienation'.[156] The classification of these particular spheres of interest as 'quasi-public'

---

twofold: first, I am not convinced that all of what I refer to as 'the public' is or can be exhausted by all conceivable instances or embodiments of common interest communities (or 'liberal commonses'); and secondly I have reservations about the (atomistic) assumption that the difference between communities and the public sphere is merely a matter of scale – the history of Grotius's atomistic view of individual and state property above is sufficiently instructive to make me hesitate about such an implication in the theory of the 'liberal commons'. Gray and Gray (n 27) certainly seem to accept without further discussion that there is more to 'the public sphere' than the communality of interests in a grouping of individuals, and I am not sure that Dagan would accept an atomistic interpretation of the liberal commons model, but going into the matter here would take the current chapter too far. There is much room for further work and discussion in this area. However, Dagan did work out a complementary and less problematic theory of property and distributive justice that illustrates the kind of public-minded property theory I have in mind here – see (n 153) and (n 154) and surrounding text below.

153 Gray and Gray (n 27) 11.

154 *Idem* 13.

155 *Idem* 16. I paraphrased the phrase in square brackets. Taggart (n 48) 195 maintains that the 'common lawyers' deep-seated distrust of statute law and the common law's innate superiority complex' help to perpetuate the unrealistic absolutist view of ownership, even against the most obvious evidence of far-reaching regulation and control over the use of property. He blames 'the failure to view the common law and [statutory] restrictions [on property use] in a holistic way' for perpetuating 'the ideology supporting the unreformed common law', which persists in denying that property rights are socially constructed (197).

156 Gray and Gray (n 27) 39. Taggart (n 48) 202 echoes this sentiment, emphasising that if the common law is to continue to play a meaningful role in controlling both private and public power it is vitally important to recognise the pervasiveness of doctrines and ideas (like Gray and Gray's 'quasi-public' property) that limit the exercise of power in the interests of neighbours, the public and the public good.

had the result, according to them, of not only mediating the relationship between public and private, but also infusing 'the decisional processes of private property with a crucial sense of social responsibility and public accountability'. They therefore emphasise the importance of distinguishing between property in the 'inherently private domain' and 'those gradations of "quasi-public" property whose acknowledgement is increasingly integral to the well-being of a civil society'.[157] In effect, Gray and Gray are demonstrating a practical way of identifying and reinforcing the existence of property forms that already embody and therefore support the notion of a public or civic element in property law.

Hanoch Dagan[158] developed a theory of takings and distributive justice that has due regard for the public aspect of property, in that it advocates a strong focus on social responsibility, civic virtues and egalitarian concerns as well as the private individual interests that are usually the sole focus of takings doctrine. First, Dagan developed a distributive criterion that accommodates the virtue of social responsibility by allowing, in a hypothetical case where an individual claims compensation on the basis of some public action, certain types of advantage that result from other public actions to act as a substitute for the strict proportionality requirement, provided the disproportionality is not too extreme.[159] Second, the conception of reciprocity of advantage is localised, so that the test is more tolerant of deviations from short-term proportionality when the

---

157 Gray and Gray (n 27) 39.

158 I concentrate on the theory as explained in Hanoch Dagan 'Takings and distributive justice' (1999) 85 *Virginia LR* 741–804. In 'Just compensation, incentives, and social meanings' (2000) 99 *Michigan LR* 134-156, Dagan responded to criticism of this theory expounded by Glynn Lunney 'Takings, efficiency, and distributive justice: A response to Professor Dagan' (2000) 99 *Michigan LR* 401, concluding that Lunney's criticisms refined but reinforced his argument in favour of a progressive takings doctrine. In 'The distributive foundation of corrective justice' (1999) 98 *Michigan LR* 138–166, Dagan set out a related project on a slightly larger scale, evaluating the corrective justice approach to private law by concentrating on the doctrine of restitution for wrongs, particularly appropriations. In this article, Dagan concluded that Ernest Weinrib 'Restitutionary damages as corrective justice' (1999) 1 *Theoretical Inquiries in Law* 1 did require a refinement of Dagan's earlier arguments (n 140), but that 'Weinrib is wrong in his claim that private law has an inner intelligibility that can be deciphered without recourse to public values. An account such as Weinrib's that attempts to explain and justify private law in isolation from its surrounding social values is question-begging at best and oppressive at worst': Hanoch Dagan (1999) 98 *Michigan LR* 166 138–139. In distinguishing between the 'social values school' to which he belongs and the corrective justice school represented by Weinrib (138), Dagan illustrates the heart of the distinction between those who think that analysis of any property dispute should begin from a private law tradition baseline (see the discussion of the three case studies, compare footnote 145 and surrounding text above), and those who think that property disputes must inevitably be analysed with reference to their social context and public values. See further (n 152) regarding Dagan's theory of the 'liberal commons', which also illustrates and expands upon the public aspect of property, but which I do not discuss here for reasons explained there.

159 Dagan 'Takings and distributive justice' (n 158) 768–777. Dagan developed this theory with reference to Michelman's notion of demoralisation costs (at 762–767). See Frank Michelman 'Property, utility, and fairness: Comments on the ethical foundations of "just compensation" law' (1967) 80 *Harvard LR* 1165–1258. The conception of long-term reciprocity of advantage is neither the narrow notion of reciprocity that requires strict proportionality nor the wide notion that considers membership of a civilised community sufficient reciprocal advantage to disallow a compensation claim. Instead, Dagan's conception 'absolves the public authority from paying compensation if, and only if, the disproportionate burden of the public action in question is not overly extreme and is offset, or is likely in all probability to be offset, by benefits of similar magnitude to the landowner's current injury that she gains from other – past, present or future – public actions (which harm neighbouring properties)' (769–770).

local community is advantaged and less so when the benefits accrue to larger social units.[160] Third, Dagan qualified the conception of long-term reciprocity of advantage with what he calls an 'egalitarian refinement'; so that the substitution of long-term reciprocity for short-term proportionality may not be available when the claimant is politically weak or economically disadvantaged.[161]

The result is a takings theory that does not ignore disproportionate individual disadvantage and the need for compensation, but still refuses to enforce strict short-term proportionality because it 'refuses to reduce citizenship and membership [of a community] to monetary exchanges, and seeks to preserve and inculcate people's sense of responsibility toward their fellow community members'.[162] Long-term reciprocity, Dagan argues, provides 'an attractive qualification of the ideal of proportionality' in that it incorporates the value of social responsibility into legal doctrine, reminding us that landowners are members of a community, that they enjoy social benefits for which they do not have to pay directly, and that they therefore also bear certain obligations toward that community. By doing so this theory avoids the 'atomistic social vision' that underplays the significance of belonging to a community and that perceives our membership of communities in purely instrumental, commodified terms.[163] The conception of long-term reciprocity of advantage 'presupposes – or, maybe, attempts to inspire – a different social vision' that 'perceives people as fundamentally social beings, situated in relation to others, embedded in communities as well as in ongoing relationships of give-and-take'.[164] As such, this alternative vision of property, community and social responsibility is not completely noncommodified – it refuses to reduce citizenship to a market relationship, but it nevertheless pays careful attention to situations where direct compensation is required on the basis of short-term disproportionality: specifically where the lack of proportion is too severe, or where the social benefit is too remote, or where the claimant is politically weak or economically disadvantaged.[165] In the process, property acquires a social, or public, or civic, meaning that is much richer than the purely private and economic traditional understanding.

In addition to his conception of long-term reciprocity of advantage, Dagan seeks to further promote the vision of property that accommodates social responsibility and solidarity by combining it with a 'takings doctrine with an equalising tendency' – a criterion that distinguishes between regulation and takings while at the same time 'giving preferential treatment to improvement in the lives of the worse-off, or, at least, … avoiding any structural privileges that favour the better-off'.[166] This part of Dagan's

160 Dagan 'Takings and distributive justice' (n 158) 771–777.

161 *Idem* 777–778. At 777 Dagan describes this 'egalitarian refinement' of his theory, with reference to Carol Rose 'Trust in the mirror of betrayal' (1995) 75 *Boston University LR* 531 at 537, as 'upholding "the bonds of civic mutuality" against the systemic threat of "corrosion by the privatisation … of politics"' – a clear example of protecting the public against the private by refusing to allow the public to be completely colonised by private (and even commonly shared multiple private) economic interests. See (n 129) and surrounding text above.

162 *Idem* 767.

163 *Idem* 771–772.

164 *Idem* 772.

165 *Idem* 768, 774, 777.

166 *Idem* 778–792.

theory is based on the Legal Realist premise that property ownership is a source of economic, social and political power, the correlative of which is duties and liabilities of non-owners. Referring to Michelman, Dagan concludes that private property is not merely a possessive proprietary principle but 'an expression of a cluster of values' – primarily privacy, security, and independence – that 'always involve the distribution as well as the retention of wealth'.[167] In Dagan's view, 'an egalitarian conception of property emerges that acknowledges and endorses the dialectic of retention and distribution [of property].'[168]

Ross Zucker[169] also developed a theory of property and distributive justice, but with a different slant. His theory is based on the argument that there is an integral relation between politics and economic justice, and that distributive justice is intimately linked to the notion of democratic rule.[170] The heart of Zucker's thesis is that a just distribution of economic resources is definitive of democratic rule, and that distributive justice demands that total social income should be distributed unequally to the extent that it is produced by individual action, and equally to the extent that it is created by joint activity of people shaped by social conditions.[171] In this view, property rights come with redistributory strings in the form of a redistributory property right to a just portion of redistributed income.

Zucker argues that neoclassical economics and liberal property theories are incomplete because they exclude the possibility of concrete common ends and concrete justice. The reason why liberals such as Nozick can interpret rights as 'side constraints' that demarcate inviolable moral spaces around individual right holders – spaces that cannot be breached without their consent – is that neoclassical theories of property distribution provide no principle of equalisation.[172] The entitlement logic of liberalism justifies unequal distribution of property on the basis of an individualist view of the person as something that developed outside and independent of society, whereas intersubjective models focus on human nature as something that is formed and sustained through interaction with others.[173] Liberal theories of property hold on to subjective individualism as their operative ontological assumption and therefore they can never develop any social view of property.[174] In contrast, an egalitarian notion of property legitimates individual, unequal property but also recognises a claim to an egalitarian distribution of part of social property,[175] and Zucker explores the distributive implications of rights

167 *Idem* 779, referring to Frank Michelman 'Tutelary jurisprudence and constitutional property', in Ellen Paul and Howard Dickman (eds) *Liberty, property, and the future of constitutional development* (1990) 127 at 150.

168 *Idem* 781.

169 Ross Zucker *Democratic distributive justice* (2001).

170 *Idem* 1.

171 *Idem* 4.

172 *Idem* 8–9. Since unanimous agreement on redistribution is practically impossible, rights practically prohibit redistribution.

173 *Idem* 29.

174 *Idem* 77.

175 *Idem* 85.

by analysing their social function with reference to two social ideals from the logic of entitlement: reward for economic contributions and membership of a community.[176]

The interesting aspect of Zucker's theory is that the dimension of community or 'concrete common ends' in economic society has implications for the just distribution of property in that it morally justifies a distribution rule that has direct normative implications for democratic rule.[177] Citizens have a right to share equally in a portion of total income and wealth, and because this distribution rule is based on common ends in the economic community it forms part of the defining characteristics of democracy, which is founded on economic justice.[178]

Perhaps the most exciting recent theory that supports a richer, public or civic notion of property is not primarily a theory of property at all, but a theory of justice in transitional contexts. Ruti Teitel[179] painted a picture of transitional justice in which I get a glimpse of the spaces that will need to open up if people are to recover their sense of the civic, that which transcends the purely private and the public as communal concern about the private, through transition. In her view, transitions open up critical space because they imply a paradigm shift in our conception of justice that undermines and destabilises traditional dualisms such as individual/collective, private/public, past/future, thereby making the function of law deeply and inherently paradoxical: in transitions, law maintains order and stability, but it also enables change and transformation; it is simultaneously constitutive of, and constituted by, the transition; it is itself a product of, but also structures and challenges the transition; it enables the transition away from past injustice and is elaborated in response to that injustice but often perpetuates the same injustice.[180] As such, law in transition is always both settled and unsettled, restrained and restraining, historically and politically contingent,[181] partial, provisional, limited and symbolic in nature; as law it both stabilises and destabilises, and it is best understood in its liminal quality as law in between regimes.[182]

The most interesting aspects of Teitel's notion of transitional justice for property theory is the destabilising role that reparatory justice plays in it by reversing traditional hierarchies of individual/collective and private/public, while combining the traditionally backward-looking focus of stabilising law[183] with the destabilising forward-looking

---

176 *Idem* 11. The problem is that the ethics of dueness for economic contribution traditionally neglects some forms of economic contribution, particularly the fact that wealth is also created by mere participation in the ongoing circulation of commodities. Zucker's contribution is to highlight the consumption side of contribution to the value of commodities, arguing that this justifies dueness and an entitlement to claim social property in the form of a redistributed portion of social wealth, proportionate to the contribution that this form of participation makes to the creation of social wealth overall: at 85-87. The economic argument is summarised at 86–87.

177 *Idem* 246.

178 *Idem* 269–270, 276–277.

179 Teitel (n 94).

180 *Idem* 6–8.

181 *Idem* 6.

182 *Idem* 215, 220. In this respect Teitel refers to the forward- and backward-looking quality of transitional law that renders it separate from its predecessor but also informed by prior injustice in forming a notion of what is just: at 6–7, 196. See also in this regard André van der Walt 'Dancing with codes – protecting, developing, limiting and deconstructing property rights in the constitutional state' (2001) 118 *SALJ* 258–311.

183 This is the Dominican perspective of pre-conventional natural (property) rights that trump whatever comes later.

perspective of transforming law.[184] By using reparatory measures as transformative alternatives to punishment, transitional justice challenges traditional distinctions between and hierarchies of civil/criminal and private/state, rejecting the truncated liberal vision of the public and expanding it to include public responsibility for civic processes such as corrective justice, redress and transformation.[185] Transitional justice also undermines the traditional vision of the private, because it 'lacks the symmetry of private law' and reconceives the traditional relation between wrongdoer/victim and between individual/collective, and develops new perspectives on individual, collective and state responsibility for redress and reparation.[186]

It is immediately apparent that this vision of transitional justice presents us with a conceptual and analytical framework that has significant critical implications for a transitional notion of property,[187] radically different from the backward-looking, natural-rights-orientated model that informed the majority opinion in *Kaiser Aetna* and the civil court *a quo*'s decision in *Groundwater*, and also dramatically richer than Grotius' atomist view of the scale differences between private and public. In such a transitional model, property cannot be a pre-constitutional, pre-societal human faculty or power that every individual carries with him or her into the social compact; it has to be a contingent, temporary, partial arrangement developed in the social context – 'in between regimes' – and therefore open for further amendment as demanded by the context, according to the principles of justice and legality that operate in that specific society at a given moment.

I do not want now to explore Teitel's description of the characteristics of law in a transitional situation, although such an analysis would no doubt be interesting. Instead, I would like to draw attention to the implications of Teitel's analysis for the traditional distinctions between, and hierarchies of, private and public. To my mind, one of the implications is that, in its transitional concern with redress, restorative justice and distributive justice – 'in between regimes' – property law is deprived of the neat distinction between private law and public law, and of the traditional private law symmetry described by Teitel; the classic paradigm of equal private individuals as the subjects of private law, and unequally balanced state and citizen as the subjects of public law does not cover all the variables any longer. In the transitional perspective private and public become blurred in the 'in-between', liminal notion of responsibility for redress and justice. A transitional perspective also means abandoning the privilege of private

---

184 Teitel (n 94) 119.

185 *Idem* 128.

186 *Idem* 146. Teitel explains that the state cannot adopt the restrictive traditional views on corrective justice in transitional situations, and that it has to include traditional corrective aims as well as transformative redistributive purposes in its vision of redress. On the one hand redress is the primary symbol of discontinuity with the past, but on the other hand it is also continuously informed by past injustices (147).

187 It is of course a different question whether law in all societies can or should be considered from the perspective of transition, but coming from a country where law is in transition I find Teitel's idea of transitional justice fascinating and instructive. It is possible to argue that all of property theory can benefit from the transformative perspective, but that is an argument for another time. See in general in this respect André van der Walt 'Property theory and the transformation of property law' in Elizabeth Cooke (ed.) *Modern Studies in Property Law vol 3* (2005) 361.

law as the source of baseline rights that are insulated against private and public interferences, the only role of public law being to guarantee and mutually balance private rights, and to patrol the boundaries where individual rights are, by way of exception and according to strict due process rules, allowed to be overridden by public interest necessities. And, finally, in venturing into the realms of responsibility for redress, reparation and reform, it means redefining the truncated and impoverished liberal vision of the public and opens up space where we could regain something of the civic that goes beyond traditional understandings of the private and the public.[188] In this view, the public inevitably involves aspects of civic or societal life without which individual life is unthinkable; aspects that transcend both purely individual interests in property and the public interest in the narrow sense of protecting and harmonising individual economic interests. This richer view of the public loses its threatening relationship with private individual interests, because it is not primarily concerned with the restriction, limitation or regulation of private use of property but rather with the custody of those 'intangible and fragile bonds' that characterise social life in a community with concrete common ends and responsibilities.[189] The protection of the public interest in this wider and richer sense may certainly have dramatic effects on private individual rights, and perhaps the losses caused in the process may have to be compensated in all or in some instances, but that is a different question altogether; not because individual interests are subjected to the public interest but because they are enabled by it and enabling of it, protected by and protective of it, secured by and security for it.

Author Jonathan Franzen[190] said that the popular desire for karaoke fame[191] reduces the public sphere to a 'coast-to-coast, shag-carpeted imperial bedroom' – a phrase that beautifully describes the unthinking and disastrous flooding of public space with the details of private intimacies, lending support to the counterintuitive notion that public life is being colonised and overwhelmed by the private. In this chapter, I argue that public life is similarly threatened by the overwhelming presence and force of private property, an equally disastrous process that could be described – with apologies to Franzen – as the reduction of property to an imperial bathroom or, better still, the Imperial Fountain.

Students used to wash at the Trinity College Fountain in the days before en suite facilities were installed in college rooms.[192] The design of the fountain made special provision for this purpose: each panel in the octagonal base of the fountain used to

---

188 In *A change of tongue* (2003) 126, author and journalist Antjie Krog echoes a similar sentiment when she argues that change is not the same as transformation – for transformation, the unit has to undergo internal change or a change of direction; the system, structure or vision has to change. In the book she uses the transformation of flatfish (depicted on the cover and described at 128–129) as a metaphor: the fish is born normal, but as it grows older the bottom eye migrates to the top flank, the mouth, nasal and gill openings move to a different position, skull bones develop asymmetrically and the top side develop a darker pigmentation, all so that the fish can lie flat on the ocean floor in perfect camouflage.

189 Gray and Gray (n 27) 39 refer to 'those intangible and fragile values which alone assure freedom from widespread exploitation, exclusion and social alienation'.

190 Franzen (n 125) 52.

191 Martin Amis's phrase (n 123).

192 See the College website (n 3).

include a water tap and a lead-lined basin.[193] Now, of course, students have access to private bathroom facilities in or near their rooms, making it unnecessary to expose the intimate details of their daily lives to relentless public visibility, allowing them to withdraw into privacy for those aspects of our lives that belong to the 'shadowy interior of the household'.[194] From one perspective, this was a victory for privacy, because intimate bathroom business has been withdrawn from the College Great Court, which is left free for more suitable occasions of being seen in public college life. From another perspective, this development illustrates an important aspect of private and public property in the construction of the Great Court. If the College Fountain were to function as an Imperial Fountain, where the intimate details of everybody's daily ablutions were displayed publicly, the Great Court would have been reduced to nothing more than a public screen around the most private aspects of college life, which would have been sadly impoverished in the process. In reality, however, the private rooms and en suite bathrooms of those living in Great Court form an enclosure within which the rich public life of the college can flourish, creating a public space where fellows and students can appear to one another as they walk by the fountain on their way to the chapel, the library, or the hall.[195]

Hannah Arendt had it right all along: the private is recognised and protected so that it could form the basis upon which public life can be built; the enclosure within which people can appear to one aother and where civic virtue can be treasured.

---

193 Royal Commission on Historical Monuments: England (n 3) 232–233. The stop-cock of the tap and the basin remain in the panel facing the Hall; in the others the places where the taps and the basins have been removed can still be seen.

194 The quotation is from Hannah Arendt (n 124), which was one of the earliest texts discussed in the Pretoria discussion group in its final composition of six members (1997). The reference to Arendt's discussion of privacy comes from an article I wrote in response to our discussions at the time, published as 'Un-Doing things with words: The colonisation of the public sphere by private-property discourse' (n 133), where I also refer to Patrick Süskind's novel *Die Taube* (1987, I used the 1990 ed.). The novel inspired my reference to the need for a private space where we can take care of intimate needs out of the public eye.

195 Hannah Arendt (n 124) 133 again inspires the rhetoric of 'appearing to each other in public'. I am well aware of the limitations of this metaphor and its potential contradiction of my view as expressed in (n 152) above – the college cannot be seen as a metaphor for public life without first entering into a fairly complex debate about common interest communities and their private and public aspects. However, I use the metaphor of the Great Court (as opposed to Trinity as a College), the Fountain and its relation to the inside and outside purely with reference to the architectural design of the court, because it illustrates the point I want to make in a visually attractive way, with no further pretensions or claims about the validity or scope of the rhetoric. Obviously, in using this metaphor I am making no statements or claims whatsoever about the nature, the life or the customs of Trinity College as an institution or its members, and I apologise in advance for any impression to the contrary. In chapter three of this collection, Wessel le Roux explores in some detail other attempts by post-apartheid legal scholars and architects to find a visually attractive spatial metaphor for the public dimension of the South African rights discourse.

BIBLIOGRAPHY: CHAPTER 4

Books and articles

Alciatus. *Omnia Opera II* (Basle 1546).

Alexander, G. 'Property as a Fundamental Constitutional Right? The German Example'. *Cornell LR 88* (2003): 733.

___. *Commodity and Propriety: Competing Visions of Property in American Legal Thought 1776–1970*. Chicago: University of Chicago Press, 1997.

Amis, M. *Experience*. New York: Vintage Books, 2000.

Arendt, H. *The Human Condition*. Chicago: University of Chicago Press, 1958.

Barnes, J. *The Lemon Table*. London: Jonathan Cape, 2004.

Benn, S. and G. Gaus, 'The Public and the Private: Concepts and Action'. In *Public and Private in Social Life*, edited by S. Benn and G. Gaus. London: St. Martin's Press, 1983.

Cicero. *De Inventione 1.2* (Loeb ed).

Dagan, H. 'Takings and Distributive Justice'. *Virginia LR 85* (1999): 741.

___. 'The Craft of Property'. *Cal LR 91* (2003):1517.

Dagan, H. 'The Distributive Foundation of Corrective Justice'. *Michigan LR* 98 (1999): 138–166.

Dagan, H. *Unjust Enrichment: A Study of Private Law and Public Values*. Cambridge: Cambridge University Press, 1997.

Dagan, H. and M. Heller, 'The Liberal Commons'. *Yale LJ 110* (2001): 549–623.

De Molina, L. *De Iustitia et Iure I* (1614).

Douzinas, C. *The End of Human Rights: Critical Legal Thought at the Turn of the Century*. Oxford: Hart, 2000.

Dovring, F. and H. Fischer, and E. Meijers, eds. *Inleidinge tot de Hollandsche Rechts-Geleertheid (1619–1621)*. Leiden: Universitaire Pers, 1952.

Franzen, J. *How to Be Alone: Essays*. New York: Picador, 2002.

Franzese, P. 'Does it Take a Village? Privatisation, Patterns of Restrictiveness and the Demise of Community'. *Villanova LR 47* (2002):553.

Gerson, J. *Oevres complétes III ed Glorieux*, 1962.

Getzler, J. *A History of Water Rights at Common Law*. Oxford: Oxford University Press, 2004.

Gray, K. 'Property in Thin Air'. *Cambridge LJ 50* (1991): 252–307.

Gray, K. and S. F. Gray. 'Private Property and Public Property'. In *Property and the Constitution*, edited by J. McLean. Oxford: Hart, 1999.

Kleyn, D. 'Die Mandament van Spolie as Besitsremedie'. *De Jur*e 19 (1986):1.

Kommers, D. *The Constitutional Jurisprudence of the Federal Republic of Germany*. Durham: Duke University Press, 1997.

Krog, A. *A Change of Tongu*e. Johannesburg: Random House, 2003.

Lunney, G. 'Takings, Efficiency, and Distributive Justice: A Response to Professor Dagan'. *Michigan LR 99* (2000):401.

Macpherson, C. B. *The Political Theory of Possessive Individualism: Hobbes to Locke*. Oxford: Oxford University Press, 1985.

Maunz, T. and G. Dürig, et al. eds. *Grundgesetz Kommentar: Vol II*. München: Beck, 2003.

Michelman, F. 'Property, Utility, and Fairness: Comments on the Ethical Foundations of "Just Compensation" Law'. *Harvard LR 80* (1967):1165.

Michelman, F. 'Tutelary Jurisprudence and Constitutional Property'. In *Liberty, Property, and the Future of Constitutional Development*, edited by E. F. Paul and H. Dickman. New York : State University of New York Press, 1990.

Ockham, W. *Opera politica II*, edited by R. Bennet and H. Offler. Manchester: Manchester University Press, 1974.

Penner, J. *The Idea of Property in Law*. Oxford: Oxford University Press, 1997.

Pevsner, N. *The Buildings of England: Cambridgeshire*. London: Penguin, 1954.

Pocock, J. *Virtue, Commerce, and History*. Cambridge: Cambridge University Press, 1985.

Radin, M. 'Market-Inalienability'. *Harvard LR 100* (1987):1849.

Radin, M. *Contested Commodities: The Trouble with Trade in Sex, Children, Body Parts, and Other Things*. Cambridge: Harvard University Press, 1996.

Rose, C. *Property and Persuasion: Essays on the History, Theory, and Rhetoric of Property*. Boulder: West View Press, 1994.

Sarat, A. and T. Kearns. 'The Unsettled Status of Human Rights'. In *Human Rights: Concepts, Contests, Contingencies*, edited by A. Sarat and T. Kearns. Ann Arbor: University of Michigan Press, 2001

Scotus. *Opera omnia XVIII*, 1637.

Singer, J. and J. Beerman, 'The Social Origins of Property'. *Canadian Journal of Law and Jurisprudence* 6 (1993):217.

Singer, J. Entitlement: *The Paradoxes of Property*. New Haven: Yale University Press, 2000.

Sonnekus, J. 'Besit van Serwituutbevoegdhede, Mandament van Spolie en Logika'. *TSAR* (1989):429.

Sonnekus, J. 'Mandament van Spolie: Kragtige Remedie by Kragonderbreking?' *TSAR* (1985):331.

Taggart, M. *Private Property and Abuse of Rights in Victorian England: The Story of Edward Pickles and the Bradford Water Supply*. Oxford: Oxford University Press, 2002.

Teitel, R. *Transitional Justice*. Oxford: Oxford University Press, 2000.

Thomas, P. *Textbook of Roman Law*. New York: North-Holland, 1976.

Trevelyan, G. *Trinity College: An Historical Sketch*. Cambridge: Cambridge University Press, 2001.

Tribe, L. *American Constitutional Law: Vol I*. New York: Foundation Press, 2000.

Tuck, R. *Natural Rights Theories: Their Origin and Development*. Cambridge: Cambridge University Press, 1979.

Underkuffler, L. *The Idea of Property: Its Meaning and Power*. Oxford: Oxford University Press, 2003.

Van der Walt , A. 'Un-doing Things with Words: The Colonisation of the Public sphere by Private-Property Discourse'. *Acta Juridica* (1998):235.

___. 'Bartolus se Omskrywing van Dominium en die Interpretasies Daarvan Sedert die Vyftiende Eeu'. *THRHR 49* (1986):305.

___. 'Bon Quelle v Munisipaliteit van Otavi 1989 1 SA 508 (A)'. *Codicillus 31* (1989):65.

___. 'Der Eigentumsbegriff', in *Das Römisch-Holländische Recht: Fortschritte des Zivilrechts im 17*. Jahrhundert edited by R. Feenstra, and R. Zimmermann. Berlin: Duncker & Humblot, 1992.

___. 'Die Funksies en Omskrywing van Besit'. *THRHR 51* (1988):276.

___. 'Die Mandament van Spolie en Quasi-Besit'. *THRHR 52* (1989):444.

___. 'Naidoo v Moodley 1982 (4) SA 82 (T)'. *THRHR 46* (1983):237.

___. 'Nog eens Naidoo v Moodley: ' n Repliek'. *THRHR 47* (1984):429.

___. 'Toepassing van die Mandament van Spolie op Onroerende Sake'. *THRHR 49* (1986):223.

___. and Sutherland, P. 'Dispossession of Incorporeals or Rights: Is the Mandament van Spolie the Appropriate Remedy?'. *SA Merc LJ 15* (2003):95.

___. ' An Overview of Developments in Constitutional Property Law since the Introduction of the Property Clause in 1993'. *SAPR/PL 19* (2004):102.

___. 'Dancing with Codes: Protecting, Developing, Limiting and Deconstructing Property Rights in the Constitutional State'. *SALJ 118* (2001):258.

___. 'Three Cases on the Mandament van Spolie'. *SALJ 100* (1983):689.

___. *Constitutional Property Clauses: A Comparative Analysis*. Lansdowne: Juta, 1999.

Van der Walt, J. 'Blixen's Difference: Horizontal Application of Fundamental Rights and the Resistance to Neo-Colonialism'. *TSAR* (2003):311.

___. 'Piracy, Property and Plurality: Re-Reading the Foundations of Modern Law'. *TSAR* (2001):524.

___. 'Progressive Indirect Horizontal Application: Towards a Co-operative Relationship between Common Law and Constitutional Law Jurisprudence'. *SAJHR 17* (2001):341.

___. 'The Critique of Subjectivism and its Implications for Property Law: Towards a Deconstructive Republican Theory of Property'. In *Property Law on the Threshold of the 21st Century*, edited by G. van Maanen and A. van der Walt. Antwerpen: MAKLU, 1996.

___. *Tangible mais intouchable, la loi du tact, la loi de la loi*. Nijmegen: Wolf Legal Publishers, 2002.

Weinrib, E. 'Restitutionary Damages as Corrective Justice'. *Theoretical Inquiries in Law 1* (1999):1.

Zimmerman, R. and Visser, D. 'Introduction: South African Law as a Mixed legal System'. In *Southern Cross: Civil law and Common Law in South Africa*, edited by R. Zimmermann and D. Visser. Oxford: Clarendon Press, 1996.

Zucker, R. *Democratic Distributive Justice*. Cambridge: Cambridge University Press, 2001.

Case law

Andrus v Allard 444 US 51 (1979).

Berman v Parker 348 US 26 (1954).

Bon Quelle (Edms) Bpk v Munisipaliteit van Otavi 1989 (1) SA 508 (A).

Fredericks v Stellenbosch Divisional Council 1977 (3) SA 113 (C).

Froman v Herbmore Timber and Hardware 1984 (3) SA 609 (W).

Kaiser Aetna v United States 444 US 164 (1979).

Lewis Blue Point Oyster Co v Briggs 229 US 82 (1913).

Loretto v Teleprompter Manhattan CATV Corp 458 US 419 1982.

Lucas v South Carolina Coastal Council 505 US 1003 (1992).

Naidoo v Moodley 1982 (4) SA 82 (T).

Nienaber v Stuckey 1946 AD 1049.

Nino Bonino v De Lange 1906 TS 120 at 122.

Penn Central Transportation Co v New York City 438 US 104 (1978) 124.

Pennsylvania Coal Co v Mahon 260 US 393 (1922).

Shoprite Checkers v Pangbourne Properties 1994 (1) SA 616 (W).

Tahoe-Sierra Preservation Council, Inc v Tahoe Regional Planning Agency 535 US 302 (2002).

Telkom SA Ltd v Xsinet (Pty) Ltd 2003 (5) SA 309 (SCA).

The Mayor, Aldermen and Burgesses of the Borough of Bradford v Pickles [1895] AC 587.

Tigon Ltd v Bestyet Investments (Pty) Ltd 2001 (4) SA 634 (N).

Yeko v Qana 1973 (4) SA 735 (A).

Zulu v Minister of Works, KwaZulu 1992 (1) SA 181 (D&C).

FIVE

Equality, Dignity and the Politics of Interpretation

Henk Botha

5.1 Introduction

The equality standard articulated by South Africa's Constitutional Court[1] is premised on a substantive concept of equality, and purports to be sensitive to context and mindful of past patterns of discrimination, systemic inequality and the role of harmful social stereotypes. However, the emancipatory potential of the court's general approach to equality is not always reflected in its judgments. In fact, the reasoning in some of these judgments strikes me as formalistic and uncritical of existing power relations.

The disjuncture between the constitutional promise and the reality of the enforcement of the equality guarantee is a recurring theme in legal scholarship.[2] According to some authors, the dignity-based approach of the Constitutional Court lies at the heart

---

1 The Constitutional Court has placed the prohibition of unfair discrimination at the centre of the constitutional equality guarantee. In this chapter, I am interested primarily in the court's interpretation of the right not be subjected to unfair discrimination. The Constitutional Court's equality jurisprudence has been developed, inter alia, in the following cases: *Brink v Kitshoff* 1996 (4) SA 197; 1996 (6) BCLR 752 (CC); *Fraser v Children's Court, Pretoria North* 1997 (2) SA 261; 1997 (2) BCLR 153 (CC); *President RSA v Hugo* 1997 (4) SA 1; 1997 (6) BCLR 708 (CC); *Prinsloo v Van der Linde* 1997 (3) SA 1012; 1997 (6) BCLR 759 (CC); *Harksen v Lane* NO 1998 (1) SA 300; 1997 (11) BCLR 1489 (CC); *Larbi-Odam v Member of Executive Council for Education* 1998 (1) SA 745; 1997 (12) BCLR 1655 (CC); *Pretoria City Council v Walker* 1998 (2) SA 363; 1998 (3) BCLR 257 (CC); *National Coalition for Gay and Lesbian Equality v Minister of Justice* 1999 (1) SA 6; 1998 (12) BCLR 1517 (CC); *Democratic Party v Minister of Home Affairs* 1999 (3) SA 254; 1999 (6) BCLR 611 (CC); *National Coalition for Gay and Lesbian Equality v Minister of Home Affairs* 2000 (2) SA 1; 2000 (1) BCLR 39 (CC); *Hoffmann v South African Airways* 2001 (1) SA 1; 2000 (11) BCLR 1211 (CC); *Moseneke v The Master* 2001 (2) SA 18; 2001 (2) BCLR 103 (CC); *Satchwell v President of the RSA* 2002 (6) SA 1; 2002 9 BCLR 986 (CC); *Du Toit v Minister for Welfare and Population Development* 2003 (2) SA 198; 2002 (10) BCLR 1006 (CC); *S v Jordan* 2002 (6) SA 642; 2002 (11) BCLR 1117 (CC); *J v Director-General, Department of Home Affairs* 2003 (5) BCLR 463 (CC); and *Daniels v Campbell* NO 2004 (7) BCLR 735 (CC).

2 The Constitutional Court's interpretation of the equality and non-discrimination guarantee has given rise to a substantial body of academic literature. My understanding of the relevant issues has been influenced by the following academic contributions, though the list is by no means comprehensive: Laurie Ackermann 'Equality and the South African Constitution: The role of dignity' (2000) 63 *ZaöRV* 537; Cathy Albertyn and Janet Kentridge 'Introducing the right to equality in the interim Constitution' (1994) 10 *SAJHR* 149; Cathy Albertyn and Beth Goldblatt 'Facing the challenge of transformation: Difficulties in the development of an indigenous jurisprudence of equality' (1998) 14 *SAJHR* 248; Gretchen Carpenter 'Equality and non-discrimination in the new South African constitutional order (1): The early cases' (2001) 64 THRHR 409; 'Equality and non-discrimination in the new South African constitutional order (2): An important trilogy of decisions' (2001) 64 *THRHR* 619; 'Equality and non-discrimination in the new South African constitutional order (3): The saga continues' (2002) 65 *THRHR* 37; 'Equality and non-discrimination in the new South African constitutional order (4): Update' (2002) 65 *THRHR* 177; Susie Cowen 'Can "dignity" guide South Africa's equality jurisprudence?' (2001) 17 *SAJHR* 34; Dennis Davis 'Equality: The majesty of legoland jurisprudence' (1999) 116 *SALJ* 398; Pierre De Vos 'Equality

of the problem. In their view, the notion of dignity is not only completely indeterminate, which allows judges to give almost any content to it, but the focus on dignity (rather than disadvantage) also results in an overly individualistic emphasis, which tends to blind judges to systemic inequality and material disadvantage. Others have countered that the notion of human dignity is not as devoid of meaning as claimed by the critics and that there is nothing inherently individualistic about it.

In this chapter, I explore the gap between the promise of the Constitutional Court's equality rhetoric and its actual judgments from the perspective of the debate between advocates and critics of a dignity-based approach. I am particularly interested in the link made in the literature between a dignity-based approach and 'neutral principles', and the way the Constitutional Court has used a dignity-based interpretation of the right to equality to negotiate some of its conflicting commitments. I argue that a dignity-based approach is incapable of containing the politics of interpretation, and propose instead a complex vision of equality which recognises multiple forms of disadvantage and openly acknowledges the constitutive role of power in social relations as well as in law

5.2 The gap between the promise and reality of the equality guarantee in the South African Constitution

The gap between the promise and reality of the constitutional equality guarantee is nowhere more evident than in the judgment of the majority of the Constitutional Court in *S v Jordan*.[3] In *Jordan*, the appellants argued that section 20(1)(aA) of the Sexual Offences Act[4] violated the right to equality and non-discrimination.[5] The section makes it an offence to have 'unlawful carnal intercourse', or to commit 'an act of indecency, with any other person for reward'. It was contended that the provision constituted unfair discrimination on the grounds of gender, to the extent that it criminalised only the conduct of the prostitute and not that of the client.

---

for all? A critical analysis of the equality jurisprudence of the Constitutional Court' (2000) 63 *THRHR* 62; Anton Fagan 'Dignity and unfair discrimination: A value misplaced and a right misunderstood' (1998) 14 *SAJHR* 220; Saras Jagwanth 'What is the difference? Group categorisation in *Pretoria City Council v Walker* 1998 2 SA 363 (CC)' (1999) 15 *SAJHR* 200; Saras Jagwanth and Evance Kalula (eds) *Equality law: reflections from South Africa and elsewhere (2002)*; André van der Walt and Henk Botha 'Coming to grips with the new constitutional order: Critical comments on *Harksen v Lane* NO' (1998) 13 *SAPR/PL* 17; Karin van Marle 'Equality: An ethical interpretation' (2000) 63 *THRHR* 595; and Tobias Van Reenen 'Equality, discrimination and affirmative action: An analysis of section 9 of the Constitution of the Republic of South Africa' (1997) 12 *SAPR/PL* 151.

3 *S v Jordan* (n 1). The case was also discussed in chapter three of this collection by Wessel le Roux as one example of the disjunction in the jurisprudence of the South African Constitutional Court.

4 Act 23 of 1957

5 There were also other challenges. The appellants argued that section 20(1)(aA) also infringed the rights to privacy and occupational freedom and further attacked the constitutionality of sections in the Act relating to brothels. These challenges were rejected by both the majority and minority and will not be dealt with here. See Wessel le Roux 'Sex work, the right to occupational freedom and the constitutional politics of recognition' (2003) 120 *SALJ* 452, for a critique of the court's reasoning in relation to the occupational freedom challenge. See also Gretchen Carpenter 'Of prostitutes, pimps and patrons – some still more equal than others?' (2004) 19 *SAPR/PL* 231.

Ngcobo J, writing for the majority, found that the section did not constitute unfair discrimination in terms of section 8(2) of the interim Constitution.[6] His reasoning rested on seven premises. One, the impugned section is gender neutral, as it applies to male prostitutes as well as female prostitutes.[7] Two, there is a qualitative difference between the prostitute, who is engaged in the business of prostitution and who is likely to be a repeat offender, and the client, 'who seeks the service of a prostitute only on occasion'.[8] Three, the client is an accomplice to the offence under common law, and is therefore not absolved from criminal prosecution. He is also liable to the same punishment as the prostitute in terms of the Riotous Assemblies Act.[9] Four, the purpose of the section is to prohibit commercial sex, not to protect the client.[10] Five, striking at the dealer and not at the client is a perfectly legitimate means of achieving this purpose, particularly in view of the fact that the client is also guilty of criminal conduct and that the distinction between merchant and dealer is often employed in criminal law.[11] Six, if and to the extent that the conviction of the prostitute carries a greater stigma than that of the client, 'that is a social attitude and not the result of the law'. Moreover, such stigma attaches to them 'not by virtue of their gender, but by virtue of the conduct they engage in'.[12] And seven, even if it is true that in practice only prostitutes are prosecuted and not clients, 'that may point to a flaw in the application of the law but it does not establish a constitutional defect in it'.[13]

Ngcobo J concluded on the first ground that penalising the prostitute only and not the client does not amount to direct discrimination on the grounds of gender. He further found, on the basis of the remaining grounds, that the impugned provision does not constitute indirect gender discrimination either. He added that, even if there is discrimination, it is not unfair, as the provision applies to male and female prostitutes (ground one), does not absolve the client from criminal liability (ground three), and pursues a legitimate and important purpose (ground four).

It is hard to square this reasoning with the court's understanding, as articulated in previous judgments, that the Constitution seeks to achieve substantive equality and aims to redress systemic discrimination and past patterns of disadvantage.[14] The majority's emphasis on the gender neutrality of section 20(1)(aA) and the way in which it divorces the law from social attitudes and separates the inquiry into the constitutionality of the provision from its enforcement, smack of a formal understanding of equality and a failure to situate its inquiry within a broader context of systemic gender discrimination. Its insistence that the stigma associated with prostitution is the result of personal choice, and

---

6 Le Roux (n 5) 453–455 criticises the court's finding that the interim Constitution, rather than the final constitution, had to be applied.

7 *S v Jordan* (n 1) at para 9.

8 *Idem* para 10.

9 *Idem* para 11–14.

10 *Idem* para 12.

11 *Idem* para 10, 15.

12 *Idem* para 16.

13 *Idem* para 19.

14 See for instance *National Coalition for Gay and Lesbian Equality v Minister of Justice* (n 1) at paras 60–62.

is unrelated to the role of law in apportioning blame and sustaining structural inequality and deeply ingrained patterns of disadvantage, is premised on ideas about individual freedom and the relationship between law and social attitudes that are highly problematic in the society in which we live in. It rests upon the idea – already discredited by the legal realists[15] – that there is a sphere of human belief and interaction that exists prior to, and independently of the law and is therefore a matter of purely personal choice, which is untouched by institutional power relations. This idea is particularly problematic in a society characterised by massive inequality, in which the impact of past discriminatory laws and policies is likely to endure long after their repeal.[16]

The dissenting judgment[17] of O'Regan and Sachs JJ exposes the sterility of the majority's approach. It situates the inquiry into the constitutionality of section 20(1)(A) within the context of women's subordination, the dire financial need confronting many women who turn to prostitution, and sexual stereotyping and double standards. Moreover, it does not shy away from the role of the law in sustaining and reinforcing material inequality and sexual stereotypes. Its finding that the impugned provision constitutes indirect discrimination on the grounds of gender is based on its 'markedly differential impact' on men and women, and the fact that, by making the prostitute the primary offender, it 'directly reinforces a pattern of sexual stereotyping which is itself in conflict with the principle of gender equality'.[18] Its rejection of the argument that the provision is not discriminatory, the client is also criminally liable in terms of the common law and the Riotous Assemblies Act, evinces a concern with the actual impact of the differentiation, rather than with merely formal equality. As the judges demonstrate, '[t]he difference between being a principal offender and an accomplice or co-conspirator may have little impact in formal legal terms. It does, however, carry a difference in social stigma and impact'.[19] This differential impact

> tracks and reinforces in a profound way double standards regarding the expression of male and female sexuality. The differential impact is accordingly not accidental, just as the failure of the authorities to prosecute male customers as accomplices is entirely unsurprising. They both stem from the same defect in our justice system which holds women to one standard of conduct and men to another.[20]

The failure of the majority to situate section 20(1)(aA) within a context of sexual double standards, material inequality and systemic discrimination against women is puzzling, given the court's insistence that the constitutional equality guarantee calls for a context-sensitive appraisal of the impact of the alleged discrimination, with due regard to the

---

15 See Joseph Singer 'Legal realism now' (1988) 76 *California LR* 465.

16 The questionable nature of the same assumption in the context of property disputes is explored in chapter four of this collection by André van der Walt.

17 Three other judges concurred in their dissent. The split between the majority and minority was thus a narrow 6:5.

18 *S v Jordan* (n 1) at para 60.

19 *Idem* para 63; see also para 64–65.

20 *Idem* para 67.

position of the complainants in society and whether they have been subject to past patterns of discrimination.[21] Their dismissal of the argument that the section constitutes indirect gender discrimination, in that it has a disproportionate impact on women, is difficult to square with the earlier judgment in *Walker*,[22] in which it was held that differentiation between historically black and historically white areas constituted indirect discrimination on the grounds of race. Moreover, the lack of sensitivity shown by the majority to the way in which the section reinforces sexual stereotypes and stigmatises those dealing in commercial sex – the overwhelming majority of which are women – and not those paying for it – the overwhelming majority of which are men – is surprising in view of the courts insistence in previous judgments that the constitution prohibits the state from basing its decisions on, or perpetuating, harmful stereotypes.[23]

And yet, at another level, the majority's failure in *Jordan* to translate the promise of its equality rhetoric into reality, and to extend the transformative potential of its judgments in cases dealing with discrimination against gays/lesbians[24] and people who are HIV positive[25] to new social contexts, is not entirely unsurprising. The court has, in the past, been criticised for what is seen as a failure to engage critically with forms of discrimination that tend to confine men and women to stereotypical gender roles, or that adhere to and reinforce outdated conceptions of marriage. Its finding in *Hugo*[26] that a presidential decision to pardon all mothers – but not fathers – in prison with children under the age of 12 did not constitute unfair discrimination on the grounds of sex/gender, could be criticised for failing to challenge sexual stereotypes that confine women to the role of primary nurturers of children. But at least in *Hugo*, the court grappled with the fact that the presidential pardon rested upon outmoded stereotypes which, in the words of the main judgment, make it 'more difficult for women to compete in the labour market' and which are among 'the root causes of women's inequality in

21 See for example *President RSA v Hugo* supra (n 1) at para 41 (Goldstone J); para 112 (O'Regan J concurring).

22 *Pretoria City Council v Walker* supra (n 1)) at paras 30–35. But see also paras 105–118 (Sachs J dissenting).

23 The Constitutional Court found in *National Coalition for Gay and Lesbian Equality v Minister of Justice* supra (n 1) that the outlawing of sex between consenting men stigmatised gay sex, reinforced existing prejudices against gays, and impaired their dignity, personhood and identity. See in particular paras 23, 28 (Ackermann J) and 108–109 (Sachs J, concurring). It was also found in *Hoffmann v South African Airways* supra (n 1) at paras 35–37 that an organ of state may not base its treatment of people who are HIV positive on prejudice and stereotyping. Compare also the finding of Sachs J in his minority judgment in *Harksen v Lane* supra (n 1) (discussed below) that s 21 of the Insolvency Act reinforced a stereotypical view of marriage which is demeaning to both spouses and the dissenting judgment of Kriegler J in *Hugo* supra (n 1), in which he described the assumption that women are the primary care givers of young children, upon which a presidential pardon to mothers in prison was based, as 'a root cause of women's inequality in our society. It is both a result and a cause of prejudice; a societal attitude which relegates women to a subservient, occupationally inferior yet unceasingly onerous role. It is a relic and a feature of the patriarchy which the Cconstitution so violently condemns' (para 80). The majority conceded that the president's act rested upon a stereotype that was harmful to women, but found that the discrimination in question was not unfair, as South African mothers still generally bear far greater burdens than fathers in the rearing of children. See paras 109–115. See also the discussion of *Hugo* below.

24 *National Coalition for Gay and Lesbian Equality v Minister of Justice* supra (n 1); *National Coalition for Gay and Lesbian Equality v Minister of Home Affairs* supra (n 1); *Du Toit v Minister for Welfare and Population Development* supra (n 1); *Satchwell v President of the RSA* (n 1).

25 *President RSA v Hoffmann* (n 1).

26 *President RSA v Hugo* (n 1). See Davis (n 2) 404–407 and Van Marle (n 2) 599–600 for criticisms of the majority judgment in *Hugo*.

society'.[27] The majority's conclusion that the discrimination in question was not unfair, rested not upon a denial of the harmful effects of this type of gender typecasting,[28] but upon the conviction that it may sometimes be legitimate for the state to rely on otherwise harmful generalisations where refusal to do so would lead to further disadvantage to vulnerable groups. As O'Regan J argued in a separate judgment (concurred with by seven judges):

> [A]lthough the long-term goal of our constitutional order is equal treatment, insisting upon equal treatment in circumstances of established inequality may well result in the entrenchment of that inequality ... In this case, mothers have been afforded an advantage on the basis of a proposition that is generally speaking true. There is no doubt that the goal of equality entrenched in our constitution would be better served if the responsibilities for child rearing were more fairly shared between fathers and mothers. The simple fact of the matter is that at present they are not. Nor are they likely to be more evenly shared in the near future. For the moment, then, and for some time to come, mothers are going to carry greater burdens than fathers in the rearing of children. We cannot ignore this crucial fact in considering the impact of discrimination in this case.[29]

But whereas the majority in *Hugo* half-grudgingly accepted the validity of the president's reliance on gender stereotypes, on the ground that it would result in further discrimination against women if the social reality of the unequal burden carried by mothers and fathers were to be simply ignored, the majority in *Harksen*[30] seemed to be blind to the ways in which section 21 of the Insolvency Act entrenches stereotypical views of marriage. Section 21 provides that, upon the sequestration of the estate of an insolvent spouse, the property of the solvent spouse vests in the Master of the Supreme Court or in the trustee of the insolvent estate. The majority held that, even though the section discriminates between the solvent spouse of an insolvent and other persons who may have had dealings or close relationships with the insolvent, such discrimination is not unfair. Their judgment not only underestimates the adverse impact of section 21 on the solvent spouse,[31] but also fails to come to terms with the power relations which underlie and are perpetuated by the provision. As Sachs J demonstrates in his dissent, section 21 is 'manifestly patriarchal in origin',[32] and promotes 'a stereotyped and outdated view of marriage' which 'inhibits the capacity for self-realisation of the spouses, affects the quality of their relationship with each other as free and equal persons within the union, and encourages society to look at them not as "a couple" made up of two persons with independent personalities and shared lives, but as "a couple" in which each loses his or her individual existence'.[33]

---

27 *Idem* para 38 (per Goldstone J).

28 Of course, it could still be argued that the majority under-estimated the negative impact of reliance on such generalisations. See Kriegler J's dissent at paras 80, 83; Davis (n 2) 405–407.

29 *Hugo* (n 1) at paras112, 113.

30 *Harksen v Lane* (n 1). See Albertyn and Goldblatt (n 2) 261–263; Davis (n 2) 409–412 and Van der Walt and Botha (n 2) for criticisms of the majority judgment in *Harksen*.

31 *Harksen* (n 1). Compare the dissenting judgment of O'Regan J at paras 88, 96–100.

32 *Idem* para 120.

33 *Idem* para 124.

In *Harksen*, as in *Jordan*, the majority failed to situate the relevant legislative provision within the context of the patriarchal society from which it emerged, and within deeply entrenched stereotypes that continue to frustrate the realisation of gender equality. This raises a number of questions. For instance, how does one explain the apparent tension between the court's readiness to challenge stereotypes that are demeaning to gays and lesbians, and its failure in *Harksen* and *Jordan* to do the same in relation to stereotypes that are inimical to the achievement of a non-sexist society? Why the reluctance to find indirect discrimination on the grounds of sex/gender, if the court was prepared to make a finding of indirect discrimination on the grounds of race in *Walker*,[34] in which a disproportionate number of white people were adversely affected by a municipality's (transitional) policy of charging differential rates in historically white and historically black areas? Could it be that the present court is just not sufficiently gender conscious? Is there something about the equality standard enunciated by the court that makes it impervious to claims based on gender equality? Or is the problem that gender discrimination is often more subtle and difficult to detect than other forms of discrimination?

It is instructive to compare the facts in *Harksen* and *Jordan* with those cases in which the impugned provisions were held to constitute unfair discrimination. In the first two cases, the provisions in question did not impose burdens or withhold benefits from persons directly on any of the enumerated grounds, such as sex or gender. This is in contrast to cases involving overt discrimination on the grounds of race,[35] gender[36] or sexual orientation,[37] in which the disadvantage to blacks, women, or gays and lesbians was far more tangible. In these cases, the impugned provisions were blatantly discriminatory – clear relics of South Africa's apartheid and sexist past which unmistakeably rested upon (and reinforced) the assumption that certain groups were inferior, or incapable of full and equal participation in economic life or of entering into meaningful sexual relationships.[38] The discrimination in *Harksen* and *Jordan*, by contrast, was more subtle, and the link between the respective legislative provisions and prevailing patterns of inequality and stigmatisation not quite so obvious.

It is perhaps, then, necessary to reformulate my initial set of questions: to ask not why the court's jurisprudence in the area of, say, sexual orientation seems to be more in line with a transformative vision of the constitution than its jurisprudence on discrimination on the grounds of sex/gender, but why the majority of judges seem to be unable to bring their supposedly substantive and context-sensitive approach to equality to bear

---

34 *Pretoria City Council v Walker* (n 1).

35 For example, *Moseneke v The Master* (n 1).

36 For example, *Brink v Kitshoff* (n 1).

37 For example, *National Coalition for Gay and Lesbian Equality v Minister of Justice* supra (n 1); *National Coalition for Gay and Lesbian Equality v Minister of Home Affairs* supra (n 1); *Satchwell v President of the RSA* supra (n 1); *Du Toit v Minister for Welfare and Population Development* (n 1).

38 Of course, the same cannot be said of the *Walker* case, in which indirect discrimination on the grounds of race was found. However, the link in *Walker* between the differentiation in question (between formerly white and formerly black residential areas) and a listed ground (race) was so obvious, that an inquiry into systemic forms of discrimination or prevailing patterns of inequality was hardly needed. In fact, such an inquiry might well have resulted in the opposite conclusion – see the minority judgment of Sachs J at paras 105–118.

on forms of discrimination that are no less pernicious, but more subtle and therefore more difficult to detect.

5.3 The dignity-based approach and its critics

The gap between the transformative potential of the Constitutional Court's substantive understanding of equality and its failure, in certain cases, to challenge forms of discrimination that are deeply embedded in social attitudes, practices and institutions, is often blamed on the Constitutional Court's dignity-based approach to the interpretation of the constitutional equality guarantee. The court has placed the value of dignity at the centre of its analysis of the equality right. In the view of the court, the idea that all human beings should be accorded equal dignity and respect is meant to guide the interpretation of the right not to be unfairly discriminated against.[39] In keeping with this emphasis, dignity features in three distinct stages in the equality test laid down in *Harksen*. In the first place, the question whether differentiation on unlisted grounds amounts to discrimination is answered with reference to the question whether 'it is based on attributes or characteristics which have the potential to impair the fundamental dignity of persons as human beings, or to affect them adversely in a comparably serious manner'.[40] Second, whether discrimination on listed or unlisted grounds is found to be unfair, turns to a significant extent on the question whether it has led to an impairment of the complainants' fundamental human dignity or constitutes an impairment of a comparably serious nature.[41] And third, if an infringement of the right to equality or non-discrimination is found to exist, a court must establish whether the limitation is reasonable and justifiable in an open and democratic society based on human dignity, equality and freedom.

In the view of some authors, the court's emphasis on the value of dignity impedes the establishment of a transformative equality jurisprudence. Albertyn and Goldblatt[42] argue that the focus on dignity tends to result in an individualised conception of equality which does not take sufficient cognisance of the groups-based nature of discrimination and systemic forms of inequality. It is concerned primarily with the infringement of personal interests, rather than with material disadvantage. Although the authors recognise that the *Harksen* test can be used to challenge groups-based disadvantage to the extent that it expressly refers to the position of the complainants in society and past patterns of disadvantage, they argue that the emphasis on dignity creates too much room for an individualised understanding of equality, and that the weight to be attached to substantive considerations of disadvantage is made to depend almost entirely on the

39 Goldstone J proclaimed in *Hugo* (n 1) at para. 41: 'At the heart of the prohibition of unfair discrimination lies a recognition that the purpose of our new constitutional and democratic order is the establishment of a society in which all human beings will be accorded equal dignity and respect regardless of their membership of particular groups'. See also *Prinsloo v Van der Linde* (n 1) at paras 31–33; *Harksen v Lane* (n 1) at paras 46, 50, 51, 53 (Goldstone J) and 91–92 (O'Regan J dissenting).

40 *Harksen* (n 1) at para. 46.

41 *Idem* para 51.

42 Albertyn and Goldblatt (n 2).

approach of an individual judge. In their view, the right to equality and non-discrimination should be interpreted in the light of the value of equality, rather than the value of dignity. Such an interpretation would place 'disadvantage, vulnerability and harm, and their connotation of groups-based prejudice'[43] at the centre of the equality right.

These concerns are echoed by Davis, who criticises the court for its failure to develop a substantive vision of equality and for collapsing *equality* into *dignity*. He also notes that the court's interpretation of dignity is internally contradictory: it sometimes examines groups-based disadvantage and systemic discrimination under the rubric of dignity, which is an inherently individualistic notion. The court, in his view, 'has given dignity both a content and a scope that make for a piece of jurisprudential Legoland – to be used in whatever form and shape is required by the demands of the judicial designer'.[44] The dignity-based conception of equality accordingly lacks justificatory power, and fails to promote reasoned debate about the meaning and application of the foundational value of equality.

Not everyone believes that the dignity-based approach espoused by the Constitutional Court is irreconcilable with the ideal of a transformative equality jurisprudence. In the view of some authors, the individualism that could potentially flow from a dignity-based interpretation of equality is held in check by the court's emphasis on contextual considerations, the position of the complainants in society and whether they have been subject to past patterns of discrimination, and the impact of the discrimination. According to de Vos,[45] the court's use of dignity is largely rhetorical and does not have a significant practical effect on the outcomes of cases.[46] Importantly, it does not detract from the court's engagement with context and disadvantage.

Others deny that dignity is an inherently individualistic notion and that it is for that therefore incapable of guiding a transformative equality jurisprudence. Cowen[47] argues that human dignity is rooted, not in abstract notions of individualism, but in the individual as a social being, whose sense of self is forged within a social and communal context. Moreover, the value of dignity is closely bound up with material considerations, and can be relied upon to challenge material inequality and to justify state intervention aimed at a redistribution of wealth.

The Constitutional Court itself had occasion to engage with its critics in *National Coalition for Gay and Lesbian Equality v Minister of Justice*.[48] In this case, it was submitted on behalf of the *amicus curiae* that the court should give a more substantive interpretation to section 9 of the final Constitution than the one given to section 8 of the interim Constitution, and that the value of equality, rather than that of dignity, should

---

43 *Idem* 258.

44 Davis (n 2) 413.

45 De Vos (n 2).

46 Fagan (n 2) agrees that the use of dignity in *Hugo* is merely a rhetorical flourish (221), but argues that this rhetoric came to haunt the court in subsequent cases.

47 Cowen (n 2) 49–54.

48 *National Coalition for Gay and Lesbian Equality v Minister of Justice* (n 1) at paras 58–64 (Ackermann J); 120–129 (Sachs J concurring).

be placed at the centre of the right. The court rejected the contention, arguing that there were no material differences between sections 8 of the interim Constitution and 9 of the final Constitution, and that its interpretation of section 8 of the interim Constitution had already evinced a commitment to substantive and remedial equality. The court clearly felt that its reasoning in this case vindicated a dignity-based approach, and made nonsense of the claim that such an approach does not take sufficient heed of groups-based disadvantage and systemic discrimination. Its analysis of the ways in which the criminal prohibition of gay sodomy had reinforced anti-gay prejudice and affected the dignity, personhood and identity of gay men, appears to give credence to its view that a dignity-based approach is not at odds with a sensitivity to systemic discrimination and past patterns of disadvantage.

5.4 Justifications for the dignity-based approach

The justices of the Constitutional Court and academic commentators who favour a dignity-based interpretation of equality have offered a number of justifications for this approach. The first justification is a historical one. It is argued that, chief among the past ills whose recurrence the constitution seeks to prevent, is the denial under apartheid of the equal worth and dignity of sections of the population. The history of the discrimination and human rights abuses that characterised apartheid is, in this view, first and foremost one of the systematic denial of people's personhood and moral agency on the basis of the colour of their skin. It is this denial of dignity that lies at the root of the denial of freedom and equality.[49] It therefore makes sense to interpret both freedom and equality in the light of the value of the fundamental dignity inherent in every human being.

A second justification which is offered for the court's dignity-based approach is the connection that is sometimes made between equality and human dignity in international law and comparative constitutional law.[50] Mention is made *inter alia* of the preamble to the Universal Declaration of Human Rights; article 1 of the Convention on the Elimination of All Forms of Racial Discrimination;[51] the historical link between the denial of dignity and equality by the Nazi regime and; the adoption of United Nations human rights instruments; the centrality of dignity to the German basic law; and the judgment of L'Heureux-Dubé J in *Egan v Canada*.[52]

49 See Ackermann (n 2) 540–542.

50 *Idem* 539–540, n 4; Cowen (n 2) 48.

51 'Discrimination between human beings on the grounds of race, colour or ethnic origin is an offence to human dignity'.

52 *Egan v Canada* 124 DLR (4th) 609. The following passage from her judgment was quoted with approval in *Hugo* supra (n 1) at para. 41: 'This court [the Supreme Court of Canada] has recognized that inherent human dignity is at the heart of individual rights in a free and democratic society … More than any other right in the *Charter*, s 15 gives effect to this notion … Equality, as that concept is enshrined as a fundamental human right within s 15 of the *Charter* means nothing if it does not represent a commitment to recognizing each person's equal worth as a human being, regardless of individual differences. Equality means that our society cannot tolerate legislative distinctions that treat certain people as second-class citizens, that demean them, that treat them as less capable for no good reason, or that otherwise offend fundamental human dignity.'

While these reasons establish a plausible historical and conceptual link between equality and dignity, they do not explain adequately why the interpretation of the equality right should be informed by the value of dignity, rather than that of equality. It is of course true that apartheid constituted a pervasive and systematic denial of the dignity of the majority of the population, and that this fact accounts, at least in part, for the central role of dignity under the Constitution of South Africa. But the denial of respect for people's dignity and personhood was not the only dimension of the inequality and discrimination of the apartheid era. There was also another side to it, which is better captured by the language of power and economic interest than by the language of morality. As much as the history of apartheid was characterised by the denial of human dignity, it was also characterised by economic exploitation and the systematic political and economic disempowerment of the majority of the population. It was a history of the establishment, through legal and other means, of the hegemony of a racial elite; of the economic dispossession of entire communities; of the relegation of the overwhelming majority of people to the fringes of the economy. It was a history of an attempt to divide and rule; to keep the black majority locked in a permanent state of serfdom; and thus to entrench white power and privilege.

To argue that equality cannot be subsumed under the value of dignity, is not to deny that there is a historical and conceptual link between violations of equality and dignity. The political and material inequality characterising South Africa's colonial and apartheid past were, after all, justified with reference to a crude racial ideology which denied that black people had the capacity for moral agency and autonomous self-realisation. Of course, economic deprivation and political disempowerment resulted in further deprivations of the fundamental human dignity of those affected. But to recognise that there is a connection between violations of equality and dignity, is not necessarily to accept that the one can be subsumed under the other. In fact, it seems relatively uncontroversial to argue that, in order to come to terms with the legacy of apartheid, the focus should be on both moral questions of personhood and individual autonomy, and on political and socio-economic considerations of power and disadvantage. It could, I think, be plausibly argued that the constitutional right to human dignity (and, possibly, related rights such as privacy and the right not to be subjected to cruel or inhuman punishment) is the proper place for addressing the former, while the right to equality is better suited to an exploration of the latter.

If the first two reasons do not provide an adequate justification for preferring a dignity-based approach to an alternative approach based on disadvantage, what then is the decisive factor which, in the view of the court, swings matters in favour of a dignity-based interpretation? I would suggest that the answer to this question lies in the third and fourth justifications, to which I now turn.

A third reason that is sometimes mooted in favour of a dignity-based approach, is based on Peter Westen's idea that equality is an empty form that has no substantive content of its own.[53] Although Cowen does not make express reference to Westen's

---

53 Peter Westen 'The empty idea of equality' (1982) 95 *Harvard* LR 537. Westen's idea is endorsed by Fagan (n 2) 222; 237–241. However, this leads him not to an endorsement of the Constitutional Court's dignity-based approach, but to an

article in her defence of the Constitutional Court's dignity-based approach, she argues that equality is a 'comparative concept' and that '[t]o value equality without saying more does not explain what outcome it is that we value. In Amartya Sen's language, it does not answer the question, "equality of what?"'[54] Cowen further suggests that, 'because of the distinctive comparative nature of equality as a concept, it does not seem to make sense to posit it and dignity against each other as two of the court's choices in this debate'.[55] In other words, the right to equality and non-discrimination necessarily has to be interpreted in the light of a value other than equality itself. In view of South Africa's history and the larger constitutionalist tradition[56] that it has embraced, it makes sense to accord that role to dignity.

The fourth justification relates to the judiciary's weak institutional position and lack of democratic accountability. In an article on the relationship between equality and dignity, Justice Laurie Ackermann – the author of some of the Constitutional Court's most important equality judgments – stresses the dangers of undue judicial subjectivity in the exercise of the power to review the decisions of democratically elected legislatures, and underscores the need for 'constitutional decision making that is neutral and principled'.[57] He then turns to a discussion of Herbert Wechsler's call for neutral principles of constitutional law[58] – a call that he wholeheartedly endorses. Ackermann takes Wechsler's thesis to mean, *inter alia*, that a judge must state reasons for a decision 'that he would be willing to follow in other situations to which it applies', and that 'the principles must be adequately general and neutral and must "reach out beyond the narrow circumstances of the case"'.[59] He further suggests that neutral principles constitute 'an indispensable bridge' on South Africa's road to a culture of justification,[60] and that 'dignity, and its relationship to equality … is an indispensable constituent in neutrally principled and correct adjudication on issues of unfair discrimination'.[61]

---

alternative understanding of the non-discrimination provision which turns it into a mechanism for enhancing the protection of independently existing rights. Davis (n 2) 400–401 also engages with Westen's argument, but notes that it 'makes somewhat disturbing reading', particularly as the 'concept of equality lies at the centre of the South African constitutional idea'. He argues that equality should not be reduced to the value of dignity or the protection of independently existing rights, and that the Constitutional Court 'should have the courage to begin its search for an equality jurisprudence afresh' (414).

54 Cowen (n 2) 40.

55 *Idem* 48.

56 It is often asserted that the value of dignity is central to the new conception of constitutionalism which informs many of the constitutions that were adopted since the end of the Second World War. See for example Ernest Weinrib 'Constitutional conceptions and constitutional comparativism', in Jackson and Mark Tushnet (eds) *Defining the field of comparative constitutional law* (2002) 3.

57 Ackermann (n 2) 554.

58 Herbert Wechsler 'Toward neutral principles of constitutional law' (1959) 73 *Harvard LR* 1. Wechsler argued that to be legitimate, constitutional judgments have to be 'entirely principled'. He defined a principled decision as 'one that rests on reasons with respect to all the issues in the case, reasons that in their generality and their neutrality transcend any immediate result that is involved'. *Idem* 19. See also *idem* 15.

59 Ackermann (n 2) 555 (quoting from Ken Greenawalt 'The enduring significance of neutral principles' (1978) 78 *Columbia LR* 982 at 985, 987).

60 *Ibid.*

61 *Idem* 556.

Justice Ackermann offers surprisingly little to substantiate his view that a dignity-based interpretation of the right to equality and non-discrimination is indispensable to a neutrally principled approach to constitutional adjudication. He does state that dignity and its relationship to equality forms part of an 'irreducible minimum of common values', the acceptance of which, in the words of Isaiah Berlin, is not only 'intrinsic to human communication' but also 'ground[s] our conception of a normal human being'.[62] However, it is unclear how this appeal to common values takes matters forward. The contention that a dignity-based approach allows for neutral and principled reason-giving, to the extent that it is grounded in inter-subjective agreement about the fundamental value of human dignity, fails to persuade in the absence of a plausible answer to the question: but how can agreement at such a high level of generality promote decision-making that is neutral and principled in a particular case?[63]

A more promising line of argument is suggested in the following passage: 'The application of neutral principles should quite obviously not be seen as a mechanical exercise nor as an infallible route to correct decisions, but rather as a form of jurisprudential discipline and morality'.[64] The concern here seems to be, not with finding a method that would render constitutional adjudication objectively determinate but with the quality of the justifications offered for constitutional decisions. This suggests that a dignity-based approach is to be preferred, not because there can be no reasonable disagreement about the meaning of dignity or the application of a dignity-based equality standard,[65] but because there is something about the concept of dignity that makes an inquiry into its meaning and possible violation more conducive to a culture of justification than an inquiry based upon the value of equality. What it is about dignity that makes it an ideal contender for this role is, however, not spelt out.

5.5 Dignity as a 'neutral principle'

'Wechsler formulated the concept of neutral principles against the background of the increasing judicial activism of the *Warren* court, and growing concern that there was no principled difference between that court's defence of personal freedom and equality and the *Lochner* court's earlier usurpation of legislative power in the name of economic freedom. For Wechsler, the challenge was to show that not all value-based reasoning rests simply upon personal preference. He sought to demonstrate that judicial decision

62 *Ibid.*

63 There are at least two problems here. First, even assuming widespread agreement about the importance of dignity and its historical link to equality, it does not necessarily follow that a dignity-based interpretation is the only plausible interpretation of the right to equality, or that it alone is capable of principled application. And second, agreement at the most general level about the importance of human dignity and its link to equality does not preclude the possibility of fundamental disagreement about the meaning of dignity and the precise nature of its relation to equality. In fact, some of the critics of a dignity-based approach seem to argue that the concept of dignity is so open to different interpretations that it can be invoked to justify almost any result. They thus suggest that a dignity-based approach is the very antithesis of neutrally principled adjudication.

64 Ackermann (n 2) 555.

65 See also Cowen (n 2) 45; 54–58.

making can be made to rest upon neutrally principled reasoning; that review on substantive grounds does not inevitably involve the substitution of a judge's will for that of the legislature. Wechsler did not believe that the *Warren* court's judgments always conformed to the ideal of neutrally principled reasoning. The challenge, in his view, was to come up with neutral justifications for the progressive outcomes of cases such as *Shelley v Kraemer*[66] and *Brown v Board of Education of Topeka*[67] to reformulate the holdings of these cases to affirm broader principles that reach beyond the narrow circumstances of the individual case.

The link established by Justice Ackermann between the Constitutional Court's equality jurisprudence and the idea of neutral principles suggests that the court's choice of a dignity-based interpretation of equality was motivated by similar concerns.[68] The Constitutional Court regularly stresses that, even when judges are called upon to adjudicate politically contentious issues and are required to do so with express reference to the values enshrined in the constitution and the context of South Africa's discriminatory and divided past, their function remains a legal and not a political one.[69] In Ackermann's view, a dignity-based approach allows judges to engage in substantive reasoning, to take due consideration of social context and past patterns of discrimination, and yet to remain faithful to the legal nature of their mandate by grounding their decisions in reasoned elaboration of the meaning of the constitution. An alternative approach, he seems to imply, would allow judges to stray too far from the constraining effects of the constitutional text and a commitment to neutrally principled reason-giving, and would be likely to give rise to decisions that rested upon 'personal subjective preference' or that were 'not demonstrably rooted in the Constitution'.[70]

Difficulties of interpretation notwithstanding,[71] a number of arguments can be derived from Justice Ackermann's lecture and from the work of other advocates of a dignity-based approach, in favour of the contention that a dignity-based interpretation of the equality

---

66 *Shelley v Kraemer* 334 US 1 (1948). Wechsler (n 57) 29–31 criticised the reasoning in *Shelley* – in which it was held that a racially restrictive covenant was contrary to the equal protection clause on the basis that judicial enforcement of such a covenant constituted state action – for lacking neutrality and generality, as the court would not possibly be prepared to extend this reasoning to all other situations in which it applied.

67 *Brown v Board of Education of Topeka* 347 US 483 (1954). According to Wechsler (n 57) 31–34, the holding in *Brown* was non-neutral to the extent that it preferred the associational interests of blacks who favoured integration over the associational interests of whites who favoured segregation.

68 Justice Ackermann develops the idea of dignity as a neutral principle within the context of a discussion of the horizontal application of the constitutional equality right. He provides a number of examples to illustrate how a dignity-based interpretation of equality can be used to mediate conflicts between equality and freedom. See Ackermann (n 2) 551–554. The first of these examples is almost identical to the factual situation in *Kraemer*, while the second, like *Brown*, involves a conflict between racial equality and freedom of association. His choice of these examples is not surprising: they all involve pronounced conflicts between equality and freedom, which are often said to be incommensurable values.

69 Compare for example *In re: Certification of the Constitution of the Republic of South Africa*, 1996 1996 (4) SA 744; 1996 (10) BCLR 1253 (CC) at para. 27; and *United Democratic Movement v President of the RSA* (1) 2002 (11) BCLR 1179 (CC) at para.11.

70 Ackermann (n 2) 554.

71 Apart from the fact that Justice Ackermann does not fully develop the suggested link between neutral principles and a dignity-based approach, he also does not directly engage with the court's critics or with suggested alternatives to the court's interpretation of the equality right. The reader who wants to make sense of his suggestion that a dignity-based approach is indispensable to neutrally principled constitutional adjudication, inevitably has to read between the lines.

right is more likely than an alternative (equality-based) approach, – to promote constitutional reasoning that is neutrally principled. First, despite the possibility of reasonable disagreement over the correct application of a dignity-based interpretation, participants in such a debate are at least constrained by a shared understanding of the types of laws and conduct that typically offend basic notions of dignity.[72] Second, that is more than one can say of an approach grounded in the value of equality, which is essentially a comparative concept that is devoid of substantive meaning.[73] Third, a dignity-based approach allows for sensitivity to context and careful attention to differences of degree, rather than sweeping generalisations that the court may be unwilling to follow in subsequent cases.[74] Fourth, a dignity-based interpretation of equality enables judges to adjudicate conflicts between freedom and equality in a principled manner, without reducing either of these constitutional values to a subordinate status. Justice Ackermann is clearly concerned that a less nuanced understanding of equality might result in a serious diminution of the sphere of personal freedom, especially in cases involving a conflict between equality and, say, freedom of association or freedom of testation. By contrast, a dignity-based approach to equality enables judges to make a principled distinction between instances of private discrimination that constitute a violation of somebody's equal moral worth and citizenship, and legitimate exercises of personal and associational freedom.[75] Fifth, by focusing on dignity, a court is able to avoid the negative consequences that may otherwise flow from a consideration of the position of the complainants in society and the group(s) to which they belong. The dignity-based approach provides a focal point that allows the court to place group membership and disadvantage in the proper perspective – as important factors to be considered alongside others, but not as dispositive of the case. As Goldstone J stated in *Hugo*:

> The prohibition on unfair discrimination in the interim Constitution seeks not only to avoid discrimination against people who are members of disadvantaged groups. It seeks more than that. At the heart of the prohibition of unfair discrimination lies a recognition that the purpose of our new constitutional and democratic order is the establishment of a society in which all human beings will be accorded equal dignity and respect regardless of their membership of particular groups.[76]

---

72 Compare Justice Ackermann's appeal to common values (discussed under 5.4 above) and Cowen's argument ((n 2) 42–45) that dignity has a determinate meaning at a general level.

73 Compare this with the discussion of the third argument in favour of a dignity-based approach under 5.4 above.

74 Compare Ackermann's discussion of the horizontal application of the equality right (n 2) at 552–554.

75 For instance, it provides a principled basis for distinguishing between a racially restrictive condition in a contract of sale, on the one hand, and the right of the owner of a private residence to refuse, on racist grounds, to entertain certain people at his home. Ackermann clearly regards the first instance as one of unfair discrimination, but seems to think that the home owner should, in the second instance, be free to choose whom to invite.

76 *President RSA v Hugo* (n 1) at para 41. Again, compare Ackermann's discussion of the horizontal application of the equality right at (n 2) 552–554. I suspect that Justice Ackermann may also have in mind a sixth, more conceptual connection, which can be expressed as follows: The concept of dignity goes to the heart of a culture of justification. A culture of justification presupposes that all individuals are worthy of equal respect; that everyone whose interests are affected by exercises of public power is entitled to reasons. By grounding its equality analysis in dignity, a court seeks to ensure that all parties that are represented before it, either directly or indirectly, are shown the basic respect of being given reasons for its judgment – reasons, that is, that are not reducible to mere expressions of personal preference or sympathy for one group rather than another.

In other words, a dignity-based approach is thought to enable judges to stay clear of two distinct dangers, which can be presented as opposite poles. At the one end, there is the danger of a formal conception of equality which insists on equal treatment despite material differences between individuals. Initial appearances notwithstanding, such an approach entrenches existing inequality and is thus skewed in favour of the beneficiaries of past discrimination. At the other end of the spectrum is the idea of an equality of outcome, which negates the differences between individuals and would be too invasive of individual liberty. A dignity-based approach, in the view of the court, requires judges both to take account of past patterns of disadvantage and systemic discrimination, and to guard against a conception of equality that tends to reduce individuals to a bland and restrictive sameness. An alternative approach based on the value of equality, is suspected of being too close to the second pole: it is feared that its focus on material and groups-based disadvantage may degenerate into a non-neutral jurisprudence which is based on judges' personal preferences for the claims of certain groups and which threatens respect for individual autonomy.

Inherent in the dignity-based approach, is an attempt to neutralise the politics of adjudication; to ground the court's equality jurisprudence in a form of substantive reasoning which is indifferent to the identity of the winner. A dignity-based approach is thought to enable judges to provide reasoned and neutrally principled justifications for their decisions, and thus to dispel suspicions that their judgments rest upon personal preference, or upon their belief that the Constitution favours one group/class over another.

5.6 Can neutral principles contain the politics of interpretation?

Justice Ackermann's reliance on Wechsler's notion of neutral principles to ground a substantive and transformative vision of equality is ironic, given Wechsler's own impoverished and highly formal understanding of equality and the proceduralism of his approach. Wechsler contested the idea that the issue in *Brown* was one of discrimination. For him, it was rather a case of the denial of black people's freedom of association, which came into conflict with the freedom of whites not to associate with them. He argued that there was inconclusive proof that black children were harmed by school segregation, that it was impermissible to inquire into the motive of the legislature, and that it was equally problematic

> to make the measure of validity of legislation the way it is interpreted by those who are affected by it. In the context of a charge that segregation *with equal facilities* is a denial of equality, is there not a point in *Plessy*[77] in the statement that if 'enforced separation stamps the colored race with a badge of inferiority' it is simply because its members choose 'to put that construction upon it'?[78]

---

77 *Plessy v Ferguson* (163) US 537, 551 (1896), the case in which the 'separate but equal' doctrine was adopted.

78 Wechsler (n 58) 33.

Not only does this statement show a blatant disregard for the disadvantage suffered by blacks and the systemic nature of racial discrimination, but it also makes it clear that Wechsler would have rejected the idea that dignity could serve as a neutral principle of constitutional adjudication. Dignity, in his view, would be far too subjective to ground a neutrally principled approach. To base a finding of racial or sexual discrimination on the impairment of the complainants' dignity, would be to privilege the subjective experience and social understanding of, say, black people or women over those of white people or men. In Wechsler's view, an inquiry into actual relations of social inequality and domination falls outside the province of reasoned judicial elaboration and should be undertaken, if at all, by the political branches of government.

Ackermann's identification of dignity as a neutral principle should perhaps, then, be seen as an attempt to strip the idea of neutral principles of the formalism and proceduralism that characterised Wechsler's thought,[79] and to conceive of it in terms that are consonant with a substantive constitutional jurisprudence and a more sophisticated understanding of the separation of powers. Ackermann, like Wechsler, is concerned about the separation of powers between the legislature and judiciary, and insists that judges should justify their decisions with reference to reasons that transcend the immediate result of the particular case. However, unlike Wechsler, he believes that an inquiry into actual relations of inequality does not invariably take judges out of the realm of law into that of politics. A judge, in his view, can consider material disadvantage and systemic power relations and still act in a principled way – as long as the judge's inquiry into these issues is filtered through the neutral principle of dignity.

Whether the dignity-based approach has been, or indeed can be, successful in grounding an equality jurisprudence that is neutrally principled is, however, debatable. Critics of such an approach are likely to point out that the court often concludes its inquiry into the question whether differentiation has the potential to impair the fundamental dignity of the complainants, or whether discrimination has led to an impairment of their human dignity, rather summarily, without engaging in a careful contextual analysis of the impact of the differentiation on those affected, and without providing reasons for its conclusion that are sufficiently general to guide judges in subsequent cases.[80] They may also point out that the identity of the applicants often does matter; that the fact that the application in a case involving discrimination on the grounds of sex, gender or marital status is brought by a prostitute or the wife of a controversial businessperson,[81] sometimes has a direct bearing on the outcome of the case.

Even if one assumes, with defenders of the dignity-based approach, that these problems are not insurmountable, that they can be overcome through greater judicial

79 See Gary Peller 'Neutral principles in the 1950's' (1988) 21 *Journal of Legal Reform* 561; Morton Horwitz *The transformation of American law*, 1870-1960 (1992) 265-268 on the formalism and proceduralism of Wechsler's appeal to neutral principles.

80 Compare Davis's argument (n 2) 413 that the dignity-based approach results in a 'Legoland' jurisprudence, 'to be used in whatever form and shape is required by the demands of the judicial designer'.

81 See Albertyn and Goldblatt (n 2) 263, who criticise the inability of the majority in *Harksen* to 'see beyond the particular litigant before it to appreciate the situation of others affected by the provision'.

elaboration of the meaning of human dignity[82] and better explication of the grounds for the courts' equality decisions, it remains difficult to escape the suspicion that there is something profoundly political about what judges do. Consider, for instance, the *Jordan* case. Both the majority and minority judgments can be justified in terms of principles that are general and neutral. For instance, the majority judgment can be explained as follows:

> Facially neutral differentiation which affects more members of one sex than the other, does not constitute indirect discrimination on the grounds of sex or gender if it serves a legitimate purpose, is rational, and does not have the potential to impair the dignity of the complainants, by virtue of the fact that it does not impose a significantly greater burden or disadvantage on one group than the other, or the fact that the impairment of the complainants' dignity is a result of their own choice.

The principle governing the minority judgment can be expressed thus:

> Facially neutral differentiation which has a disproportionate impact on either males or females, constitutes indirect discrimination on the grounds of sex or gender if it has the potential to impair the dignity of the complainants, by virtue of the fact that it is based on and reinforces sexual stereotypes which are demeaning to either of the sexes.

Not only are both principles general and neutral, but both seem unobjectionable – even from the other side's perspective. However, the crunch comes within the application of these principles. The majority, I think, would deny that the provision in question reinforces stereotypes that are demeaning to either sex. The minority would contest the finding that it does not impose a significantly greater burden or disadvantage on women, or that the impairment of the complainants' dignity is simply a result of their own choice. Underlying and informing the split between the majority and minority are not irreconcilably different principles or differences in methodology, but widely divergent assumptions about power, individual choice and responsibility, social stigma and moral blame, and the relation between law and social attitudes.

It is difficult to see how neutral principles can serve as a significant constraint on judicial reasoning if, as in *Jordan*, the split between the majority and minority has more to do with different social visions and underlying moral and political assumptions than with differences about the appropriate principle governing the case. The idea that the politics of law can be contained through reliance on neutral principles seems rather fanciful if opposite outcomes are the result, not of reliance on significantly different principles but of different ways of looking at actual situations and of perceiving the social world.

The inability of neutral principles to neutralise the politics of law should not come as a surprise. In fact, the very idea of 'neutral principles' is not as ideologically innocent as it may at first appear. It has been pointed out by various authors that what is considered general, neutral and principled is itself a function of a particular legal culture and is historically and socially contingent. There is therefore something circular

82 See for example Cowen (n 2) 54.

about neutral principles: to qualify as neutrally principled, a decision must rest on 'the conventional understandings and values that characterise the culture'.[83] Those understandings themselves reflect a particular hegemony, and may serve to render certain forms of disadvantage 'invisible', to 'naturalise' and 'neutralise' them. In the words of Patricia Williams:

> Racial discrimination is powerful precisely because of its frequent invisibility, its felt neutrality ... Racism inscribes culture with generalized preferences and routinized notions of propriety ... It empowers the mere familiarity and comfort of the status quo by labelling that status quo as 'natural'.[84]

The point therefore is not only that judges are often able to appeal to the same 'neutral principles' to justify opposite outcomes but, more fundamentally, that the perceived generality and neutrality of those principles are themselves a function of social power. Seen thus, the politics of law is not only at work when judges base their decisions simply on their own, subjective, preferences, but also manifests itself in judges' reliance upon 'neutral principles'. In fact, as Steven Winter[85] argues, the politics of law 'is most pronounced precisely when judges are acting in good faith, unaware of the normative entailments of the conceptual materials with which they work'.

5.7 Moral and political conceptions of equality

The belief that a dignity-based interpretation of equality is indispensable to neutrally principled adjudication, must be seen against the background of the Constitutional Court's struggle to establish its institutional legitimacy through a combination of courage *and* restraint, tough-minded independence *and* co-operation with, and deference to, the other branches of government, and, most pertinent to the present discussion, a commitment to a substantive and transformative vision of the constitution and a resolve not to be seen to stray from its judicial mandate into the realm of politics.[86] A dignity-based approach seems to enable the court to reconcile some of the conflicting normative and institutional commitments embodied in the constitution. It allows judges to make sense of the commitment to social *and* individual justice; substantive and remedial equality *and* respect for the individual, regardless of her membership of particular social groups; and the ideal of a nonracist and non-sexist society *and* the recognition that the adoption of race-conscious and gender-conscious measures is indispensable to the creation of such a society. It does so by requiring judges to consider past patterns of discrimination and systemic forms of disadvantage, yet to situate their inquiry within the broader framework of a dignity-based approach. It does not deny the possibility of reasonable

---

83 Steven Winter *A clearing in the forest: Law, life, and mind* (2001) 325, with reference to Jan Deutsch 'Neutrality, legitimacy, and the Supreme Court: Some intersections between law and political science' (1968) 20 *Stanford LR* 169.

84 '*Metro Broadcasting, Inc v FCC*: Regrouping in singular times', in Kimberle Crenshaw et al. (eds) *Critical race theory: The key writings that formed the movement* (1995) 198.

85 Winter (n 83) 331.

86 See Heinz Klug *Constituting democracy: Law, globalism and South Africa's political reconstruction* (2000) for an incisive analysis of the ways in which the court has negotiated these conflicting normative and institutional commitments.

disagreement or the role played by judges' own convictions and life experience, but seeks to contain such political disagreement within acceptable bounds by structuring the inquiry in terms of a unifying discourse centred around the concept of dignity.

Central to the dignity-based approach is the assumption that, unless translated into moral harm, judicial consideration of material disadvantage and structural power is bound to lapse into politics, which is by definition non-neutral and unprincipled. However, critics of a dignity-based approach are concerned that material and groups-based disadvantage may not always be capable of being expressed in moral terms. Even though the minority judgment in *Jordan* suggests that a dignity-based inquiry can be stretched to allow for a consideration of these forms of disadvantage, the moralism of the majority judgment points to serious problems inherent in a dignity-based approach.[87] Because they conceive of harm in moral and individual terms, the majority assume that it must consist, if at all, in an impairment of the prostitute's reputation. However, since prostitutes knowingly accept the risk of lowering their social standing in the eyes of the community when they offer sex for reward, they cannot complain about the stigmatising effects of legislation that punishes only the prostitute. In the view of the majority, the stigma attaching to prostitutes is the product of their own choice and of social attitudes, and cannot be imputed to legislative distinctions.

The key to the majority judgment lies in the shift from a consideration of disadvantage to a discourse on moral agency, choice and reputation. This shift is facilitated by the focus on moral harm which is inherent in a dignity-based interpretation of the right to equality. The dignity-based approach, it could be argued, is at least partly to blame for the moralism, individualistic conception of power and disregard for systemic inequality characterising the majority judgment in *Jordan* – even if this approach is flexible enough to allow for a more transformative jurisprudence, as is evidenced by the minority judgment.

In an essay on racial justice in the United States, Kendall Thomas[88] criticises the dominant discourse of racial moralism and proposes instead a political understanding of racial equality. According to Thomas, the moral model of racial justice, with its emphasis on moral consensus, neutral rules and the reputation of different race groups,

> fails to capture the distinctive and constitutive role of the political in racial claims-making … The moral concept of racial justice tries to capture and control the explosive, agonistic conflicts that characterize American racial politics. If it cannot altogether remove questions of racial power from its agenda, the racial moralism model can aspire to confine them within the dispassionate discursive boundaries of juridical settlement, bureaucratic administration, and deliberative legislation. If contemporary history teaches us anything about our racial dilemma, it is that conflicts over the forms and substance of racial injustice have been primarily contests about access to the means of political power, about social relations of domination, subordination, and

---

87 The danger which 'moralism' posed to the work of the South African Truth and Reconciliation Commission and poses to post-apartheid constitutionalism in general is also discussed in chapter one of their collection by Johan van der Walt and chapter two by Karin van Marle.

88 Kendall Thomas 'Racial justice', in Austin Sarat et al. (eds) *Looking back at law's century* (2002) 78.

> resistance. These distinctively political dimensions of race in America resist the normative logic of the moral view that continues to predominate in public debates about racial justice.[89]

Thomas shows how a preoccupation with the moral dimensions of racial justice blinds analysts to the ways in which forms of discrimination that are facially neutral, such as the sentencing disparity between crack and powder cocaine violations, diminish the political power of African American civic publics.[90] In his view, the best way of responding to the political dimension of racial justice is by openly confronting it, not by seeking to contain it within supposedly neutral decision-making procedures. A political understanding of racial equality concerns itself with questions of racial subjugation, political citizenship, and the capacity of vulnerable racial groups to form 'oppositional counterpublics' which are able to develop 'oppositional ideas about racial justice'.[91]

Thomas's critique of a moral understanding of racial equality resembles the criticism that a dignity-based interpretation of the constitutional equality right is overly individualistic and not sensitive enough to material and groups-based disadvantage. The political concept of racial justice that he proposes, resists attempts to ground equality in moral consensus or neutral principles, or to reduce it to individual dignity, personhood or (group) reputation. Instead, it seeks to ground the equal protection right in the Constitution of the United States in the values of equality and democratic citizenship. It is rooted in a radical pluralist conception of democracy, which views conflict as constitutive of social relations and seeks to remind one that any apparent agreement on the rules of the political game or the correct interpretation of political values such as freedom, equality and democracy is the result of a particular hegemony which always remains (and should remain) open to challenge. In fact, these values can be kept alive only to the extent that they are the subject of an open and robust political discourse which precludes any particular consensus from ossifying into a 'final' understanding of social relations.[92]

The majority judgment in *Jordan* illustrates the way in which relations of subordination can be legitimated in the name of supposedly 'neutral' principles that rest upon social understandings that are themselves the result of a particular hegemony. The majority's insistence that the stigma associated with prostitution is the result of the prostitute's own choice, rests upon a highly conventional understanding of sexual relations. 'Normal' sexual relations, on this understanding, occur within a sphere of intimacy that is far removed from the world of money and power. The prostitute, in this view, chooses to take her sexuality out of this intimate sphere, to enter a world in which sexual relations are mediated by the cold and impersonal calculus of money.

By rejecting Jordan's claim, the majority legitimated this conventional discourse of sexuality and prevented oppositional ideas from entering mainstream public dis-

---

89 *Idem* 84.

90 *Idem* 91–98.

91 *Idem* 87.

92 See Chantal Mouffe *The return of the political* (1993). A more radical expression of the same idea is presented in chapter one of this collection by Johan van der Walt.

course.[93] I can only speculate about what such an oppositional discourse of sexuality might look like, but it seems fairly certain that it would challenge the construction of autonomy, choice and consent that informs conventional thinking;[94] provide alternative interpretations of gender equality and the relation between sex, power and poverty; promote understanding of alternative lifestyles; and contest the idea that all 'legitimate' expressions of sexuality should be based on the same standard. Instead of encouraging the emergence of 'counterpublics' which are able to develop such oppositional ideas, the majority effectively drove them underground by portraying their sexuality as aberrant and their plight as exceptional and the product of their own choice.

5.8 Complex equality

The minority judgment in *Jordan* suggests that a dignity-based interpretation of the right to equality need not necessarily result in the moralism and conservatism characterising the majority judgment. In one view, the majority judgment is simply a perversion of the dignity-based approach. From this perspective, the majority's failure to situate the inquiry within a context of systemic gender inequality points not to serious problems inherent in the dignity-based approach, but to flaws in its application. It could, moreover, be argued that, far from being a natural outgrowth of the dignity-based approach, the moralism of the majority judgment flows from a failure to recognise the intrinsic dignity of every human being, regardless of the circumstances in which she may find herself.[95]

Others believe that the dignity-based approach should not be let off the hook too easily – that even if it does not necessarily result in a moralistic and overly individualistic approach, there may be something about it that makes it easier for judges to fall back uncritically onto conventional understandings and 'commonsense' assumptions, which may themselves be problematic in view of the constitution's transformative aspirations. Even if dignity can be rooted in a conception of the self as a social being, even if it can be interpreted to encompass both public and private autonomy and be used to chal-

---

93 Of course, there is a long history of state attempts to confine prostitution to the margins of society, and thus to prevent such oppositional ideas from entering mainstream discourse. This history includes the regulation of prostitution, as in nineteenth-century Great Britain and France. Drucilla Cornell quotes a nineteenth-century French social scientist as saying: 'prostitutes are as inevitable, in an agglomeration of men, as sewers, garbage-heaps, and refuse-dumps; the conduct of the authorities ought to be the same with regard to one as to the other; the duty is to watch over, to diminish by all possible means the inconveniences inherent in them, and, certainly, to hide them, to relegate them to the darkest corners, to make their presence as unnoticed as possible.' Drucilla Cornell *At the heart of freedom: Feminism, sex, and equality* (1998) 48.

94 It would not only challenge the view that money and power play a negligible role in 'normal' sexual relations, but would also question the assumption that prostitutes surrender their autonomy by engaging in sex work. Cornell argues, on the basis of interviews conducted with prostitutes, that for some women prostitution is 'a representation of [their] sexuate being, a persona that [they have] to live out'. *Idem* 55. '[I]n a world of abuse some women will take on the life of a prostitute in order to work though their incestuous and violent pasts'. *Idem* 56. It would therefore be wrong simply to equate prostitution with sexual slavery and to treat it as an abandonment of the self. Even though sex workers are subjected to degradation and alienation, they have not renounced their right to establish their own autonomous identity. 'State-enforced moralism hinders what we as feminists should seek: the psychic, political, and ethical space for women to represent themselves.' *Idem* 58.

95 As Drucilla Cornell pointed out at a seminar held in Pretoria in August 2004, the majority conflated the ideal of human dignity with the notion of a dignified existence.

lenge material inequality, these are not the connotations that have traditionally been attached to it. Traditionally, in South African law, the concept of dignity has carried more individualistic meanings and has been taken to refer to personality interests, such as personal reputation. That these connotations continue to inform legal discourse, is evident from legal fields as diverse as equality litigation and the law of defamation.

My own analysis of *Jordan* and of the idea of dignity as a neutral principle suggests that the dignity-based approach facilitates the moralism and subjectivism of the majority judgment – even if it does not necessarily lead to them. It further suggests that the quest for neutral principles of adjudication may be misconceived and that a more political understanding of equality is called for.

However, simply calling for the abandonment of the dignity-based approach and its replacement with an alternative approach may not be the best way forward. In the first place, it seems unlikely that the Constitutional Court will abandon its dignity-based interpretation of equality in the foreseeable future. Second, even though the limits of a dignity-based approach have been revealed in certain areas, this approach has, in the majority of cases, resulted in context-sensitive and transformative judgments. Third, it may be possible to exploit the tensions inherent in the court's equality jurisprudence to allow for a greater focus on material and political disadvantage.

What needs to be done, is to infuse the court's equality standard with an understanding of the complexity of equality. This understanding should rest, *inter alia*, on the following premises: first of all, equality cannot and should not be reduced to a single value, such as human dignity. An awareness of the interrelatedness of equality and dignity can, admittedly, assist in giving content to the right to equality, and in subjecting certain forms of discrimination to a transformative critique. But the same is true of the relationship between equality and democracy, or between equality and social justice. What is needed, is a more adequate understanding of the moral, political *and* material dimensions of equality.

Second, such an understanding of equality must recognise the possibility that different forms of discrimination may require different types of analysis. It is, for instance, likely that certain forms of discrimination can be more easily captured in the language of moral harm than others. It appears that discrimination on the grounds of sexual orientation can often be expressed quite powerfully in terms of this type of moral analysis, as discrimination against gays and lesbians is usually rooted in moral disapproval and results directly in an affront to their dignity and identity.[96] In other areas, like gender, a focus on moral issues may be less helpful and may serve to obscure the power relations at work. Here, it could be argued, questions of political disempowerment and material disadvantage should loom large in the court's inquiry. Rather than focusing predominantly on issues of personhood and identity, the court should concentrate on questions of domination and access to the means of political and economic power.

---

96 As Sachs J wrote in *National Coalition for Gay and Lesbian Equality v Minister of Justice* (n 1) at para. 128, with reference to an article by Edwin Cameron: '[P]recisely because neither power nor specific resource allocation are at issue, sexual orientation becomes a moral focus in our constitutional order. For this same reason, the question of dignity is in this context central to the question of equality.'

Third, a vision of complex equality would not be satisfied merely with generalisations about the different types of analysis that are best suited to different grounds of discrimination. It would resist the conclusion that a single criterion is suitable to a particular ground of discrimination, such as gender, and would require sensitivity to the concrete life experiences of those affected, the intersectional nature of disadvantage,[97] and the different considerations that may be applicable in different spheres, such as education, employment, welfare and citizenship.[98]

What is likely to emerge from such a vision of equality, is a complex web of factors and principles that relate differently to different forms of disadvantage.[99] Not only may gender discrimination require a different focus from racial discrimination, but the focus may also vary, depending on whether the women affected are black or white (or rich or poor), and whether the alleged discrimination occurred in the field of employment or welfare. Judges would be required to explain the relevance of different factors and criteria to the factual situation at hand. In doing so, they would have to articulate and substantiate their own understandings of different forms of disadvantage, the intersections between them and the ways in which they are manifested in different areas of life.

Such an approach has several advantages. First place, its recognition of multiple forms of disadvantage is likely to result in a nuanced approach, which would make it easier to detect and interrogate forms of discrimination that are more subtle, or that are not easily captured in the language of moral harm.

Second, it would deepen understanding of the relation between equality, dignity, democracy and social justice. By asking, for instance, whether a particular differentiation diminishes the capacity of vulnerable groups to form oppositional counter-publics which are able to develop oppositional ideas, one should be able to get a clearer vision of the ways in which systemic forms of disadvantage impede access to the means of political power and impoverish democratic debate. One should also be able to gain important insights into the relation between public and private autonomy, between democracy and dignity, and between collective and individual self-realisation. People would become more sensitive to the ways in which individual autonomy and the right to organise collectively hang together. Returning to *Jordan*, one would be better able to

---

97 This refers both to the ways in which economic disadvantage, political invisibility and moral stigma intersect to constitute relations of domination, and the ways in which patterns of subordination, such as racism, sexism and poverty intersect to subordinate black or poor women (or poor black women) in ways experienced by neither white women nor black men. See Kimberle Crenshaw 'Mapping the margins: Intersectionality, identity politics, and violence against women of color', in Kimberle Crenshaw et al. (eds) *Critical race theory* (n 84).

98 See Michael Walzer *Spheres of justice: A defense of pluralism and equality* (1983).

99 Writing from a political-theory perspective, Nancy Fraser argues that gender equity is best understood as 'a complex notion comprising a plurality of distinct normative principles'. (Nancy Fraser 'Gender equity and the welfare state: A postindustrialist thought experiment', in Seyla Benhabib (ed.) *Democracy and difference: Contesting the boundaries of the political* (1996) 218 at 221). She identifies seven such principles: the anti-poverty principle, the anti-exploitation principle, the principles of income equality, leisure-time equality and equality of respect, the anti-marginalisation principle and the anti-androcentrism principle. She notes that she developed this account of gender equality with the specific purpose of evaluating alternative pictures of a postindustrial welfare state', and recognises that '[f]or issues other than welfare a somewhat different package of norms might be called for'. *Idem* 222.

see how material disadvantage, sexual double standards and an official policy of relegating sex work to the darkest corners of society,[100] combine to deprive women of their dignity and to keep them locked in a state of vulnerability and disadvantage.

Third, the concept of complex equality advocated here, could enable a more nuanced understanding of the relationship between equality and difference. Proponents of a dignity-based approach are concerned that other interpretations of the right to equality would negate the differences between individuals, and impose upon them a dull and mindless conformity. However, it is my contention that a focus on questions of access to the means of political and economic power – in addition to the question whether there has been an impairment of the complainants' human dignity – may result in even greater sensitivity to difference and respect for diversity. This is so because the vision of complex equality developed in this section is concerned with the protection of difference, not merely as a 'private' attribute, but as a means of creating and safeguarding a public space which is characterised by robust political debate and the existence of a plurality of democratic visions.

Despite its focus on the material position and social power of groups, this concept of equality does not presuppose a homogeneity of viewpoints and/or interests among particular racial, cultural or religious groups, or among gays or women. However, it acknowledges that members of disadvantaged and marginalised groups are likely to have certain experiences, outlooks, tastes, world views and survival strategies in common, which may appear curious, immoral, irrational or bizarre from the perspective of the dominant culture. These departures from middle-class sensibilities are often branded as illegitimate in the name of a supposedly universalistic philosophy which asserts the equal moral worth of all individuals. However, on closer inspection, it appears that this philosophy is itself the expression of a particular set of contingent assumptions and experiences; that what appears to be a celebration of the differences between individuals, may really amount to the imposition of a 'corporate group identity, radically constraining any sense of individuality, and silently advancing the claims of that group identity'.[101] The complex vision of equality proposed in this section, recognises that every individual is entitled to a 'psychic, political and ethical space' within which she can develop her own autonomous identity.[102] It further recognises that the creation of such spaces is the stuff of political action as much as of personal growth and discovery, and depends on the ability of a plurality of groups to participate in an ongoing process of democratic contestation.[103]

---

100 See (n 93) above.

101 Williams (n 84) 194.

102 Cornell (n 93) 58.

103 This recognition also underlies the concerns which Karin van Marle expresses in chapter two of this collection about the threat which constitutional law (in the guise of neutral principles and a dignity -based concept of equality, for example) poses to action, politics and revolt in post-apartheid South Africa. It is also central to André van der Walt's understanding of the public aspect of property as it is developed in chapter four.

104 As indicated in (n 1), I am interested here in the court's approach to the question of unfair discrimination (in terms of s 9(3)). Whether criticisms of the court's interpretation of s 9(1) (equality before the law and equal protection

Finally, the approach advocated here does not require a rejection of the equality standard enunciated in *Harksen* but, rather, its modification and re-interpretation.[104] The *Harksen* test should be re-interpreted to allow for a consideration of different forms of disadvantage – it should be 'opened up' to enable a careful, contextual evaluation of the factors and normative principles that are relevant in a particular area of discrimination. This could be done by exploiting the tensions and ambiguities in the *Harksen* test. For instance, the references in *Harksen* to the impact of the differentiation/discrimination and the question whether it has led to an impairment of the complainants' fundamental human dignity *or an impairment of a comparably serious nature* (or has the potential to do so), could be utilised to create more room for the consideration of material disadvantage and political disempowerment.[105] Moreover, the references to the social context and the nature of the provision or power in question, could be used to elaborate different factors and principles which are relevant to different forms of discrimination and different life spheres.

5.9 Concluding remarks

The concept of equality proposed in the previous section is in many respects similar to the Constitutional Court's dignity-based interpretation of the equality right. However, there are also important differences. While the two approaches share a commitment to substantive equality and an engagement with context and disadvantage, they differ on the best way of conceptualising such an approach. Drawing, *inter alia*, on the criticisms and proposals of Davis and Albertyn and Goldblatt, as well as the political conception of racial equality proposed by Thomas, I argue for a conception of equality that stresses its moral, political and material dimensions, which does not seek to reduce material disadvantage and political disempowerment to moral harm, and which recognises the ways in which economic disadvantage, political invisibility and moral stigma intersect to constitute relations of domination.

Furthermore, the two conceptions of equality are informed by different understandings of the politics of interpretation.[106] The idea of dignity as a neutral principle is based on the fear of judicial subjectivity – a fear that has shaped much of the discourse on the 'counter-majoritarian dilemma', and has resulted in a quest for adjudicative methods that would defuse the politics of legal interpretation. My own view is that the quest for 'neutral' methods of adjudication both over-estimates and under-estimates the politics of interpretation. The fear that constitutional adjudication would, in the absence of a

---

and benefit of the law) are justified, and whether any deficiencies in the court's interpretation of that subsection can be cured by means of a re-interpretation and modification of the existing test, are questions for another day. The same goes for the court's understanding of the relation between ss 9(3) and 36(1) (the general limitation clause).

105 It is true that the current formulation 'privileges' the impairment of human dignity, as it is held up as the standard against which other forms of harm should be measured. However, material disadvantage and political disempowerment could be given an independent status through judicial elaboration of the meaning of the phrase 'or an impairment of a comparably serious nature'.

106 See Henk Botha 'Democracy and rights: Constitutional interpretation in a postrealist world' (2000) 63 *THRHR* 561; 'Freedom and constraint in constitutional adjudication' (2004) 20 *SAJHR* 249.

neutral method underpinning it, rest simply on the subjective preferences and prejudices of individual judges, exaggerates the dangers of judicial subjectivity and fails to account for the constraints to which judges are subject by virtue of their socialisation into a legal universe. At the same time, the assumption that the politics of law can be defused through neutral adjudicative methods or procedures, under-estimates the extent to which legal interpretation is – inevitably – informed by ideological presuppositions and contestable normative assumptions.

An approach that is more overtly 'political' and which does not seek to filter the consideration of material disadvantage and political power through 'neutral' principles, is not necessarily more 'subjective' than one based on dignity. Such an approach requires judicial candour and a willingness to explain the reasons for decisions as fully as possible. It openly acknowledges the ubiquity of power, and is ready to confront the ways in which the discourses are themselves shaped by power relations.

BIBLIOGRAPHY: CHAPTER FIVE

Books and articles

Crenshaw, K., N. Gotanda, G. Peller and K. Thomas. eds. *Critical Race Theory: The Key Writings That Formed the Movement*. New York: New Press, 1995.

Ackermann, L. 'Equality and the South African Constitution: The Role of Dignity'. *ZaöRV* 63 (2000):37.

Albertyn, C. and B. Goldblatt. 'Facing the Challenge of Transformation: Difficulties in the Development of an Indigenous Jurisprudence of Equality'. *SAJHR* 14 (1998):248.

Albertyn, C. and J. Kentridge, 'Introducing the Right to Equality in the Interim Constitution'. *SAJHR* 10 (1994):149.

Botha, H. 'Democracy and Rights: Constitutional Interpretation in a Postrealist World'. *THRHR* 63 (2000):561.

Botha, H. 'Freedom and Constraint in Constitutional Adjudication'. *SAJHR* 20 (2004):249.

Carpenter, G. 'Equality and Non-Discrimination in the new South African Constitutional Order 1: The Early Cases'. *THRHR* 64 (2001):409.

___. 'Equality and Non-Discrimination in the New South African Constitutional Order 2: An Important Trilogy of Decisions'. *THRHR* 64 (2001):619.

___. 'Equality and Non-Discrimination in the New South African Constitutional Order 3: the Saga Continues'. *THRHR* 65 (2002):37.

___. 'Equality and Non-Discrimination in the new South African Constitutional Order 4: Update'. *THRHR* 65 (2002):177.

___. 'Of Prostitutes, Pimps and Patrons: Are Some Still more Equal than Others?' *SAPR/PL* 19 (2004):231.

Cornell, D. *At The Heart of Freedom: Feminism, Sex, and Equality*. Princeton: Princeton University Press, 1998.

Cowen, S. 'Can Dignity Guide South Africa's Equality Jurisprudence?' *SAJHR* 17 (2001):34.

Crenshaw, K. 'Mapping the Margins: Intersectionality, Identity Politics, and Violence Against Women of Color'. In *Critical Race Theory: The Key Writings That Formed the Movement,* edited by K. Crenshaw, N. Gotanda, G. Peller and K. Thomas. New York: New Press, 1995.

Davis, D. 'Equality: The Majesty of Legoland Jurisprudence'. *SALJ* 116 (1999):398.

De Vos, P. 'Equality For All? A Critical Analysis of the Equality Jurisprudence of the Constitutional Court'. *THRHR* 63 (2000):62.

Deutsch, J. 'Neutrality, Legitimacy, and the Supreme Court: Some Intersections Between Law and Political Science'. *Stanford LR* 20 (1968):169.

Fagan, A. 'Dignity and Unfair Discrimination: A Value Misplaced and a Right Misunderstood'. *SAJHR* 14 (1998):220.

Fraser, N. 'Gender Equity and the Welfare State: A Postindustrialist Thought Experiment'. In *Democracy and Difference: Contesting The Boundaries of The Political* edited by S. Benhabib. Princeton: Princeton University Press, 1996.

Greenawalt, K. 'The Enduring Significance of Neutral Principles'. *Columbia LR* 78 (1978): 982.

Horwitz, M. *The Transformation of American Law, 1870–1960*. Oxford: Oxford University Press, 1992.

Jagwanth, S. 'What Is the Difference? Group Categorisation in *Pretoria City Council v Walker* 1998 2 SA 363 CC'. *SAJHR* 15 (1999):200.

Jagwanth, S. and E. Kalula, eds. *Equality Law: Reflections from South Africa and Elsewhere*. Lansdowne: Juta, 2002.

Klug, H. *Constituting Democracy: Law, Globalism and South Africa's Political Reconstruction*. Cambridge: Cambridge University Press, 2000.

Le Roux, W. 'Sex Work, the Right to Occupational Freedom and the Constitutional Politics of Recognition'. *SALJ* 120 (2003):452.

Mouffe, C. *The Return of the Political.* London: Verso, 1993.

Peller, G. 'Neutral Principles in the 1950's'. *Journal of Legal Reform* 21 (1988):561.

Singer, J. 'Legal Realism Now'. *California LR* 76 (1988):465.

Thomas, K. 'Racial Justice'. In *Looking Back at Law's Century*, edited by A. Sarat, B. Garth and R. Kagan. Ithaca: Cornell University Press, 2002.

Van der Walt, A and H. Botha, 'Coming to Grips with the New Constitutional Order: Critical Comments On *Harksen V Lane NO*'. *SAPR/PL* 13 (1998):17.

Van Marle, K. 'Equality: An Ethical Interpretation'. *THRHR* 63 (2000):595.

Van Reenen, T. 'Equality, Discrimination and Affirmative Action: An Analysis of Section 9 of the Constitution of the Republic of South Africa'. *SAPR/PL* 12 (1997):151.

Walzer, M. *Spheres of Justice: A Defense of Pluralism and Equality.* Oxford: Martin Robertson, 1983.

Wechsler, H. 'Toward Neutral Principles of Constitutional Law'. *Harvard LR* 73 (1959):1.

Weinrib, E. 'Constitutional Conceptions and Constitutional Comparativism'. In *Defining the Field of Comparative Constitutional law,* edited by V. Jackson and M. Tushnet. Westport: Praeger, 2002.

Westen, P. 'The Empty Idea of Equality'. *Harvard LR* 95 (1982):537.

Winter, S. *A Clearing in the Forest: Law, Life, and Mind.* Chicago: University of Chicago Press, 2001.

Case law

Brink v Kitshoff 1996 (4) SA 197; 1996 (6) BCLR 752 (CC).

Brown v Board of Education of Topeka 347 US 483 (1954).

Daniels v Campbell NO 2004 (7) BCLR 735 (CC).

Democratic Party v Minister of Home Affairs 1999 (3) SA 254; 1999 (6) BCLR 611 (CC).

Du Toit v Minister for Welfare and Population Development 2003 (2) SA 198; 2002 (10) BCLR 1006 (CC).

Egan v Canada 124 DLR (4th) 609.

Fraser v Children's Court, Pretoria North 1997 (2) SA 261; 1997 (2) BCLR 153 (CC).

Harksen v Lane NO 1998 (1) SA 300; 1997 (11) BCLR 1489 (CC).

Hoffmann v South African Airways 2001 (1) SA 1; 2000 (11) BCLR 1211 (CC).

In re: Certification of the Constitution of the Republic of South Africa, 1996 1996 (4) SA 744; 1996 (10) BCLR 1253 (CC).

J v Director-General, Department of Home Affairs 2003 (5) BCLR 463 (CC).

S v Jordan 2002 (6) SA 642; 2002 (11) BCLR 1117 (CC).

Larbi-Odam v Member of Executive Council for Education 1998 (1) SA 745; 1997 (12) BCLR 1655 (CC).

Moseneke v The Master 2001 (2) SA 18; 2001 (2) BCLR 103 (CC).

National Coalition for Gay and Lesbian Equality v Minister of Home Affairs 2000 (2) SA 1; 2000 (1) BCLR 39 (CC).

National Coalition for Gay and Lesbian Equality v Minister of Justice 1999 (1) SA 6; 1998 (12) BCLR 1517 (CC).

Plessy v Ferguson (163) US 537, 551 (1896).

President RSA v Hugo 1997 (4) SA 1; 1997 (6) BCLR 708 (CC).

Pretoria City Council v Walker 1998 (2) SA 363; 1998 (3) BCLR 257 (CC).

Prinsloo v Van der Linde 1997 (3) SA 1012; 1997 (6) BCLR 759 (CC).

Satchwell v President of the RSA 2002 (6) SA 1; 2002 9 BCLR 986 (CC).

Shelley v Kraemer 334 US 1 (1948).

United Democratic Movement v President of the RSA (1) 2002 (11) BCLR 1179 (CC).

CONCLUSION

Spectres of 'Communism' in Post-Apartheid South Africa

Stewart Motha

> One name for another, a part for the whole: the historic violence of Apartheid can always be treated as a metonymy. In its past as well as its present. By diverse paths (condensation, displacement, expression, or representation), one can always decipher through its singularity so many other kinds of violence going on in the world. At once part, cause, effect, example, what is happening there translates what takes place here, always here, wherever one is and wherever one looks, closest to home. Infinite responsibility, therefore, no rest allowed for any kind of good conscience.[1] — Jacques Derrida

On April 9, 1993, a few days before Jacques Derrida gave his lecture to open a colloquium titled 'Whither Marxism?' at the University of California, Riverside, Chris Hani was assassinated in Boksburg, South Africa. The epigraph above is taken from Derrida's dedication of his lecture, later published as *Spectres of Marx*, to this man who was killed as a communist. The proper name Chris Hani, Derrida warned us, must not be invoked as a symbol of a certain paradigm inflated through the rhetoric of martyrdom. However, he reminded us that this man was put to death *as a communist* – that was the proclaimed intent of his assassins.[2] At the time people wondered if the delicate negotiations to inaugurate what has come to be called the 'transition to a non-racial democracy in South Africa' would be blown off course. That fear subsided. A compromise was reached in the form of an interim Constitution. In-finite responsibility for the crimes of the apartheid era and its legacy of unequal wealth was given a new heading called *reconciliation*.

Reconciliation was at once a delimitation of responsibility and an infinite opening of a post-racist future for South African law and society. Hence the notion of *in-finite* responsibility invoked here. The possibility of a spacio-temporal event called 'post-apartheid' requires that responsibility for a form of sociality called apartheid be delimited, be made finite. Through the Truth and Reconciliation Commission and the new Constitution it was imagined that apartheid could be converted to a memory. That

1 Jacques Derrida 'Dedication', in Jacques Derrida *Spectres of Marx: The State of the Debt, the Work of Mourning, and the New International* (1994) xv.

2 *Idem* xvi.

memory, if the juridico-political can be given the luxury of such mastery of time, would convert the racial Republic to a thing of the past. Memory was thus supposed to be the founding event of the new South Africa. All the chapters in this collection attest to the reasons why such 'post-apartheid' time and sociality is yet to come.

This problem of in-finite responsibility is not a concern for South Africans only. This is signalled with characteristic acuity by Derrida in the epigraph above: 'there is no rest allowed for any kind of good conscience'. Let us not forget the question 'whither Marxism?' posed in 1993. Chris Hani was not a paradigm lost only to South Africa. Fukuyama had announced his distortion of Kojeve.[3] The possibility of political struggle and social transformation was being stilled worldwide as obituaries were written for communism. The 'post-ideological new world order' (yet another misleading periodisation of politics) has now turned out to offer the two poles of 'full spectrum dominance' (*pax Americana*) or 'full spectrum governance' (*pax Europeana*). Democracy, the rule of law, a capitalist market economy, harmonisation with global markets, that is, the neo-liberalisation of the juridico-political, was all that was on offer for the post-communist and post-apartheid era. Those who subscribed to vanquished old orders and ideologies or struggled for actual transformation of the conditions of economic and social production were offered an abstraction: human rights. The realm of the possible was at best reduced, then, to 'equal opportunity' or 'duty'.

The 'new South Africa' and the 'new world order' have much in common. The shift from totalitarianisms to what is called *democracy* has taken the form of a shift from politics to law. 'Negotiated revolutions' have ushered in new hegemonic systems. As Karin van Marle points out in chapter two of this collection, the liberal constitution is a 'monument' for a democratic sociality that is still marked by poverty, the crushing of dissent, and massive economic disparity. The new 'Hobbesian pact' described by Mamdani allowed a minority to secure their privilege in South Africa. The compromise, which was largely economic, preserved the accumulated wealth of the few by granting 'equal citizenship', which was already robbed of content for the many newly admitted to its ranks. Van Marle speaks of spectres, of being 'haunted by the seeming absence of action, thinking and revolt and ultimately a politics of becoming'. How will systems and their subjects undergo a radical transformation, she asks, when political struggle is disciplined and controlled through the rhetoric of rights? She eschews violence and militancy yet does not want the struggle to be reduced to what is legitimate. This is the aporia of all systemic transformation – how to sustain the possibility of radical transformation, but not constrain such change by determining the legitimacy of action/revolt in advance.

'Memory', drawing from Du Plessis,[4] is the device that Van Marle seeks to adopt for the passage from past to future. Memory, the archive, is the space of possibility, the ground of transformation. The Constitution shares with the archive a failure that is

3 *Idem* 72–75.

4 Lourens du Plessis 'The South African Constitution as memory and promise', in Charles Villa-Vincencio (ed.) *Transcending a century of injustice* (2000) 63.

actually its success. They both fail to delimit or render finite the possibility that memory will always return as a haunting that unsettles the negotiated truce and the disciplined confines of the rule of law. Through the notion of the 'archival sliver', Van Marle joins Verne Harris in proclaiming the potential of all iterations of memory – memory is and will be a fractured and shifting ground. This Van Marle contrasts with the monumental constitution, that symptom of the 'death drive'. The question she finally poses is whether the constitution as memorial, the potential marked by the unstable archive, is yet another way of being 'framed' (disciplined and set up).

I agree with Van Marle that the choice is not between law and politics. I want to suggest that Van Marle's project, and indeed the concern provoked by all the chapters in this collection, is the possibility of another sociality. If I can be permitted to ask, then, why is this concern for a reconciled sociality – the demand for a political community of action, thinking and revolt, where beings seek a community free of economic and social deprivation — not called *communism*? Is it this name that drives equivocation? Or is it all the thinking, and indeed action and revolt, needed to reinvigorate this sullied term, or devise another that re-presents its many potentialities? The chapters in this collection certainly seem to have as their common concern the possibility of another 'political community'. Each chapter also raises the concern of the urgent need for material transformation. Material transformation, they all seem to acknowledge, cannot be legislated. It will not be brought about by a collection of decisions of the Constitutional Court, which, as we observed through Wessel le Roux in chapter three, is busy establishing its own place as the paradigm of the new South Africa. Radical transformation cannot be legalised.

The limit of legalising political transformation is taken up in chapter four by André van der Walt. He poses a pressing question: 'is it possible in law to take deeper social, political or civic contextual factors into account, or do they fall outside the scope of what property law can and ought to do?' He asks this question with the conviction that there is something beyond the individual, some 'transcending' sense of the public, a civic republicanism perhaps. He is asking what form or kind of community will offer the material conditions for a sociality where the fate of the individual is not sealed by a social contract which affirms the privilege of a minority. Drawing on Ruti Teitel, he sees the potentiality in the space and time of in-finite responsibility. This is the liminal space/time *in between* regimes where traditional distinctions can be challenged. The possibility of unsettling or undermining the public/private, individual/community, civic/state oppositions becomes possible, according to this view, because law is itself nothing but 'transition'. Law has no secure position other than in the responsive, liminal space in-between regimes (one could also say precedent, rule, concept).[5] As far as it concerns private property – and in South Africa and other contexts where the hegemony of ill-gotten gains remains to be undone – this in-between presents the possibility of a sense of the 'public' that can supersede narrow 'private' interests in a transitional proc-

---

5 For an account of law occupying the place in-between determination and responsiveness, law as movement, see Peter Fitzpatrick *Modernism and the grounds of law* (2001).

ess of 'redress, reparation, and reform'. This sense of the 'public' or 'new common' will sustain and inform transition and transformation.

The difficulty with this sense of a 'new common' is that it is immanent in a space/time, a 'transition', that cannot be held open if it is to succeed. By contrast, the new common must always be an opening; it must be permanently held open. The new 'we' lingers between the past and some common future that is also here now, here in the in-between. But there are dangers too – such lingering will soon become the time of the 'lost opportunity'. There is the haunting of the generations that are passing; the ones who can justly call themselves 'the generation that waited for what did not arrive'. Their haunting is here now. What has to be outlined more explicitly, then, is what material transformations, refusal of identities and re-presentations, what singularities and multiplicities, will inaugurate this new 'public'. Property is always already hierarchy. What remains to be thought and elaborated is what sense of public property/propriety, what sense of being-in-common, will deliver a political community where being-together is not presupposed by a sovereign subject and her property.

The task of elaborating a concept of political community in South Africa involves departing from an apartheid form of sociality to 'post-apartheid sociality'. This is a task taken up by Johan van de Walt in chapter one of this collection. He is right to conceive of apartheid sociality as a sovereign intensification – in the language of the German jurist Carl Schmitt, a state of exception. Apartheid was the exception as the norm. But it is important to stress that apartheid was not an exception among exceptions. The West has overstated the exceptionality of apartheid for its own ends. There is no room for such 'good conscience' (Derrida) so soon after colonialism was brought home to Europe in the form of the Holocaust. Indeed, centuries of ethno-racial conflicts, pogroms and genocides to secure Euro-American political dominance and economic affluence means that South African apartheid must not be allowed to become a 'figure' that sustains yet more moralising from the West. Let us not forget that the concentration camp is a British invention from the Boer War (South African War), and 'reserves' and 'Bantustans' were a crime visited on indigenous people throughout the many European empires before that technology of sovereign rule was acquired by South Africa.

In his exploration of two (possibly) distinct forms of sovereign sociality termed in-tensionality/intentionality, Johan van der Walt considers the 'time of reconciliation' through the tension between, on the one hand, a sovereign (resistant) determination of the political (associated with Schmitt), and on the other, a sense of the political as a plural exposure of 'being together' (which resonates with Arendt but is also drawn through Nancy). The Schmittian political moment is an abyssal event, the encounter with the enemy. The brinkmanship of this sovereign encounter, like the resistance of the patient in psychoanalysis, is a patriarchal disruption of 'regular sociality'. The distinction between the Schmittian and Arendtian moments of the political assumes that there is 'regular sociality' with *in-tensional* intensifications (e.g. commerce, culture and religion), distinct from the traumatic disruption of such relations by *intentional* sovereignties (presumably apartheid, ethno-cultural grounds for community and so on). The concern then is to articulate a concept of the political that is in between 'regular' sociality and its Schmittian intensification.

This thought of community or the political is addressed to the 'traumatic breach' of apartheid. How is reconciliation possible after such a breach? Responding to this, the concern for Johan van der Walt is how 'society returns to in-tensionality after a disastrous slip into intentionality'. This recovery of sociality has as its constant disruptive companion the eternally returning sovereign intensification that is the condition of concepts of the political, including liberal democracy.[6] In the 'new' South Africa the attempt to return to regular sociality took the form of a non-ethnic, non-racial democracy. Bringing the schism between in-tensional/intentional sociality to bear on this heading of reconciliation, Van der Walt argues that:

> [t]he insistence on non-ethnicity in a unitary state itself then turns into a mode of resistance to real reconciliation. It itself then comes to represent an exclusively or predominantly Schmittian return to unitary political sovereignty. It thus takes leave of the Arendtian concern with plurality that initially appeared to mark it so clearly. It thus turns into a form of inverse ethnicity that certainly does not bode well for the future of the reconciliation process in South Africa.[7]

It is not clear to me what such 'real reconciliation' would entail. To name a heading or direction that insists on non-ethnicity hardly warrants the Schmittian mantle. What is more interesting is Johan van der Walt's implication that there is a new host in South Africa. The implication is that this is the African National Congress. But does this not return us to the questions posed by André van der Walt – is it not the person with property that is still in a position to be the host? Who is the guest, who is the host; to whom *must* hospitality be extended – Johan van der Walt certainly alerts us to these pressing questions.

According to him, though the principle of non-ethnicity was crucial at the moment of transition to democracy, it has unsurprisingly produced yet another state that enforces a clerically administered communion, with more symbols, and another unification that flattens the singular-plural exposure of all being. The question this opens is 'from whom and from where does reconciliation ultimately come?'[8] Reconciliation gives time. The responsibility of the individual and the common is to determine what to do with this time. This responsibility, moreover, cannot be demanded but must be given. Given the in-finitude of time, responsibility must also be given, in-finitely.

Let me make my concern here explicit – is there not too much attention being given to ethno-cultural formations such as an Afrikaner ethno-racial-language-identity that is historically no less of a sovereign intensification? Johan van der Walt has done much to question this emerging Afrikaner identity politics – the evidence is there in his chapter. However, I find the opposition between ethnicised identity and the 'state-as-communion' surprising. Why entertain abyssal sociality when the point is to think beyond such identifications, beyond such unions, unities and the paradigms they present? It is more pressing to pose the question of community differently. Such a thought of community

---

6 Johan van der Walt 'The time of reconciliation', chapter one in this collection, 21.

7 *Idem* 27.

8 *Idem* 28.

would question the presence of ethnicity, place its appearance in 'old' colonialisms and neo-imperial enterprises – but importantly, challenge the presence that is claimed by any identification, any re-presentation of being. It is this line of questioning that should reinvigorate a thought of communism.

Can 'we' conceive of a 'communism' not as a predetermined path, a scientific process, or certain destination, but a 'new International' as Derrida called it?[9] This would be a communism that would confront what all the chapters in this collection identify as a persistent problem – communal, sovereign, material intensifications of the political. This would be a communism that would require a history which has all the uncertainties, all the disruptions of memory and none of the hypostatisations of monumental constitutions.[10]

All the chapters in this collection in some way grapple with the question of community or the political. Henk Botha makes the point in chapter five that the question of the political cannot be thought or addressed without attending to the problem of economic equality:

> As much as the history of apartheid was characterised by the denial of human dignity, it was also one of economic exploitation and the systematic political and economic disempowerment of the majority of the population. It was a history of the establishment, through legal and other means, of the hegemony of a racial elite; of the economic dispossession of entire communities; of the relegation of the overwhelming majority of people to the fringes of the economy. It was a history of an attempt to divide and rule; to keep the black majority locked in a permanent state of serfdom; and thus to entrench white power and privilege.[11]

This account by Botha eloquently sets out what remains to be (un)done. Eschewing the purportedly neutral view that equality can be given content through the amorphous notion of 'dignity', Botha proposes a vision of 'complex equality'. He calls for a better understanding of the relation between moral, political and material dimensions of equality. The character of material disadvantage looms large in his attempt to give content to how the Constitutional Court should address the notion of equality. Drawing on the arguments of Kimberle Crenshaw and others, he advances an 'intersectional' approach to what he terms 'complex equality'. This would involve, for instance, exploring:

> the ways in which economic disadvantage, political invisibility and moral stigma intersect to constitute relations of domination, and the ways in which patterns of subordination, such as racism, sexism and poverty intersect to subordinate black or poor women (or poor black women) in ways experienced neither by white women nor black men.[12]

The subject who comes before the law, this account tells us, should not be received through some 'neutral' notion of dignity. While the subject should not be regarded as over-determined by any one or a combination of social, economic and political posi-

---

9 Derrida (n 1) 29.

10 I will later return to sketch what can be, at this point, only a tentative opening of this line of questioning.

11 Henk Botha 'Equality, dignity and the politics of interpretation', chapter five in this collection, 157.

12 *Idem* 170.

tions, these are nonetheless constitutive of a distinction/difference to which the law must be open.

How the law should be open to the subject that comes before it – not least the actual opening of the Constitutional Court as the 'paradigmatic institution of 'post-apartheid' South Africa – is the concern of Wessel le Roux's evocative discussion in chapter three. Aptly for this age, the Constitutional Court has a logo. And why not – it is marketing something. A new gathering, a stable society for a regular and predictable market, a new republic with counter-majoritarian checks, a 'bridge' that will enable the traversal of space/time from the evils of the past to the democratic future – all this it seems is captured in the design of the court, and in the logo of a big tree providing shelter to all in the community. In Le Roux's account, the logo captures the sense of law as organic, dialogic, facilitating relations between people. Nothing holds people around the tree, perhaps other than the pull of its shelter. The law is thus a dialogic community – the tree embodying the sense of unforced plurality. But as Le Roux, Botha and Van Marle point out, this plurality is an enforcement of a form of dialogic republicanism where rights are the language, and judges perceive themselves to be the 'self-governing' guardians of a legalised politics.

Transformative constitutionalism needs more than a new image. It requires that the materiality of the political community be confronted. Community cannot be about its presentation and re-presentation. The constitution can have no ground. What does Le Roux propose for this coming community and constitution without ground? He suggests a labyrinthine postmodern constitution derived from Derrida's reading of Kafka's fable, 'Before the law'. The place of the law in this fable, indeed even its architecture, reveals a non-place – what Le Roux calls an 'atopology'. There is no itinerary, method or path to gain access to the law. The impossibility of gaining entry to the law is an 'interruption' or 'deferment of passage' rather than an impenetrable obstacle. Here the emphasis is on keeping the law open, indefinitely. The implications of this for a constitutionalised attempt to launch a new political community is this: there is no 'proper place' for 'gathering' the community, for setting its destination and choosing its path. For instance, the Constitutional Court as the paradigmatic institution of the new South Africa is beset by the ambivalence of the inscription '*welkom*' in its foyer. What kind of hospitality is this? Who is (still) the host? Has a clear demarcation been drawn between past and future? Has apartheid time/space been rendered finite, and is this the place from which an infinite future of responsibility will be opened? If this is the place from which the future will be opened, can we trust its gatekeepers? These are some of the very pertinent questions raised by Le Roux in his interrogation of the constitutional framing of the new South Africa.

Tentatively, then, what might be an approach to conceiving at least the opening of a new International? Here I will draw briefly from Derrida's reading of Blanchot's chapter 'Marx's three voices'. This is perhaps the pivotal moment in *Spectres of Marx*.[13] It is the turning toward a future, but always with the spectres that disrupt the linear unfolding of time. It is precisely this turning to the future, along with the returning

13 Derrida (n 1) 29 ff.

of spectres, that we have observed through the chapters in this collection. What then should orientate the thought and revolt that Derrida has called a new International?

There is first the promise of a future, but one that must be made urgent, an injunction for justice now. This is a concern that those who have some regard for material transformation must take seriously. This, Derrida tells us, must not be a reception of Marx, a fashionable gesture, particularly in the university, where Marx is 'set off against Marxism'.[14] To do so would be to depoliticise, to rein in the potential and the immediacy of the revolt that is needed. There cannot just be a 'deciphering' of the problem. There must be revolt and action, as Van Marle put it. Derrida made the same point about the need: 'to do everything we can so as to avoid the neutralising anaesthesia of a new theoreticism, and to prevent a philosophico-philological return to Marx from prevailing.'[15]

This is not to say that the philosophico-philological is not a necessary gesture, but there must be some priority given to political action and revolt.

The second concern is not to make the mistake, when responding to the urgency of transformation and the demand for a rupture, of conceiving the rupture as a substantial presence. The demand, Derrida tells us, will always be excessive. The excess will not be captured in the moment of decision, but will disrupt any permanence, any essence to the political community. This is what will always defy the permanence of a 'permanent revolution'.

The third concern is the mode and in-felicity, if I can call it that, of theoretical thinking. Derrida argues that while a certain scientific Marxism was always privileged – if for no other reason than that its mode of knowledge was science – we must guard against the homogeneity of the 'guaranteed translation'. All inheritance, and especially knowledge, must be interrupted.[16] Interrupting the exercises of thinking is indeed an urgent requirement. Theoretical thinking, particularly within the movement of critical legal studies, must, as this collection of essays suggests, carry out an urgent discussion of what passes for engagement with politics and the related but distinct question of the political.

BIBLIOGRAPHY: CHAPTER 6

Books and articles

Derrida, J. *Spectres of Marx: The State of the Debt, the Work of Mourning, and the New International*. New York: Routledge, 1994.

Du Plessis, L. 'The South African Constitution as memory and promise'. In *Transcending a century of injustice*, edited by C. Villa-Vincencio. Cape Town: IJR, 2000.

Fitzpatrick, P. *Modernism and the Grounds of Law*. Cambridge: Cambridge University Press, 2001.

14 *Idem* 31.
15 *Idem* 32.
16 *Idem* 35.

INDEX